Building Workforce Competencies in Career and Technical Education

A volume in
Adult Education Special Topics: Theory, Research and Practice in Lifelong Learning
Kathleen P. King, *Series Editor*

Library of Congress Cataloging-in-Publication Data

Wang, Victor C. X.
  Building workforce competencies in career and technical education / Victor
C.X. Wang, Kathleen P. King.
      p. cm. – (Adult education special topics)
  Includes bibliographical references and index.
  ISBN 978-1-60752-029-0 (pbk.) – ISBN 978-1-60752-030-6 (hardcover)
1. Career education. 2. Technical education. 3. Labor
productivity–Effect of education on. I. King, Kathleen P. II. Title. III.
Series.
  LC1037.W36 2009
  370.11'3–dc22

                                                                    2008048551

Printed in the United States of America

Dedication

From Dr. King:

To the millions of CTE educators who have the vision to think and teach "outside the box" and advance our society, thank you for serving our students and schools so faithfully and well. The intellectual and innovation future of our world is dependent on your work; you are never appreciated enough. In this work, we celebrate each of you.

To those who support and teach me daily—thank you for your support and belief, in good and hard times, Sharon, Seamus and Bill. You bring me joy.

From Victor Wang:

To the CTE instructors and CTE students, colleagues and friends from around the globe, this book would not be a reality without your support.

To my family (Katie, Anni and Anthony), a heart felt thank you for your continued support and tolerance.

To our series editor, Dr. King, not only do you produce great books in adult education, but also you help produce scholarly books in career and technical education! Together with our readers, we extend a huge thank you to you, Dr. King.

From both authors:

To our publisher, George Johnson, your innovative approaches to publishing highly academic books have benefited our readers far and wide.

CONTENTS

PREFACE

Victor C. X. Wang
California State University, Long Beach

PREFACE

The history of vocational education parallels the efforts of humanity from the Stone Age to modern civilization (Wang, 2008, p. 3). Its contemporary name, "career and technical education," has come a long way. First, vocational education emerged in the form of "manual training." In an address to the 1903 meeting of the National Education Association (NEA), James P. Haney suggested the term "manual arts" (Bennett, 1917) be used instead of "manual training" (Ham, 1900) as a means of placing emphasis on the artistic elements of manual activity. Just a year later, in 1904, Charles R. Richard of Teachers College, Columbia University, suggested in an editorial in October 1904 issue of Manual Training Magazine that the term "industrial arts" be used instead of "manual training" or "manual arts" as more descriptive of this changing point of view (Wang, 2003). With the passage of the Smith-Hughes Act of 1917 (Douglas, 1921, p. 293), trade and industrial vocational education emerged as a major education program. This also gave rise to the Industrial Arts (IA) movement.

Starting in the 1980s, many industrial arts teachers began to change their course offerings. Industrial arts was replaced by technology education (Dyrenfurth & Blandow, 1994). As teachers, learners and practitioners entered the 1990s, they felt the term "vocational education" did not reflect the nature and characteristics of the field; in addition, the term is associ-

Building Workforce Competencies in Career and Technical Education, pages ix–xi

ated with the image of the skilled tradesperson and it does not appeal to a number of high school students. Hence career and technical education replaced vocational education.

The name changes during the past 20th century arose directly from the cultural needs of people in a growing technological society. Leaders in the field of career and technical education constantly debate its educational and intellectual values. Despite bitter opposition, career and technical education has gained strength and improved its educational acceptability. In fact, the field is not only surviving, but also thriving in spite of continuous budget cuts by the state and federal levels. No one is to underestimate the power of organized programs that are closely and explicitly related to preparing people, young and old, for the world of work. The rise or fall of a nation depends on its workforce competencies. Career and technical education has been designed to:

- Meet the manpower needs of society,
- Increase the options available to individuals, and
- Provide a motivating force to enhance all types of learning (Evans & Herr, 1978).

While designed to meet the basic objectives of career and technical education, at the same time, in this post-Sputnik era, career and technical education's challenge extends far beyond preparing students for the world of work. As e-learning has become an essential component of career and technical education in the new century, it poses important questions on the nature of work, work ethics, relationship between people and work, and the relationship between the traditional "journeyman" and "master craftsman."

In this new edition we attempted to update the book with a new philosophy to meet the needs of students in this knowledge-based society. Each of the chapters was revised and new chapters were added. Chapters on curriculum development in CTE, e-learning and Human Resource Development (HRD) are essential components of CTE and are considered much needed chapters for students and teachers in the field. Thus, the new edition proved somewhat cumbersome to both students and practitioners desiring an up-to-date overview of career and technical education.

While we have made these major changes in this new edition, we have maintained the original organization of each chapter in that we review the history of career and technical education, principles and philosophy of career and technical education, historical perspectives of the different components of career and technical education, current instructional programs, and other original chapters. We then present new chapters on curriculum development, e-learning and training and development. We thank Gregory

Petty and Ernest Brewer for giving us permission to reprint their journal article as another chapter. Their article first appeared in *International Journal of Vocational Education and Training.*

This book is intended for those presently functioning as career and technical education instructors and those preparing for such roles. Its central intent is to provide such readers with the knowledge and the skills needed to exercise leadership in career and technical education at several levels and in many roles. The book has been revised at the request of our undergraduate and graduate students. The aim of this important book is to prepare prospective career and technical education leaders to meet the challenge of today's changing globally connected classroom. We hope that you, as readers of this new edition, will find it useful and helpful in providing insights into the practice of career and technical education, and most importantly, in examining your knowledge, skills, and attitudes of career and technical education in order for you to better serve your students in the field.

REFERENCES

Bennett, C. A. (1917). *The manual arts.* Peoria, IL: The Manual Arts Press.

Douglas, P. H. (1921). *American apprenticeship and industrial education.* New York: Columbia University.

Dyrenfurth, M. J., & Blandow, D. (Eds.). (1994). *Technology education in school and industry: Emerging didactics for human resource development.* New York: Springer.

Evans, R. N., & Herr, E. L. (1978). *Foundations of vocational education.* New York: Macmillan.

Ham, C. H. (1900). *Mind and hand manual training: The chief factor in education.* New York: American Book Company.

Wang, V. C. X. (2003). *History and philosophy of career and technical education: The definitive classic in occupational education and human resource development.* Boston, MA: Pearson.

Wang, V. C. X. (2008). The history of vocational education up to 1850 and a rationale for work. In V. C. X. Wang, & K. P. King (Eds.), *Innovations in career and technical education: Strategic approaches towards workforce competencies around the globe* (pp. 3–20). Charlotte, NC: Information Age.

INTRODUCTION

BUILDING ON THE PAST TO MEET THE FUTURE

Kathleen P. King
Fordham University

NEWSFLASH

Join me in reading the pages of the global career journal. As I leaf through the pages, I note a full-page advertisement which is written in bold letters. Each of the first twenty or so words are all printed in capital letters. Oddly, these words are scattered across the page in seeming chaos. Ah, but look lower there is a traditional 3-line adveristment below. What is this all about?

EDUCATIONAL PROGRAMS NEEDED TO SERVE THE WORLD TOADY AND TOMORROW: MUST BE ABLE TO COPE WITH THE FOLLOWING

GLOBAL WARMING --- BANK CLOSINGS --- MASSIVE EMPLOYEE LAYOFFS
NATURAL DISASTERS --- NEW OPERATING SYSTEMS --- TERRORIST INVASIONS
CLOUD COMPUTING --- FUEL CRISES --- HOME FORECLOSURES
DROPPING DOW JONES --- CIVIL WARS --- MOBILE COMPUTING
FOREIGN INVASIONS --- EMBARGOES --- EMERGENCY RELIEF
INFLATION --- GNP UP, DOLLAR DOWN, YEN UP

WANTED: Flexibility, responsiveness and global perspectives in career development, demonstrated skills, motivated, self-directed educational programs. Others need not apply. Please call the Global Hotline as soon as possible: GLO-BAL-0911

Building Workforce Competencies in Career and Technical Education, pages xiii–xxi
Copyright © 2009 by Information Age Publishing

In a worldwide society, changes in supply and demand in one Hemisphere result in changes in the economy in another. We cannot deny the fact that global interactions impact our lives moment by moment. Because of this inter-connectedness, our rapidly changing global community, and educational orientations, which focus on relevance to current commerce and technologies, and develop self-directed learners and life-long learners can take center stage for cultivating success (eSchool News, 2008; Partnership for 21st Century Skills, 2008). Career and technical education (CTE) or vocational education (Voc Ed) has exactly this critical role in the Digital Age. Yet how will we continue to navigate our way successfully?

While having roots in agricultural field and championing of the apprenticeship system of education, CTE's diverse, skills-focused educational field has a long history that continues to profoundly impact humanity's livelihood and education. In addition, partly due to its ability to adapt quickly to changing economic, industrial, and socioeconomic demands, it has continued to be a leader in regards to educational *innovation*.

When one considers the need to successfully and simultaneously lead the way in the educational realm, key phrases related to vocations and careers emerge such as:

Think Outside of the Box,
Keep Up with Technology
Keep Your Options Open
Re-Invent Your Career Opportunities

Whether discussing in formal and informal education, CTE as a whole has proactively confronted critical challenges such as

- Surviving fluctuating and changing economic needs,
- Integration of new technologies into traditional and new careers,
- Providing career flexibility (enabling adults to retrain for multiple successive careers), and
- Developing new instructional strategies, and options for study.

With rapid technological, global change, the standard of our world, future educational efforts need the capability to embrace even more radical and frequent transformations. This book, *Building Workforce Competencies in Career and Technical Education,* provides a powerful experience and resource for educators across many grade levels and content areas to be able to do exactly that by "Building upon the past, to meet the future."

AUDIENCE AND USES OF THE BOOK

The beginning chapters of this volume provide a compelling platform of the historical, theoretical and philosophical foundations of the book, while the second section covers a one-of-a-kind detailed discussion of critical topics in the history and practice of vocational education. These critical topics range from global perspectives of CTE, to e-learning, instructional perspectives to program planning, foundations in training to work ethics. The volume read as a whole volume provides a foundational introduction to the history and breadth of this vast field.

Building Workforce Competencies in Career and Technical Education can be used in several ways and for several purposes. While it was primarily designed with CTE instructors who are pursuing a program of personal and professional development in mind, it can also be used in many other settings and applications. Teachers of CTE can use this book to ensure competency in the specialty of the foundations and global applications of the field for their formal and informal development. While some may be engaged in in-service, others may be seeking a resource for self-directed study or lifelong learning in the field. In addition, the book provides a valuable balance of practical and academic perspectives and writing so that it can also be used as a text for foundation courses in vocational education. Finally, the comprehensive scope of the text serves the needs of both new and experienced professionals and academics in the field and will no doubt provide rich findings upon multiple readings.

OVERVIEW

The historical section of this volume begins with an eye-opening and comprehensive discussion of *The History of Vocational Education Up To 1850 and a Rationale for Work* in Chapter 1. Much more than a chronology of the history of the field, we provide a thought provoking analysis of the development and evolution of the meaning of work for humankind and its interrelationship with vocational education. Across geographies, political, religious and cultural realms, the reader gains a multi-faceted perspective of the breadth and depth of humankind's understanding and need for work and the related training and learning that developed to support those needs. This chapter does us a great service to a richer understanding of the CTE field by interweaving the story with the history of vocational education, teaching, learning and the greater questions of humanity. From Egypt to Europe, the Chaldeans to the Romans, it includes vignettes of the contributions of individuals such as Luther, Comenius, Locke, Rousseau, Pestalozzi and Della Vos, to name a few. In addition, as the chapter traces the relationship of vocational education to academic education and practical arts, a thesis emerges which provides new direction for vocational education or CTE. Knowing the breadth of development of the field in thought and practice is vital in guiding practitioners, administrators, scholars, lawmakers and students in continuing to shape the future.

Chapter 2, *Principles and Philosophy of Career and Technical Education and Federal Funding*, is a vital contribution to the literature in providing a concise presentation of two critical themes in career and technical education—principles and funding—and how the historical pathways of vocational education informs it today and provides a solid basis for building its future. This chapter, concentrates on the 19th and 20th century historical roots of the principles and philosophy of career and technical education. Starting with the principles advanced by Prosser in 1925, the work of Roberts in the 1970s and then Miller in the 1980s, one gets a close up look at the development of the field. In addition, this chapter provides a valuable examination of the critical federal funding acts and how they formatively shaped vocational education since the Morrill Act of 1862 through such familiar ones as the Manpower Act and the Perkins Act. Because of their impact on education and student lives, we effectively bring these vital legislations to life for the reader, surely this chapter is a must read.

Not shying away from the difficult questions, Chapter 3, *Historical Perspectives of the Different Components of Vocational Education,* takes on the task of tracing the historical roots of the varied components within the field of vocational education. From the more traditional manual training, manual arts, industrial arts or trade and industrial education, agriculture education, business education, health occupations education, family and consumer science (formerly known as home economics), vocational-industrial education, technology education, technical education and vocational education, CTE has a much broader scope than that to which many people are accustomed. By providing an understanding of the historical development of the different components of CTE, educators who have come from different contexts and meet different needs can broaden their understanding of this vast field. This chapter is another one that proves the richness and depth of this field and can swiftly and significantly impact the understanding of current and prospective CTE teachers who read it. Be ready for an "Aha" experience when you read Chapter 3.

With more than one fourth of high school students taking three or more CTE courses and 40 million adults participating in short-term postsecondary occupational training (U.S. Department of Education, 2006), Chapter 4, *Current Instructional Programs in Career and Technical Education* provides much needed information to understand the current state of the field. In

Partnership for 21st Century Skills. (2008). *21st century skills, education & competitiveness: A resource and policy report.* Retrieved September 15, 2008, from http://www.21stcenturyskills.org/documents/21st_century_skills_education_and_competitiveness_guide.pdf

U.S. Department of Education. (2006). *Career and technical education.* Retrieved September 20, 2008, from http://www.ed.gov/about/offices/list/ovae/pi/cte/index.html

CHAPTER 1

THE HISTORY OF VOCATIONAL EDUCATION UP TO 1850 AND A RATIONALE FOR WORK

Victor C. X. Wang
California State University, Long Beach

Kathleen P. King
Fordham University

The history of vocational education parallels the efforts of humanity from the Stone Age to modern civilization. Humans learned early in history that they could improve their lot by means of work (Roberts, 1965, p. 31). Some of the following information will give the reader some ideas of the growth of this system. Thus, knowing the history of vocational education gives the practitioner useful "feed-forward" signals about the present condition of the field (Gray & Herr, 1998, p. 5). David (1976) argued that the usefulness of history lies in its potential to explain why things are the way they are. Practitioners, scholars and students cannot achieve an objective under-

Building Workforce Competencies in Career and Technical Education, pages 1–16
Copyright © 2009 by Information Age Publishing
1

standing of the current status of vocational education without first looking into its history.

Another discussion in this chapter focuses on the rationale for work. It is commonly understood that one's rationale for work stems from people's economic, psychological, creative, expressive and social needs. This chapter also reveals an interesting discussion of how prominent leaders in the field view work and its relationship with career and technical education.

THE EARLY BEGINNING OF VOCATIONAL EDUCATION

Survival is the act to remain alive or continue in existence. This was the main concern during the Stone Age because most skills were learned as a result of the need for survival (Roberts, 1965). These skills were gained from watching one's elders at the campsite, and could consist of making an axe, building a fire, heating flint so it would chip in order to make a sharp instrument, and similar skills (Bennett, 1926). Learning is an act to gain knowledge or skill by observation. During the Stone Age period, there were no written documents and the way one could learn their survival skills was to observe someone performing them (Boyd, 1921).

A second type of learning is to gain knowledge or skill with language (Roberts, 1965). As humans progressed and language developed, instruction could be given and learning was accomplished by more than observation. The use of language allowed people to learn to improve one's ways to accomplish tasks. The ways that were productive and those that were unproductive could be documented and passed from generation to generation. Through this documentation, humans were destined to not continuously repeat earlier mistakes (Breasted, 1916).

Discoveries in Europe have indicated that humans used stone implements more than 50,000 years ago. This period lasted approximately 40,000 years. During this period, improved stone instruments were developed, wooden boats were constructed, animals were domesticated, pottery was made, and grain was grown (Erman & Blackman, 1927).

The following describes how ancient peoples in the Middle East Region and in Europe contributed to vocational education during the early part of human history. Thus some international perspectives can be formed for our readers. As Grey and Herr (1998) describe it, the history of vocational education gives the practitioner useful "feed-forward" signals about the present condition of the field. Indeed, so many practitioners teach in the field of vocational education now without knowing where it comes from.

The recorded history of the Egyptians might mark the Beginning of Civilization, or people with a higher social order. Humans continued to make progress through learning and work. About 6000 years ago the ancient

Egyptians began to develop a civilization based on scientific knowledge, government, and religion in the valleys of the Nile, Tigris, and the Euphrates rivers (Good, 1962). The Egyptians developed a form of picture writing called hieroglyphics. They also developed a paper called papyrus and started schools to teach scribes how to write and make the papyrus paper. The schools were of two types: (1) schools to teach reading and writing and (2) apprenticeships where the students learned on-the-job with an experienced scribe. During this time scribes were trained through apprenticeships, however, being a scribe was considered a noble occupation (West, 1931).

When humans began to reduce copper ore to copper metal, the Metal Age began. Roads were built, buildings were constructed of bricks, and fields were irrigated. They began to grow modern day grains like barley and wheat and use domesticated animals for work. The Nile dwellers learned how to measure time and established a calendar (Roberts, 1965).

The Persian Gulf from the northern borders of Arabia to the Mediterranean Sea was the first home of the people of Western Asia. The people of this area had reclaimed the marshes and produced barley and wheat long before 3000 B.C. During the Babylonian Age, which extended for 3200 B.C. to 2100 B.C., people constructed houses of brick and fashioned arts and crafts from stone and metal. Vocations became specialized and apprenticeship-training programs were organized and legalized (Roberts, 1965). The first historical reference to apprenticeship was in the Babylonian Code compiled about 2100 B.C. The Assyrians conquered the Babylonians, brought cotton and iron to the fertile land, and organized a postal service. However, they in turn were conquered in 612 B.C. by the Chaldeans (Roberts, 1965, p. 35). The Chaldeans conquered the Assyrians in 612 B.C. Under their influence, commerce and business flourished, religion and literature were cultured and notable progress was made in the science of astronomy (Erman & Blackman, 1927, p. 198). The Persians came into prominence in approximately 561 B.C. They maintained an organization of government controlled by one man. The farmland was divided into large tracts and held by powerful landowners. Silver and gold were coined into money and excellent roads were maintained. The Persian Empire, which lasted until about 330 B.C., has provided documents which have enabled present-day humans to read the cuneiform inscriptions of Western Asia (Breasted, 1916, p. 137).

Ancient Jews recognized the value of education. They felt that everyone should possess skill in a manual trade so that they could contribute to the society rather than become a parasite, which is dangerous to any community. Jewish law placed the duty of teaching a son a trade upon the parents (Breasted, 1916). The fundamental focus of ancient Jewish education was religion. Religious teaching was known as the Law. Next to instruction in the Law, instruction in vocations was of high esteem. Children were taught the Law and to follow it. The father taught each of his sons a trade, usually the trade he followed. Boys attended school in the morning, which were taught by rabbis and worked with their father in the afternoon. This was a similar format to our current cooperative program (Roberts, 1965).

Education in both Athens and Sparta was for the purpose of training both strong and courageous soldiers and citizens. The chief objective of education in Sparta was strength, courage, endurance, patriotism, and obedience (Roberts, 1965, p. 37). During the early Greek days, handicraft occupied a place of respect, but in later times, the work of handicraftsmen was designated as merely mechanical and was frowned upon. A person with callused hands was scorned (Roberts, 1965, p. 38). Apprenticeship instruction was approved for the lower class. Boys were taught drawing quite similar to the way orators, lawyers, physicians, and cooks were trained (Seybolt, 1917, pp. 91–92). The Romans were a practical and conservative people. They were especially noted for their codes of law and plans for public administration. Their civilization, much of which was borrowed from the Greeks, has had a strong influence on present day civilization (Roberts, 1965).

Early Roman education was carried on in the family. The father provided a practical education for his sons. The sons were taken to the fields and to the forums where they learned by observation and participation. In terms of schooling, three distinct levels were provided: elementary, secondary and higher. Elementary covered reading, writing, conduct, and memorization of laws. Secondary covered literature in Latin and Greek, and Higher covered rhetoric, oratory, mathematics, music, history, and law. Public funds were used by the Romans to pay teachers of grammar and rhetoric from about 75 A.D. Most of the other funds for education were private funds.

With the fall of Rome in the fifth century, the influence of Roman culture declined, and the teaching in the schools became formal and superficial. This type of education began to have little appeal and by the sixth century most of the universities were closed. Western civilization at that time entered the Dark Ages of the medieval period. The Christian Monks devoted an excessive amount of care and attention to manual labor. Labor was required of everyone that was associated with the monasteries. St. Benedict (480–543) founded the order of the Benedictines at Monto Cassinor in Italy about 529. He made labor one of the cardinal principles of his rule. He felt that seven hours a day should be expended in labor and two hours per day should be used for reading. This reading was done from manuscripts since books were not printed until about 1450. Scribe work was accepted as equivalent to out-of-doors work, so copying manuscripts become a favored occupation with the monks. Benedictines drained marshes, built roads and bridges and introduced new methods of farming. The Benedictines' enthusiasm carried them north of the Alps. Germany was filled with monasteries, which became centers of civilization. The Benedictines became the civilization of the region (Roberts, 1965). Monastic schools attracted men both young and old, who sought an opportunity for a life of reflection and study. Thus the monasteries came to be the schools for teaching, the place of professional training, the universities of research, the only publishers of books, and "the only libraries for the preservation of learning; they produced the only scholars; they were the sole educational institution of this period."

The transition from medieval to modern times, which occurred in the 14th and 15th centuries, is known as the Italian Renaissance. One phase of the transition, the scholarly phase, is referred to as the "Revival of Learning." This revival was a return to the ancient literature of the Greeks and Romans that had been discarded at the beginning of the Dark Ages (Roberts, 1965). The invention and early development of the art of printing, and the Protestant Reformation with its center in Germany, beginning early in the 16th century, unfolded new educational possibilities and put new life into teaching methods. This new instruction was based upon two fundamental ideas: (1) sense impression is the basis for thought and consequently of knowledge and (2) the support of manual arts training with "learning by doing."

HISTORIC FIGURES WHO HELPED SHAPE VOCATIONAL EDUCATION

Many of the present-day views on vocational education still reflect the insights and philosophies of early historic leaders in the field. It is these historic leaders who helped shape vocational education. Their influences are still felt to this day. If you have never heard of these historic figures, this is a good opportunity to study their ideas and philosophies that offered the formative directions for vocational education throughout our history. Gordon (2003) argued that some of their philosophies of vocational education encompassed enduring ideas and concepts that have transcended the ravages of time (p. 34).

Martin Luther (1483–1546) objected to the system used by the Monastic school. He compared them to prisons. He indicated that the boy was like a "bird in a dark cage" or like "a young tree required to grow in a flower pot." Luther felt that schooling should be given to "all people, noble and common, rich and poor, and it should include both boys and girls." Schooling should be compulsory and it should be held two hours per day and arranged so those older children could carry on the ordinary economic duties of life uninterruptedly. Luther advocated that the curriculum should include Latin, Greek, Hebrew, logic, mathematics, music, history and science (Monroe, 1905, pp. 410–412).

Rabelais (1494–1553) also disagreed with the way that the churches and schools were being conducted. Rabelais would approach knowledge through the use of objects and the observation of processes (Hodgson, 1908). His ideals were later brought out by Montaigne, Locke, and Rousseau.

Francis Bacon (1561–1626) felt that new learning could be obtained from nature and the arts of daily life. Bacon felt that to learn new things one must go straight to nature and learn through the senses. He held that all knowledge must be obtained by a careful and unprejudiced induction from facts, hence the importance of the experiment. Bacon's philosophy of realism gave support for applied science in our schools (Manzo, 2006).

John Amos Comenius (1592–1670) agreed with Rabelais in regard to the combination of words and things, which should be integrated in instruction. He would have children learn "as much as possible, not from books, but from the book of nature, from heaven and earth, from oaks and beeches." He also believed the learning should be pleasant with the learner. He felt that both sexes should be sent to school. He felt that the schools should be divided as follows: (a) infant school, (b) Elementary, (d) Secondary School, (e) University. Comenius has been called the "father of modern pedagogy" because he formulated principles and methods of instruction that were in harmony with the main current of pedagogical development (Comenius, n.d.).

John Locke (1632–1704) became a chief proponent of the idea that education should fit a boy for practical life, whether it be a trade or a profession (Fieser & Dowden, 2007). In 1697 when he was a commissioner of trade and plantations, he advocated that a system of "working schools" for all pauper children between three and 14 years of age should be available to teach spinning and knitting or some other part of the woolen manufacture. Locke advocated the learning of manual trades because (a) they afford good physical exercise, (b) the skill gained is worth having-it may be useful, and (c) they provide diversions or recreations.

Jean Jacques Rousseau (1712–1778) was the author of *The Social Contract* (Carrin, 2006), which has been blamed for the French Revolution (Mandler, 2007). He also authored *Emile,* which is said to have caused the author to flee from France to avoid arrest. This book is also said to have broken down the walls of educational formalism and initiated a new approach in education in which the student or child is the center of teaching. Rousseau believed profoundly that experience is the best teacher and he felt that everything possible should be taught by actions and that words should only be used for those things that cannot be taught by actions. Rousseau's statements concerning the value of the manual arts in education placed him ahead of his predecessors and many of those who came after him. His recognition of the fact that the manual arts may be a means of mental training marked the beginning of a new era in education. It prepared the way for the education methods of Pestalozzi and those who followed.

In the study of manual arts, **John Henry Pestalozzi** (1746–1827) is referred to as the "father of manual training." Pestalozzi was impressed by the writing of Rousseau. He originally studied the ministry, then began a study of law, but settled for the quiet life of a farm in Birr, Switzerland where he attempted to teach a group of poor children how to farm. The farming operation was not a financial success and he had to abandon it. On the other hand, the education of the children was successful. He went on to other areas of hands-on instruction. The instruction always seemed to be successful. Pestalozzi felt there were two ways to instruct: (1) from things to words and (2) from words to things. He used the first method. He was never in a hurry for the students to study books. He always wanted them to become actively involved in their learning by hands-on experiences so that the written material would have greater meaning. He also believed that children in school should learn to work not only because of the economic value of skill and the habit of labor, but because this experience gives sense-impressions which like the study of objects, becomes the basis of knowledge (Beyer, 2004, p. 3).

Just as Pestalozzi was the new and vital force in the realm of educational philosophy and methods during the early part of the 19th century, **Phillip Emanuel Von Fellenberg** (1771–1844) was the force in practical school organization and administration during the same period (Beyer, 2004). Von Fellenberg believed in the separation of people in different social levels and organized a series of schools and classes for these various social levels at Hofwyl, Switzerland beginning in 1800. The educational establishment at Hofwyl attracted more attention and exerted a wider influence than any one institution in Europe or America at that time. It was visited and studied by many educators and statesmen. It especially attracted an American, William C. Woodbridge; editor of the *American Annals of Education*, which featured many issues "Sketches of Hofwyl" which brought to American educators a wealth of information concerning this noble experiment in education. These ideas influenced the development in vocational education in the United States. Von Fellenberg demonstrated the importance of school organization and business management in the operation of a school system (Beyer, 2004). The chief characteristic of this system was manual labor. Von Fellenberg proved that manual activities, when properly organized and directed; could contribute both financially and educationally to the success of the student and the school system.

Victor Della Vos and his shop instructors developed a new system to teach manual trades in 1867. He developed a system where the students could learn entry-level skills for a craft or trade in a school setting (Anderson, 1926). The following were crucial for him to develop this system:

- Each art or distinct type of work was required to have its own separate instruction shop; e.g., joinery, woodturning, blacksmithing, locksmithing, etc.
- Each shop was equipped with as many working places and sets of tools as there were pupils to receive the instruction at one time.
- The courses or models were arranged according to the increasing difficulty of the exercises involved, and were given to the pupils in strict succession as arranged.
- All models were made from drawings. Copies of each drawing were supplied in sufficient number to provide one for each member of a class.
- The drawings were made by the pupil in the class for elementary drawing, under the direction of the teacher of drawing with whom the manager of the shops came to an agreement concerning the various details.
- Pupils were not allowed to begin a new model until they had acceptably completed the previous model in the course.
- First exercises were accepted if dimensions were approximately correct; later exercises were required to be more exact according to the dimensions.
- Every teacher was required to possess more knowledge and skill of the specialty taught than were necessary to merely perform the exercises in the course of instruction. The instructor must also keep in practice so that demonstrations to students indicate a high level of skill.

Victor Della Vos exhibited his system of instruction at the Centennial Exposition in Philadelphia in 1876. As a result of this presentation, The School of Mechanic Arts was opened in connection with the Massachusetts Institute of Technology in Boston. Also, the St. Louis Manual Training School, in St. Louis, Missouri, adopted the principles of his system in 1880. These schools gave Manual Training in the high school, an impetus that spread over the United States in a short period of time (Schenck et al., 1984).

A RATIONALE FOR EDUCATION FOR WORK

Now that we have knowledge of how vocational education came into being and who helped shape it during the early part of human history, it is time to study the rationale for education and for work. Marx defined work as a process going on between humans and nature, a process in which humans, through their own activities, initiate, regulate, and control the material reactions between themselves and nature. (as cited in Wang, 2006, p. 39)

According to Marx (1890/1929), work produces surplus value. Wang (2006) interprets this surplus value as "added value" in vocational education and training. As noted by Gordon (2003, p. 247), career and technical education generally has focused on helping people to understand the relationship between education and work and to acquire employment skills. People often ask the question, "Why education for work?" There are a number of reasons to educate for work in a modern society. In exploring why people work, Wenrich, Wenrich and Galloway (1988) recognized that:

People Need to Work: There is ample evidence that people need to work and need assistance in learning to work and to appreciate work, and Career and Technical Education is one phase of educating individuals for work.

Perceptions of Work: Each of us has a different perception of work depending upon our experiences. It may be a joy or a burden depending upon our idea about its place in our lives.

Work vs. Leisure/Vocation vs. Avocation: What is work for one person may be leisure or play for another or vice versa. For example, for a golfing professional, golf is work, but for an editor of a magazine, golf is play or leisure.

Work Through the Ages: Work has changed through the ages. For example, in early Christianity, work was viewed as punishment laid on man by God. The ancient Hebrews and Greeks thought of work as painful drudgery. During the Reformation Age work was thought of as the right and moral thing to do. Later, the Puritan Work Ethic promoted work as good and leisure or idleness as bad. (as cited in Petty & Brewer, 2005, pp. 95–98)

People work because they need to work: For income, for activity, for self-respect and the respect of others, for social contacts and participation, and to express themselves creatively (Friedmann & Havighurst, 1954).

Work and Leisure: The shift from a labor intensive to a machine or robotic led society should provide more time for leisure. Society in America has gone from a 60-hour workweek to a 32–40 hour workweek (Friedmann & Havighurst, 1954).

Developing Work Ethic: Experiences must be provided in elementary, secondary, and post secondary education to help individuals understand and appreciate the value of work and its functions in life and to help them develop their potential to become satisfied workers.

Individuals Want to Work: The old assumption that "people do not want to work," has not proved to be true. Individuals enjoy doing those things they are good at. This supports the idea that individuals need vocational education in order to become skilled in an area they would like to pursue, whether for work or for pleasure.

Equal Educational Opportunity: with public education in a democratic society, career and technical education should be available to all secondary and postsecondary students. This is an important part of the process of developing the individual's potential for work.

Relationship of Work and Education: As noted by Wenrich, Wenrich and Galloway (1988, p. 16), primitive people did not need much formal education in order to work. Even in the early history of the nation (USA), most people learned to work by associating with experienced workers (apprenticeship). With the advent of the industrial revolution and the shift to an industrialized society, more formal education was necessary to work. The technological, or information society is requiring even more formal or technical education. Most individuals participate in formal education based on the expectation that it adds quality to their life. Fewer than 100 years ago in the United States, formal education for most individuals ended at the eighth grade. Economics was one of the main reasons why parents did not keep their children in school: it was not seen as increasing one's ability to earn money. Only when the promise of better-paying jobs was connected to more education did attending school longer become a motivating factor in education.

Gray and Herr (1998) defined workforce education (please note workforce education is the most current name for vocational education. Vocational education has had different names during different parts of human history) as follows:

> Workforce education is that form of pedagogy that is provided at the pre-baccalaureate level by education institutions, by private business and industry, or by government-sponsored, community-based organizations where the objective is to increase individual opportunity in the labor market or to solve human performance problems in the workforce. (p. 4)

They also suggested that workforce education has two functions: (a), Promote individual opportunity by making students more competitive in the labor force, and (b), Make a nation economically strong and firms internationally competitive by solving human performance problems of incumbent workers.

VOCATIONAL EDUCATION AND LIBERAL EDUCATION

Vocational ("Vocational Education," 2007) or career and technical education is education specifically designed to prepare one to enter into or advance in a specific vocation or career. Liberal education ("Liberal Arts," 2007) should assist persons to follow a number of vocations or careers. However, it does not provide them with specific skills for these vocations or careers. Instead, a liberal education prepares more for living or life in general rather than for work. Liberal education includes such disciplines as mathematics, physical sciences, natural sciences, biological sciences, and rhetoric, history, languages, and philosophy. Note that a person who works in practicing mathematics is making a vocational or career use of their education. The same can be true of virtually all subjects.

Evans and Herr (1978) wrote that some objectives of career and technical education that may be considered include:

- Meeting the manpower needs of society,
- Increasing the options available to individuals, and
- Providing a motivating force to enhance all types of learning.

All other objectives of career and technical education may revolve around the above three basic objectives.

Meeting the Manpower Needs of Society: industry, government, the schools, and indeed all institutions of society require trained people if they are to survive. As Evans and Herr (1978) noted, while the needs of family are almost invariably ignored in statements of needs for workers, society is gradually recognizing that consumer education and homemaking education of high quality are essential to the survival of the family as well. As we live in this Information Age and knowledge society, the need for trained workers has become more pronounced.

Career and Technical Education can broaden the options of an individual: an individual can pursue a career and technical education, but will not necessarily be limited to that specific vocation or career. Many individuals who pursue a vocational curriculum take general education courses to broaden their horizons. They may also learn skills that can transfer to other work areas. For example, an individual may major in auto mechanics but obtain competencies and obtain employment as a mechanical maintenance person in an industrial plant (Evans & Herr, 1978).

Career and Technical Education increases options: for an individual who attends secondary and post secondary schools, career and technical education provides skills which will give individuals more options than if they pursued a liberal education (Evans & Herr, 1978).

John Dewey and Occupational Education: John Dewey, America's first philosopher/educator, felt that occupations should be used as vehicles of instruction in elementary and secondary education. Dewey's philosophy was based upon the idea of a total organism interacting with its environment. He conceived of the mind as the process by which organisms and environment become integrated. He believed that occupations excite the interest of the student and cause them to be better students (Dewey, 1944, 1966). Dewey opposed vocational education which was limited only to the acquisition of job skills. He believed that the underlying principles of the work processes and social significance of work must be included. He further believed that through vocational studies, culture might be made truly vital for many students.

NEED FOR CAREER AND TECHNICAL EDUCATION

Wenrich, Wenrich and Galloway (1988) make the point that career and technical Education as a responsibility of the public school system can be justified only if it is planned and organized so as to achieve its objectives to the maximum degree possible. The following will address the objectives as stated earlier:

Needs for Trained Personnel: Educators must be knowledgeable about the personnel needs within their service area in order to ascertain whether the programs they implement and conduct actually serve these needs. Continual research is needed in order to determine the needs and the fulfillment of those needs by the respective career and technical programs. Programs may need to be implemented, revised, or closed as needs change in the program service area.

Individual Options: The opportunity to choose from a number of alternatives is an important concept in a democratic society and in education. Education should provide for these alternatives. Options may include choices from among different occupations, kinds and levels of education, income, employment and many other areas (Evans & Herr, 1978).

Project Talent, a study of students in United States' high schools in 1966 by Flanagan and Cooley, found that the general curriculum enrolled 25% of the students, yet it produced 76% of the high school dropouts. The study also showed that graduates of the general curriculum ranked behind the college preparatory and the vocational graduates on nearly every measure of success including:

- Proportion who go on to college
- Annual earnings
- Job satisfaction
- Length and frequency of unemployment.

Individual options are increased when:

- A larger variety of specialized career and technical programs are available from which individuals may choose.
- Career and technical programs are offered by public schools, as opposed to the vocational training provided by employers.

- High school programs are broadened so that youth are prepared for clusters of occupations, thereby giving greater flexibility in the labor market.
- Adult programs are readily available for the upgrading and retraining of employed person.
- Job placement services are provided by the schools to assist youth in finding suitable employment.

Learning Enhancer: Career and technical education can serve as a motivating force to enhance all types of learning. Employment-bound youth in secondary and post secondary programs can be challenged by the occupation of their choice and the job-entry requirements. Subject areas take on new meaning when a student begins studying an occupation and discovers they are necessary for satisfactory completion of the program. Subject areas such as mathematics, science, reading, writing, and spelling suddenly take on new meaning since the student can now see relevance in pursuing them.

CAREER AND TECHNICAL EDUCATION VERSUS PRACTICAL ARTS EDUCATION

Perhaps it is safe to say that it is Wenrich, Wenrich and Galloway (1988) who provided the similarities and differences of career and technical education and practical arts education. Their insights are still widely cited today. Wenrich, Wenrich and Galloway (1988) recognize that:

> Career and technical education and practical arts education are special subject matter areas in which applied instruction is given. That is to say that a lot of hands-on or applied learning takes place where psychomotor skills are involved. Career and technical education is job specific in order to produce students with job entry skills. Much time is devoted to practice and application of job skills needed for the occupation. Practical arts is skill-oriented instruction, however, the purpose of this training is more for consumer knowledge than for job entry. It is more for a vocational use rather than for vocational use. For that reason, practical arts education is considered general education. That is, it is useful for anyone to take no matter what their career ambitions are. Practical arts could be considered pre-vocational since many students who enroll in practical arts decide to follow one of the career and technical areas as a result of their hands-on experiences with the psychomotor skills. (pp. 5–6)

CAREER AND TECHNICAL EDUCATION
AND DROPOUT PREVENTION

Educators and parents are always concerned with the large number of youth who leave school before completing the usual 12 grades of secondary education. Studies show that from 30 to 40% of the youth who enter the first grade drop out before the completion of high school. The junior high school, grades 8, 9, and 10, show an unusually large number of dropouts. The larger schools with a greater variety of course offerings have a higher holding power than the smaller schools.

Some advocate that more students would complete the secondary school if they felt that the offerings were more interesting and relevant. Many suggest that practical arts and career and technical education could decrease the dropout rate. However, practical arts and career and technical education cannot effect much of a change unless the students enroll in the programs. Many students drop out of school before they ever enroll in practical arts and career and technical education courses. Since the "Nation At Risk" report (National Commission on Excellence in Education, 1983) was released in the early 1980s many school districts have raised graduation requirements for the non-practical courses, math, science, reading and English. This change in requirements is making it difficult for secondary students to enroll in practical arts or career and technical education courses. Since the 1976 Vocational Education Amendments were passed, the practical arts and career and technical education teacher has been involved with a number of "mainstreamed" disadvantaged and handicapped students some of whom may have difficulty in completing the work for the program. This could have an influence on the dropout rate of vocational students.

CONCLUSION

A closer examination of the history of vocational education and the rationale for work reveals that vocational education has been developed to meet the three objectives of vocational education in any form of society. The workforce needs of any society are even greater today than any previous part of human history as human beings have entered the so-called Information Age and globalization. No longer can we view vocational education just as education for work! It is also education for life, not just the preparation for life. During the primitive era, little formal education was needed for work; now for the full range of work much more formal education is needed in order to work. The relationship between vocational education and work is getting closer and closer given the nature of our technological society. The influences advanced by those early vocational educators in the field are still being felt today. In fact, their principles and philosophies will continue to guide the field of career and technical education into the future. Although federal legislation indicated that vocational instruction is designed to enable people to succeed in occupations requiring less than a baccalaureate degree, evidence shows many vocational education students are college bound students today. In other words, the distinction between vocational education and academic education is not that clear. At the same time to integrate vocational education in academic education does seem to be a viable option.

REFERENCES

Anderson, L. F. (1926). *History of manual and industrial school education.* New York: Appleton-Century-Crofts.

Bennett, C. A. (1926). *History of manual and industrial education up to 1870.* Peoria: Manual Arts.

Beyer, C. K. (2004). Manual and industrial education for Hawaiians during the 19th century. *Hawaiian Journal of History, 38,* 1–34.

Boyd, W. (1921). *The history of Western education.* London: Black.

Breasted, J. H. (1916). *Ancient times, A history of the early world.* New York: Ginn.

Carrin, G. J. (2006). Rousseau's "social contract": Contracting ahead of its time? [Review of the book The social contract]. *Bulletin of the World Health Organization, 84*(11), 917–918.

Comenius Foundation. (n.d.) *About John Amos Comenius.* Retrieved May 3, 2007, from http://www.comeniusfoundation.org/comenius.htm

David, H. (1976). *Education manpower policy.* Paper presented at the Bicentennial conference sponsored by the National Advisory Counsel on Vocational Education. Minneapolis, MN.

Dewey, J. (1944). Challenge to liberal thought. *Fortune, 30*(2), 155–190.

Dewey, J. (1966). *Democracy and education.* New York: The Free Press.

Encyclopedia Britannica online. (2007). *Liberal arts.* Retrieved January 7, 2007, from http://www.britannica.com/eb/article-9048113/liberal-arts

Encyclopedia Britannica online. (2007). *Vocational education.* Retrieved January 8, 2007, from http://www.britannica.com/eb/article-9075632/vocational-education

Erman, A., & Blackman, A. (1927). *The literature of the ancient Egyptians.* New York: Dutton.

Evans, R. N., & Herr, E. L. (1978). *Foundations of vocational education.* New York: Macmillan.

Fieser, J., & Dowden, B. (Eds.). (2007). *Educational writings.* Retrieved May 2, 2007, from http://www.utm.edu/research/iep/l/locke.htm#Educational%20Writings.

Flanagan, J. C., & Cooley, W. W. (1966). *Project talent: One-year follow-up studies.* PA: University of Pittsburgh.

Friemann, E. A., & Havighurst, R. J. (1954). *The meaning of work and retirement.* University of Chicago Press.

Good, H. G. (1962). *A history of Western education.* New York: Macmillan.

Gordon, H. R.D. (2003). The *history and growth of vocational education in America.* Long Grove, IL: Waveland Press.

Gray, K. C., & Herr, E. L. (1998). *Workforce education.* Boston: Allyn and Bacon.

Hodgson, G. (1908). *Studies in French education from Rabelais to Rousseau.* London: Cambridge University Press.

Mandler, P. (2007). The idea of the self: Thought and experience in Western Europe since the seventeenth century. *American Historical Review, 112*(2), 575–576.

Manzo, S. (2006). Francis Bacon: Freedom, authority and science. *British Journal for the History of Philosophy, 14*(2), 245–273.

Marx, K. (1929). *Capital: A critique of political economy. The process of capitalist production* (E. Paul & C. Paul, Trans). New York: International. (Original work published in 1890)

Monroe, P. (1905). *A textbook in the history of education.* NY: Macmillan.

National Commission on Excellence in Education. (1983). *A nation at risk: The imperative for reform.* Washington, D. C.: Author. (ERIC Document Reproduction Service No. ED 251 622)

Petty, G. C., & Brewer, E. W. (2005). Perspectives of a healthy work ethic in a 21st-century international community. *International Journal of Vocational Education and Training, 13*(1), 93–104.

Roberts, R. W. (1965). *Vocational and practical arts education* (2nd, ed.). New York: Harper and Row Publishers.

Seybolt, R. F. (1917). *Apprenticeship and apprenticeship education in colonial New England and New York,* Contributions to education, No. 85, Bureau of Publications. New York: Columbia University.

Schenck, J. P., & Others. (1984). *The life and times of Victor Karlovich Della-Vos.* Washington, D. C.: Education Resources Information Center. (ERIC Document Reproduction Service No. ED297 137) Retrieved May 3, 2007, from http://eric.ed.gov/ERICWebPortal/custom/portlets/recordDetails/detailmini.jsp?_nfpb=true&_&ERICExtSearch_SearchValue_0=ED297137&ERICExtSearch_SearchType_0=eric_accno&accno=ED297137

Wang, V. C. X. (2006). A Chinese work ethic in a global community. *International Journal of Vocational Education and Training, 14*(1), 39–52.

Wenrich, R. C., Wenrich, J. W., & Galloway, J. D. (1988). *Administration of vocational education.* Homewood, IL: American Technical.

West, W. M. (1931). *The story of man's early progress.* Boston: Allyn & Bacon.

CHAPTER 2

PRINCIPLES AND PHILOSOPHY OF CAREER AND TECHNICAL EDUCATION AND FEDERAL FUNDING FOR VOCATIONAL EDUCATION UP TO THE PRESENT

Victor C. X. Wang
California State University, Long Beach

Kathleen P. King
Fordham University

The principles of career and technical education emerged as vocational education was beginning in the late 19th and early 20th centuries. The original principles were a reflection of circumstances, thinking and needs specific to a time in history (Snedden, 1920). The fundamental concepts behind these principles were influential in shaping the early development of career and technical education. In most instances, these concepts are still evident in contemporary restatements of principles of career and technical educa-

Building Workforce Competencies in Career and Technical Education, pages 17–41

tion. However, in some cases the concepts have been revised or dropped. The first person to have advanced the principles of career and technical education was Dr. Charles Prosser. Prosser, the first National Director of Vocational Education, developed and publicized 16 theorems in the early days of vocational education in the United States. It is believed that Prosser also helped draft federal legislation to recognize and fund vocational education (Foster, 1997). Federal funding was available for vocational education as early as 1862 when the Morrill Act supported agriculture, engineering and military science in land-grant colleges (Allen, 1950, p. 72). Subsequently, federal legislation stimulated vocational education in many different ways. Vocational education was developed and shaped largely due to favorable guiding principles and philosophy and federal support.

PRINCIPLES AND PHILOSOPHY OF CAREER AND TECHNICAL EDUCATION

Prosser (1925) advanced these theorems as a basis for sound and successful programs of vocational education, but he did not classify the theorems as he advanced them. The language in these theorems has been changed to reflect 21st century sensibilities, but the meaning has not been changed. Prosser's Theorems (Prosser & Allen, 1925) include:

1. Career and technical education will be efficient in proportion as the environment in which the learners are trained is a replica of the environment in which they must subsequently work.
2. Effective career and technical training can only be given where the training is carried on in the same way with the same operations, the same tools and the same equipment as in the occupation itself.
3. Career and technical education will be effective in proportion as it trains the individual directly and specifically in the thinking habits and the manipulative habits required in the occupation itself.
4. Career and technical education will be effective in proportion as it will enable individuals to capitalize their interest, aptitudes, and intrinsic intelligence to the highest possible degree.
5. Effective career and technical education for any profession, calling, trade, occupation or job can only be given to the selected group of individuals who need it, want it and are able to profit by it.
6. Career and technical training will be effective in proportion as the specific training experiences for forming right habits of doing and thinking are repeated to the point that the habits developed are those of the finished skills necessary for gainful employment.

7. Career and technical education will be effective in proportion as the instructors have had successful experience in the application of skills and knowledge to the operations and processes they undertake to teach.

8. For every occupation there is a minimum of productive ability, which an individual must possess in order to secure or retain employment in that occupation. If career and technical education is not carried to that point with an individual, it is neither personally nor socially effective.

9. Providers of career and technical education must recognize conditions as they are and must train individuals to meet the demands of the "market" even though it may be true that more efficient ways of conducting the occupation may be known and those better working conditions.

10. The effective establishment of process habits in any learner will be secured in proportion as the training is given on actual jobs and not on exercises or pseudo jobs.

11. The only reliable source of content for specific training in an occupation is in the experiences of masters of that occupation.

12. For every occupation there is a body of content, which is peculiar to that occupation and which has practically no functioning value in any other occupation.

13. Career and technical education will render efficient social service in proportion as it meets the specific training needs of any group at the time that they need it and in such a way that they can most effectively profit by the instruction.

14. Career and technical education will be socially efficient in its methods of instruction and in its personal relations with learners; it takes into consideration the particular characteristics of any particular group, which it serves.

15. The administration of career and technical education will be efficient in proportion as it is elastic and fluid rather than rigid and standardized.

16. While every reasonable effort should be made to reduce per capita costs, there is a minimum below which effective career and technical education cannot be given, and if this minimum of per capita cost is not available for a course or a program, the program should not be attempted.

Prosser believed that the more nearly a career and technical program can approach the full realization of these theorems in its operation, the higher the quality of the program. Any attempt to disregard any of these basic and fundamental concepts can only result in undermining and destroying career and technical education for the citizens of the community. Prosser's views were criticized for lacking the qualities of a formal philosophic system (Miller & Gregson, 1999). Rojewski (2002) indicated that Prosser's major goal of school was not individual fulfillment but meeting the manpower needs of society. Others such as Lewis (1998) criticized Prosser's views on vocational education as being class-based and tracking certain segments of society—based on race, class, and gender—into second-class occupations and second-class citizenship. Prosser's views are in striking contrast with Dewey's in that Dewey believed that the principal goal of public education was to meet individual needs for personal fulfillment and preparation for life. Rojewski (2002) cited Hyslop-Margison by noting:

> Dewey rejected the image of students as passive individuals controlled by market economy forces and existentially limited by inherently proscribed intellectual capacities. In his view, students were active pursuers and constructors of knowledge, living and working in a world of dynamic social being. (Hyslon-Margison, 2000, p. 25)

As time goes on, other leaders in the field of vocational education and training have created different principles of vocational education. For example, Roberts (1971) further developed and classified the principles into three broad categories: Organization, Administration, and Instruction.

Organization: Principles of organization are concerned with definitions, functions, needs and procedures. They may be used to assist in arriving at decisions concerning the advisability of establishing programs of career and technical education.

- Federal aid for career and technical education is justified as a means of stimulating the further development of career and technical education and as a device for maintaining acceptable standards in it.
- The need for career and technical education in a specific area should be determined from the results of a community survey.
- Occupational information and guidance should be provided for career and technical students.

Administration: Career and technical and practical arts education present some problems of administration more complex than those of academic subjects. The use of federal funds causes some of the problems. Robert's principles for administration include:

- Representative laypersons should be appointed to boards of education concerned with the administration of career and technical education on federal, state, and local levels.

- Each state should maintain a complete program of career and technical and practical arts teacher education.
- Career and technical and practical arts educators should be technically competent and professionally qualified.
- Career and technical and practical arts education programs should be based on continuous research.

Instruction: Materials and methods of instruction in career and technical education and practical arts education differ from those of other educational areas, due to such factors as the interest and purpose of the learner, the demands of business and industry, the standards of achievement and performance, and the technological changes that are constantly occurring in a changing society.

- Career and technical instruction should be available for those who need, want, and can profit by it.
- The standards in career and technical education should be as high or higher than the accepted standards in the occupation concerned.
- Instructional programs in career and technical and practical arts education should be characterized by flexibility.
- Career and technical and practical arts instruction should include information and activities designed to protect and conserve human life.

Miller (1985) grouped the principles of career and technical education into three headings: People, Programs, and Processes as a matter of convenience. According to Miller (1985), these headings are arbitrary, although well-reasoned.

People: Miller (1985) reasoned that the individual is the focal point for the activities for career and technical education:

- Guidance is an essential component of career and technical education.
- Lifelong learning is promoted through career and technical education.
- The needs of the community are reflected by programs of career and technical education.
- Career and technical education is open to all.
- Placement in the next step is a responsibility of career and technical education.
- Elimination of sex bias and sex-role stereotyping is promoted through career and technical education.

- Individuals with special needs are served through career and technical education.
- Student organizations are an integral feature of career and technical education.
- Teachers of career and technical education are both professionally qualified and occupationally competent.
- A positive work ethic is promoted through career and technical education.

Programs: The distinguishing characteristics for these principles are that they emphasize instructional activities in career and technical education.

- The career awareness and pre-career and technical education components of career education complement career and technical education.
- Career and technical education is a part of the public system of comprehensive education.
- Curricula for career and technical education are derived from requirements in the world of work.
- Families of occupations are a basis for developing curricula for career and technical education at the secondary level.
- Innovation is stressed as a part of career and technical education.
- Persons are prepared for at least entry level jobs through career and technical education.
- Safety is paramount in career and technical education.
- Supervised occupational experience is provided through career and technical education.

Processes: Principles in the process group emphasize procedures that career and technical educators prefer in their efforts to effect change and improvement in career and technical education.

- Advice from the community is sought in providing programs of career and technical education.
- Articulation and coordination are central to the purposes of career and technical education.
- Evaluation is a continuous process in career and technical education.
- Follow-up is a vital extension of career and technical education.
- Federal legislation for career and technical education is a reflection of national priorities.
- Comprehensive planning is stressed in career and technical education.
- Research on a continuing basis is fundamental to the dynamics of career and technical education.

Many scholars and practitioners in the field have pointed out that the principles of career and technical education carry philosophical implications. The principles represent the preferred practices in career and technical education and may be characterized as representations of values held by career and technical educators. It is possible to translate the principles of career and technical education into a philosophy of career and technical education. The inductive process may be used to develop a philosophy from principles. Miller (1996) defined philosophy as making assumptions and speculations about the nature of human activity and the nature of the world...ultimately, philosophy becomes a conceptual framework for synthesis and evaluation because it helps vocational educators decide what should be and what should be different (p. xiii). It is this philosophy that has prompted vocational educators to answer the following questions:

- What is the nature of the learner?
- What is the role of the teacher?
- How do we decide what should be taught?
- What is the role of schooling in America?
- Who should pay for the schooling?

These questions can be used to inductively arrive at a philosophy for career and technical education. The principles of career and technical education can be used to provide responses to these issues. Philosophy provides a framework for thinking about career and technical education. It helps the educator sort out competing alternatives and provides a basis for a final course of action. Philosophy also provides guidelines for practice, contributing to decisions about program development, selection of learning activities, curriculums, goals, resource utilization, and identification of other essential needs and functions in career and technical education. Action without philosophical reflection leads to a mindless activism (Elias & Merriam, 2005, p. 4). Philosophies of teaching lead to meaningful practice.

Good principles and philosophies do guide the field of vocational education. However, these are not enough. For career and technical education to thrive, federal funding has played a major role. Rojewski (2002) noted that since the beginning of federal support for public vocational education, the federal government has been a predominant influence in determining the scope and direction of secondary, and to a lesser extent postsecondary, vocational and technical training. Without federal funding, career and technical education would not have been developed to this day. A glimpse of federal funding and federal legislation can provide our readers and learners information regarding what contributions federal funding has made to vocational education. Readers and learners can also find out in what ways federal legislation can enhance the three objectives of vocational education, especially the very first objective, "meet the manpower needs of society."

1862—Morrill Act

The Morrill Act gave Federal Support for the Agricultural and Mechanical Colleges, it (Land-Grant Colleges) (Allen, 1950) supported Colleges that offered instruction for Agriculture, Engineering and Military Science. Named for senator was Justin A. Morrill of Vermont who introduced the Morrill Act in 1857, but it failed to pass the Senate, reintroduced it in 1859, and it passed both houses of Congress. The bill was vetoed by President James Buchanan who said it was unconstitutional. The president feared the states would depend upon federal support for their own education systems (McClure, Chrisman & Mock, 1985). The bill was reintroduced in 1862 and it was supported by Senator Benjamin Wade who took advantage of national wartime concerns, saying it would be ideal to train officers and engineers. The bill was passed and signed into law by President Lincoln and resulted in the rapid expansion of agriculture and engineering schools. The bill became a keystone of higher education in the mid and far west. The principal objective was to develop schools to teach agriculture and mechanical arts. The bill enabled higher education to open to a broader public and improve agriculture technology. The concept of integrated academics was first identified. 30,000 acres of land was granted to states for each senator and representative in congress for the purpose of endowing colleges for agriculture and mechanical arts. 106 land grant colleges were established. As a result of the 1862 Morrill Act, Kansas State University was established in 1863. Kansas State Agricultural College developed a system of "industrials", in which shop work was more on the trade level in 1874. Victor Della Vos, from the Imperial Technical Institute in Moscow (Ham, 1990), exhibited at the Centennial Exposition in Philadelphia. The method of teaching mechanic arts was well received and it gave impetus to similar types of offerings in the U.S in 1876 (Schenck et al., 1984). The first manual training school in the U.S. was established in St. Louis, Missouri. by Calvin Woodward 1880. Col. Richard Tylden Auchtmuty founded the New York Trade School in 1881.

Hebrew Technical Institute was founded in New York City in 1883. The first manual training school to be supported by public expense was located in Baltimore in 1884. Hatch Act provided Federal Funds for state agriculture experiment stations in 1887. The second Morrill Act provided $15,000.00 annually for each of the land-grant colleges in 1890. In 1905, the Douglas Commission, led by Governor William L. Douglas of Massachusetts, investigated the need for trade training in specific areas. In 1914, a Presidential Commission authorized by the Congress was appointed to study national aid for vocational education. The summary of the commission indicated that there was a need for federal funding for Vocational Education.

1917—Smith-Hughes Act

Smith-Hughes Act was passed to provide federal support for Vocational Education. Funding began in 1918 with increments each year until 1926 (See Table 2.1):

The Smith Hughes Act of 1917 created a Federal Board for Vocational Education. It gave Federal Board control over state programs. The act designated funds given to states annually to promote programs in agriculture, trade and industry, and home economics. The passage of this act was the fruition of a long legislative campaign to secure federal aid for vocational education (Douglas, 1921, p. 293). It provided annual appropriations for (a) salaries to teachers, supervisors, and directors of vocational education areas—50/50 with states; (b) teacher preparation in areas of agriculture, home economics, and trade and industry; (c) support for activities of the Federal Board for Vocational Education. According to the general standards of this act, teacher training should be given only to those who had had adequate vocational experience in line of work they were preparing to teach (Douglas, 1921). Further, to prevent the undue slighting of any subject, it was specified that not less than 20% nor more than 60% of the quota of any state for training teachers should be spent for agriculture, for the trades and industries, and for home economics (Douglas, 1921, p. 297). The act mandated the creation of a State Board and it required a development of a state plan. In addition, it required annual reports of State System to the Federal Board. The act required states to designate 50/50 salaries for Vocational Education personnel

TABLE 2.1   Federal Support for Vocational Education (Smith-Hughes Act)

Year	Agriculture	Trade & Industrial and Home Education	Teacher Education
1918	$ 500,000.00	$500,000.00	$500,000.00
1919	$ 750,000.00	$ 750,000.00	$700,000.00
1920	$1,000,000.00	$1,000,000.00	$900,000.00
1921	$1,250,000.00	$1,250,000.00	$1,000,000.00
1922	$1,500,000.00	$1,500,000.00	$1,000,000.00
1923	$1,750,000.00	$1,750,000.00	$1,000,000.00
1924	$2,000,000.00	$2,000,000.00	$1,000,000.00
1925	$2,500,000.00	$2,500,000.00	$1,000,000.00
1926	$3,000,000.00	$3,000,000.00	$1,000,000.00

and cooperate with local schools to provide funds to support high quality instruction in vocational programs—facilities, equipment and materials. Federal funds had to be under public supervision and control. It required vocational training to be provided to persons who: (a) have selected a vocational area and desire preparation in it; (b) have already been employed and seek greater efficiency in that employment; (c) have accepted employment and wish to advance to positions of responsibility; (d) vocational education was to be less than college grade for persons over 14 years of age in day time training and over 16 who seek evening class training. Many of the vocational education issues addressed in the Smith-Hughes Act endure to this day. The three salient parts of the Smith-Hughes Act of 1917 that are worth noting may be summarized as follows:

- The Act provided an appropriation of $1.7 million for the year 1917–1918, with funding increasing at intervals to $7.2 million for 1925–1926.
- The Act also created a federal board for Vocational Education to administer the new law's provisions. The members included the Secretaries of Commerce, Agriculture and Labor, the Commissioner of Education and three appointed citizens.
- States were required to create state boards for vocational education, which would prepare a plan, to be approved by the federal board, for operation of state vocational education programs. The state or local community was required to match each dollar of federal money appropriated to the state.

After the Smith-Hughes Act was successfully implemented, Congress recognized a need for additional funds for vocational home economics and vocational agriculture. In 1929, the George Reed Act was passed.

In 1934, the George Ellzey Act replaced the George Reed Act and more appropriations were provided for vocational education. In 1937, the George Deen Act increased the vocational funding for Agriculture home economics and trade and industry and included new funding for distributive education. In 1940, vocational training was provided for war production workers and trained workers were to assist with the war effort. Time did not permit the schools to produce finished craftsmen and training was limited to job units that could be learned quickly. In 1946, the George Barden Act provided more funds for earlier areas of support and provided more flexibility in the use of these funds.

The 1958 National Defense Education Act amended the George Barden Act of 1946. Funds were used to train highly skilled technicians or occupations necessary for national defense. The act was passed as a result of Russia launching Sputnik into space in 1957. The act supported education by providing special institutes to train high school mathematics, science and foreign language teachers as well as high school guidance counselors (Anderson, Walker & Beame, 1981). In 1961, Congress passed the Area Redevelopment Act and this act enabled the federal government together with the states to help areas of substantial and persistent unemployment and under employment to better plan and finance their redevelopment. The act authorized occupational training in courses such as auto mechanics, carpentry, drafting, farm equipment, heavy equipment operation, sewing machine operation, needle trades, stenography, upholstering, and welding.

The Manpower Development and Training Act (MDTA) (1962)

This act authorized the Secretary of Labor to appraise the manpower requirements and resources of the nation while working with the Secretary of Health, Education and Welfare and with state agencies to provide training programs for the unemployed and underemployed (Manpower Development, 2006). These training programs were provided through the state vocational agencies. The original programs were 100% funded, however, after four years the funding level was reduced to 90%. The training was free to the participants and training allowances were available to eligible trainees to defray educational expenses. These allowances, which could be paid up to 104 weeks, could not exceed $1000 more than the average weekly unemployment compensation payment with adjustments for other income received. Trainees under the MDTA were required to fit within in the following Categories:

- Unemployed
- Underemployed
- Part-time workers
- Workers with skills that are obsolete
- Members of farm families with less than $1200.00 annual net family income.
- Ages 16 through 22 and in need of occupational training.

The MDTA was amended in 1963, 1965, and 1968. The 1968 amendment consolidated the MDTA and the ARA. The MDTA enrolled more than a million trainees from its beginning in 1963 through 1968. About 70% of these were in institutional programs and most of the remaining were in on-the-job training. More than 600,000 trainees completed training during the period and 90% of these were employed at some time during the first year after they completed training.

The 1963 Vocational Education Act

In 1963, Congress enacted legislation designed to extend present programs and develop new programs for vocational education; encourage research and experimentation; provide work-study programs to enable youth to continue vocational education (Anderson, Walker, & Beame, 1981). The 1963 Act also amended the Smith-Hughes, George-Barden, and the National Defense Education Act. As seen in Table 2.2, the following authorizations were made in the 1963 Act.

Funds from the 1963 VEA could be used to provide training for persons of all ages, levels of achievement, and all occupations except those requiring a baccalaureate degree.

Funds could be expended for the following: (a) Teacher training, (b) Administration and supervision of programs, (c) Instructional supplies and equipment, (d) Development of instructional materials, (e) Program evaluation, (e) Construct Area Vocational School facilities.

State Boards for Vocational Education administered the 1963 VEA program. A State plan was required in order to receive the Federal funding. Table 2.3 illustrates the work-study authorizations.

The 1968 Vocational Education Amendments

The Amendments of 1968 provided changes and additions to the 1963 VEA Act. The amendment amounted to changes in the amount of funds authorized and some new authorizations for new areas to be considered. New funding authorizations for the Act are listed in Table 2.4.

TABLE 2.2   VEA Authorization

Fiscal Year 1964	$160,000,000.00
Fiscal Year 1965	$118,500,000.00
Fiscal Year 1966	$117,500,000.00
Fiscal Year 1967	$225,000,000.00
Fiscal Year 1968	$225,000,000.00

TABLE 2.3   VEA Work-Study Authorizations

Fiscal Year 1965	$30,000,000.00
Fiscal Year 1966	$50,000,000.00
Fiscal Year 1967	$35,000,000.00
Fiscal Year 1968	$35,000,000.00

TABLE 2.4   New Funding for 1968 VEA Amendment

Fiscal Year 1969	$355,000,000.00
Fiscal Year 1970	$565,000,000.00
Fiscal Year 1971	$675,000,600.00
Fiscal Year 1972	$675,000,000.00
Fiscal Year 1973	$565,000,000.00

In addition, new funding for disadvantaged and handicapped were included:

FY 1969   at $40,000,000.00 and
FY 1970   at $40,000,000.00

This new funding was to pay the cost of the development and administration of state plans, advisory councils, evaluation and dissemination. This new funding could be used for: (a) National and State Advisory councils, (b) Research and training, (c) Exemplary Programs and Projects, (d) Residential Vocational Education, (e) Consumer and Homemaking Education, (f) Cooperative Vocational Education Programs, (g) Work-study programs, (h) Curriculum Development, and (i) Training and Development for Vocational Education Personnel.

1972 Vocational Education Amendments

The 1972 Act was actually Title II of the Public Law 92–318 which amended the Higher Education Act of 1965, the Vocational Education Act of 1963, the General Provisions Act and the Elementary and Secondary Act of 1965 (Anderson, Walker, & Beame, 1981), Title II just amended the 1963 Act and the 1968 Amendments.

Comprehensive Employment Training Act (CETA) of 1973

CETA was an extension of the 1962 MDTA. This Act superseded the 1962 Act. Source of funding was from the Department of Labor (DOL).

Public Law 94-482

The 1976 Vocational Education Amendments (Anderson, Walker, & Beame, 1981) are contained in Title II of this Act. This Title was an Amend-

TABLE 2.5   Public Law 94-482 Authorizations

Total Funds

Fiscal Year 1978	$80,000,000.00
Fiscal Year 1979	$1,030,000,000.00
Fiscal Year 1980	$1,180,000,000.00
Fiscal Year 1981	$1,325,000,000.00
Fiscal Year 1982	$1,485,000,000.00

Funds for Subpart Four for Disadvantaged

Fiscal Year 1978	$35,000,000.00
Fiscal Year 1979	$40,000,000.00
Fiscal Year 1980	$45,000,000.00
Fiscal Year 1981	$50,000,000.00
Fiscal Year 1982	$50,000,000.00

Funds for Subpart Five for Consumer and Homemaking Education

Fiscal Year 1978	$55,000,000.00
Fiscal Year 1979	$65,000,000.00
Fiscal Year 1980	$75,000,000.00
Fiscal Year 1981	$80,000,000.00
Fiscal Year 1982	$80,000,000.00

ment and an extension of the 1972 Amendments. The authorizations listed in Table 2.5 were supported by these amendments

In addition, $24,000,000.00 was authorized each year in FY 1979–1982 for States to prepare five year plans; prepare annual plans and accountability reports; conduct evaluations as required; administer vocational education programs. New funds were authorized for the following: (a) Sex equality programs, (b) Program evaluation and accountability reports, (c) State Advisory Councils, (d) Five-year plans, (e) Work-study programs, (f) Cooperative Vocational Education Programs, (g) Energy Education, (h) Residential vocational Schools, (i) Curriculum Development, (j) Vocational Guidance and Counseling, (k) Program Improvement, (l) Bilingual Vocational Training. It was not until the Carl Perkins Vocational Education Act of 1984 that this Act and related funding was suspended.

The Job Training Partnership Act of 1982 (JTPA)

This act replaced and superseded the 1973 CETA. Some new guidelines were developed to administer the funds differently (Workforce Investment,

2001). The source of funding for the JTPA was from the Department of Labor (DOL).

The 1984 Carl Perkins Vocational Education Act

This was the first new Act passed since the 1963. The emphasis of this Act extended from of supporting existing programs to funding new, innovative and expanding vocational offerings (Weizenbaum, 1986). The major portion of the funds were directed to the unserved or the underserved populations. The following were listed as purposes of the Act:

- Assist the states to expand, improve, modernize and develop quality vocational education programs in order to meet the needs of the nation's existing and future workforce for marketable skills and to improve productivity.
- Assure that individuals who are inadequately served under vocational education programs are assured access to quality vocational education programs, especially individuals who are disadvantaged, who are handicapped, men and women who are entering non-traditional occupations, adults who are in need of training and retraining, individuals who are single parents or homemakers, individuals with limited English proficiency, and individuals who are incarcerated in correctional institutions.
- Promote greater cooperation between public agencies and the private sector in preparing individuals for employment, in promoting the quality of vocational education in the states and in making the vocational system more responsive to the labor market in the states.
- Improve the academic foundation of vocational students and to aid in the application of newer technologies (including the use of computers) in terms of employment or occupational goals.
- Provide vocational education services to train, retrain, and upgrade employed and unemployed workers in new skills for which there is a demand in that state or employment market.
- Assist the most economically depressed areas of a state to raise employment and occupational competencies of its citizens.
- To assist the state to utilize a full range of supporting services, special programs, and guidance counseling and placement to achieve the basic purposes of this act.
- Improve the effectiveness of consumer and homemaking education and to reduce the limiting effects of sex-role stereotyping on occupations, job skills, levels of competency and careers.

- Authorize national programs designed to meet designated vocational education needs and to strengthen the vocational education research process.

TITLE II: Part A Funds—Unserved and underserved populations. This comprised 57% of the basic grant to the state. Table 2.6 depicts the division of these funds.

TITLE II: Part B Funds—Vocational Education Program Improvement, Innovation and Expansion. This comprised 43% of the basic grant to the state. The following are purposes of this section:
- Improvement in quality of vocational programs
- Expansion of vocational education activities
- Introduction of new vocational programs
- Training to revitalize business and industry in a state
- Exemplary and innovative programs
- Improvement and expansion of postsecondary and adult programs
- Improvement and expansion of career counseling and guidance services
- Curriculum development including basic skills training
- Expansion and improvement of programs at area vocational schools
- Acquisition of equipment and renovation of facilities
- Conduct special courses and strategies to teach the fundamentals of mathematics and science through practical applications
- Assignment of personnel to coordinate efforts to insure vocational programs are responsive to labor market needs and supportive of apprenticeship programs
- Vocational Student Organization activities
- Prevocational programs
- Programs of modern industrial and agricultural arts
- State Administration
- Stipends for students in vocational education programs

TABLE 2.6   Carl Perkins Vocational Education Title II Part A Funds

Handicapped	10.0%
Disadvantaged	22.0%
Adult Training and Retraining	12.0%
Single Parents	8.5%
Sex Bias	3.5%
Corrections	1.0%

- Placement services
- Day care services for children of vocational education students
- Construction of Area Vocational School facilities
- Acquisition of high technology equipment
- Vocational education programs in private schools and institutions
- Preservice and in-service teacher education

TITLE III: Special Programs—The following are areas which are covered under this section;
- Community Based Organizations
- Consumer and Homemaking Programs
- Adult Training, retraining, and employment development
- Career Guidance and Counseling Programs
- Industry-education partnerships. For training in high technology occupations

TITLE IV: National Programs—The following are covered under this section:
- Research activities;
- Demonstration programs;
- Model Programs;
- State equipment pools;
- Demonstration centers for retraining dislocated workers;
- Model centers for vocational education for older individuals;
- Occupations information data systems;
- National Council for Vocational Education; Bilingual vocational training.

Guidelines for the State Board in the Administration of the Act include: Coordination of the development, submission and implementation of the state plan and evaluation of the program services and activities; Development of the state plan in consultation with the state council on vocational education, and submission of this document to the secretary; Consultation with the state council and other appropriate groups and individuals involved in the planning, administration, evaluation and coordination of programs funded under the act; Convening and meeting as a state board at such times as necessary to carry out its functions under the act; Adoption of procedures to implement state level coordination with the state job training coordinating council to encourage cooperation in the conduct of the respective programs.

The Carl D. Perkins Vocational and Applied Technology Act of 1990

The Carl D. Perkins Vocational and Applied Technology Act of 1990 amended and extended for five years the original Carl D. Perkins Vocational Education Act of 1984. This Act authorized the United States government to spend up to $1.6 billion a year on State and local programs that teach the "skill competencies necessary to work in a technologically advanced society." The addition of "Applied Technology" to the name of this legislation suggests that Congress designed the new Carl Perkins legislation to improve America's high-tech competitiveness. Another focus of this new Carl Perkins Act is to provide greater vocational education opportunities to disadvantaged people. The following information gives a breakdown of areas covered under this legislation and the amount authorized under each section.

Basic State Grants
More than $940 million of the authorization: 75% of the $1.25 billion that has been authorized to go to states in the form of basic grants, is specifically earmarked for programs that address the vocational education needs of poor and handicapped, students and those of limited English-language proficiency (Office of Vocational and Adult Education, 2005). States are obligated to spend this money on schools, area vocational-technical centers and postsecondary institutions serving the greatest number of disadvantaged students. The Act requires that states be more accountable for the programs they are operating. States must be able to show that disadvantaged people have the chance for full and equitable participation in vocational education programs. States must set up extensive systems of evaluating programs and effects of Carl Perkins money on these programs. Each state must set up a core of standards and performance measures that will form the basis for Perkins-mandated evaluations. Each State must submit to the Secretary of Education a three-year plan detailing how it will administer Perkins funds.

Carl Perkins Vocational Education Act of 1998

This act replaces 1990 Carl Perkins Act and gives states and local districts greater flexibility to develop programs (Carl D. Perkins, 2003). It makes them more accountable for student performance and more money at the local level. The act eliminates set-asides for gender equity and gives vocational education separate authorizing legislation. The act ensures that education authorities, not governors or labor officials will oversee vocational education. It includes a separate authorization for tech prep and creates 10% reserve of local funding. Finally the act strengthens academic and vocational technical instruction, places more emphasis on professional development and supports career guidance activities (Hayward & Benson, 1993, p. 3). According to Lynch (2000), the two most recent reauthorizations of the 1984 Perkins legislation are essentially grounded in school reform and the mandate to use federal funds to improve student performance and achievement (p. 10).

Other Programs

In addition to basic state grants, the reauthorized Perkins Act funding is divided into eleven 11 other categories, which will be covered:

1. Tech Prep—The new Perkins Act authorizes $125 million to fund tech prep programs—cooperative arrangements that combine two years of technology-oriented preparatory education in high school with two years of advanced technology studies at a community college. These programs are to integrate academic and vocational education, which is a major emphasis of the new Act.

2. The national Tech Prep initiative establishes goals which may give all of education an opportunity to implement change. A major goal is to allow students to move from one level of learning to another without unnecessary repetition or duplication of coursework. Another major goal is to prepare students to assume the roles of a highly skilled workforce. The aim of the Tech Prep initiative is to help break down barriers between secondary and postsecondary institutions, resulting in a coordinated, integrated, focused and challenging education program. Tech Prep is a program consisting of two years at the secondary level and two years at the postsecondary level in higher education or apprenticeship training, which includes a common core of mathematics, science, communications, and technologies and leads to an associate degree or a certificate in a specific career. It is considered a dual-purpose program, which means that students are prepared to enter a vocational or technical program, a college prep program, or a combination of the two. Tech Prep does not undermine the academic system; in fact, research shows that the Tech Prep program of study can strengthen the academic achievement of all students.

3. Supplementary Grants for Facilities and Equipment—Up to $100 million has been authorized to improve vocational education facilities and equipment in economically depressed areas. These funds will flow to states and school districts with the highest concentrations of disadvantaged students.

4. Consumer and Homemaking Education—The Act authorizes $38.5 million for states to develop or improve instruction in nutrition, health, clothing, consumer education, family living and parenthood, child development, housing and homemaking;

5. Career Guidance and Counseling—The law authorizes $20 million for career development programs that assist people to make the transition from school to work, maintain current job skills, develop skills needed to move into high-tech careers, develop job-search skills and learn about other job training programs.

6. Community-based Organizations—Up to $15 million in Perkins funding may go to local non-profit and other community groups providing vocational education services to disadvantaged people.

7. Bilingual Vocational Education—The Act authorizes $10 million to fund programs specifically designed to provide bilingual vocational education and English-language instruction.

8. Business/labor/education Partnerships—$10 million has been authorized to help fund state grants to cooperative partnerships that team schools, local agencies, or state departments with business, industry or labor groups to provide vocational education.

9. Community Education/Lighthouse Schools—The Act authorizes $10 million to establish and evaluate model high school community education employment centers serving low-income urban and rural youth. So-called Lighthouse Schools—model vocational education institutions that provide information and assistance to other programs—are also eligible to receive the funding.

10. State Councils on Vocational Education—Up to $9 million may go to the state councils, established by the original Perkins Act. These groups advise and make recommendations to state agencies that set vocational education policy. Tribally Controlled Postsecondary Institutions—$4 Million may go to postsecondary vocational institutions operated by Native American tribes.

11. National Council on Vocational Education—The law authorized $350,000 to fund the activities of the National Council through September 30, 1991. This advisory group created by the original Act was disbanded on October 1, 1991.

While it appears that the Perkins Act authorization was generous, it is important to remember that the law set maximum spending limits. Congress may and usually does, appropriate less than the amount set. For Fiscal Year 1991 Congress appropriated $1,003 billion, which is about 63% of what the Act allowed.

School-to-Work (1994)

When the School-to-Work Opportunities Act (STWOA) was initiated in 1994, it was envisioned as a "systematic, comprehensive effort to help all young people (a) prepare for high-skill and high-wage careers, (b) receive top quality academic instruction, and (c) gain the foundation skills to pursue postsecondary education and lifelong learning" ("School to Work," 1994). Because school-to-work (STW) approaches to teaching and learning were seen as most appropriate for students not designed for college, however, it was considered by many to be just another vocational program. STWOA did call for the development of three main components in a STW system: School-based learning, work-based learning, and connecting activities. School-based learning consists of integrated academic and vocational courses that focused on a career area or industry with links to postsecondary education. Partnerships are created with business to develop opportunities for students to take part in worksite learning; these work-based activities coordinate with students' school-based learning. Connecting activities are developed to coordinate the school-based and work-based activities. STW is learner centered, provides authentic learning opportunities, and is based on principles that can benefit all students, including a focus on active learning, exploration of career possibilities and interests, and supervised experiences outside of the classroom. STW offers a seamless educational system that offers as many options as possible. STW begins at the elementary level with career awareness activities, progresses to career exploration in the middle grades and early high school and finally to career preparation during the later high school years. In summary, the following are key elements of STWOA:

- Collaborative partnerships
- Integrated curriculum
- Technological advances
- Adaptable workers
- Comprehensive career guidance
- Work-based learning
- Step by step approval
- Grades K–6: develop Career Awareness
- Grades 7–10: Career Exploration
- Grades 11–12: Career Preparations

In addition, the respective work based, school based and connecting activities components of STW are:

Work Based Learning Components of STW
- Job shadowing
- Job training
- Work experience (paid or nonpaid)
- Workplace mentoring
- Instruction in workplace competencies
- Instruction in all elements of industry

School Based Learning Components of STW
- Career counseling
- Career pathways
- Rigorous program of study
- Integration of academics and vocational education
- Evaluation
- Secondary/postsecondary articulation

Connecting Activities Components of STW
- Matching students with employers
- Establishing liaisons between education and work
- Technical assistance to schools, students and employers
- Assistance to integrate school-based and work based learning
- Encourage participation of employers
- Job placement, continuing education or further training assistance
- Collection and analysis of post-program outcomes of participants
- Linkages with youth development activities and industry

The Workforce Investment Act of 1998

This act provides the framework or a unique national workforce preparation and employment system designed to meet both the needs of the nation's businesses and the needs of job seekers and those who want to further their careers (U.S. Department of Labor, 2006). Title I of the legislation is based on the following elements: (a) Training and employment programs must be designed and managed at the local level—where the needs of businesses and individuals are best understood; (b) Customers, potential participants, must be able to conveniently access the employment, education, training, and information services they need at a single location in their neighborhoods; (c) Customers should have choices in deciding the training program that best fits their needs and the organizations that will provide that service—they should have control over their own career development; (d) Customers have a right to information about how well training provided succeed in preparing people for jobs. Training providers will provide information on their success rate; and (e) Business will provide information, leadership, and play an active role in ensuring that the system prepares people for current and future jobs.

The Act builds on the most successful elements of previous Federal legislation. Just as important, its key components are based on local and State input and extensive research and evaluation studies of successful training and employment innovations over the past decade. Federal funding has been available for all vocational-technical program areas since the 1963 VEA was passed. It has served well in stimulating vocational education in the United States for a number of years. Agriculture, Home Economics, and Trade and Industrial Education have been stimulated ever since the 1917 Smith Hughes Act was passed.

CONCLUSION

Developed during the late 19th and 20th centuries, principles of career and technical education were instrumental in shaping the early development of vocational education in our country. The concepts behind these principles are still evident in guiding today's career and technical education although in some cases, these principles need to be reinterpreted given the new contexts in our society. For the most part, federal funding has stimulated career and technical education in many ways. For example, the federal government has been obliged to use various types of agriculture programs to improve farm incomes during periods of declining prices and poor weather conditions. Although business education was not covered specifically in any federal legislation, the 1963 VEA, the Carl Perkins Act of 1984 and the 1990 Amendments provided monies for upgrading or expanding the business area.

As Health Occupations education was considered part of the Trade and Industrial (T&I) education, the Smith-Hughes Act of 1917 supported Health Occupations Education. Later, a number of federal legislation supported Health Occupations Education. The same can be said about Family and Consumer Science. The Carl Perkins funding was used to purchase equipment as well as computers, which can be used to operate Computer Assisted Design (CAD) and Computer Assisted Manufacturing (CAM). This funding was also used to integrate math and science in the vocational curriculums and to support student organizational activities as an integral part of the instructional process. Federal funds have been used to support vocational guidance since 1938. The first funds used were not directly for vocational guidance but for supporting teacher training and indirectly assisting vocational guidance. In short, while principles and philosophy guide the development and direction of vocational education, federal legislation stimulated it in many different ways. Rather than defying one another, the two complement and supplement each other. Both were and continue to be necessary and important in shaping the further development of career and technical education.

REFERENCES

Allen, H. P. (1950). *The federal government and education: the original and complete study of education for the Hoover Commission Task Force on Public Welfare.* New York: McGraw-Hill.

Anderson, W. F., Walker, D. B., & Beame, A. D. (1981). *The federal role in the federal system: The dynamics of growth.* Washington, DC: Diane.

Douglas, P. H. (1921). *American apprenticeship and industrial education.* New York: Longmans, Green, & Co.

Elias, J. L., & Merriam, S. B. (1995). *Philosophical foundations of adult education* (3rd ed.). Malabar, FL: Krieger.

Foster, P. N. (1997). Lessons from history: Industrial arts/technology education as a case. *Journal of Vocational Technical Education, 13*(2), 1–14.

Ham, C. H. (1990). *Mind and hand: Manual training the chief factor in education.* New York: American Book.

Hayward, G. C., & Benson, C. S. (1993). *Vocational-technical education: Major reforms and debates 1917-present.* Washington, DC: U.S. Department of Education, Office of Vocational and Adult Education. (ERIC Document Reproduction Service No. ED 369 959)

Hyslop-Margison, E. J. (2000). An assessment of the historical arguments in vocational education reform. *Journal of Career and Technical Education, 17,* 23–30.

Lewis, T. (1998). *Toward the 21st century: Retrospect, prospect for American vocationalism* (Information series No. 373). Columbus: Ohio State University, ERIC Clearinghouse on Adult, Career, and Vocational Education.

Lynch, R. L. (2000). *New directions for high school career and technical education in the 21st century* (Information series No. 384). Columbus: Ohio State University, ERIC Clearinghouse on Adult, Career, and Vocational Education.

Manpower Development. (2006). *Manpower Development and Training Act.* Retrieved December 29, 2006, from http://en.wikipedia.org/wiki/Manpower_Development_and_Training_Act

McClure, A. F., Chrisman, J. R., & Mock, P. (1985). *Education for work: The historical evolution of vocational and distributive education in America.* London, Toronto: Farleigh Dickinson University Press.

Miller, M. D. (1985). *Principles and philosophy for vocational education.* Columbus: Ohio State University.

Miller, M. D. (1996). Philosophy: The conceptual framework for designing a system of teacher education. In N. K. Hartley & T. L. Wentling (Eds.), *Beyond tradition: Preparing the teachers of tomorrow's workforce* (pp. 53–72). Columbia, MO: University Council for Vocational Education.

Miller, M. D., & Gregson, J. A. (1999). A philosophic view for seeing the past of vocational education and envisioning the future of workforce education: Pragmatism revisited. In A. J. Paulter, Jr. (Ed.), *Workforce education: Issues for the new century* (pp. 21–34). Ann Arbor, MI: Prakken.

Office of Vocational and Adult Education. (2005). *State plan guide for the Carl D. Perkins Vocational and Technical Education Act.* Retrieved December 26, 2006, from http://www.ed.gov/about/offices/list/ovae/pi/cte/memo2004.html

Prosser, C. A., & Allen, C. R. (1925). *Vocational education in a democracy.* New York: The century Co.

Roberts, R. W. (1971). *Vocational and practical arts education: History, development and principles* (3rd, ed.). New York: Harper & Row.

Rojewski, J. W. (2002). Preparing the workforce of tomorrow: A conceptual framework for career and technical education. *Journal of Vocational Education Research, 27*(1), 1–27.

Schenck, J. P., & Others. (1984). *The life and times of Victor Karlovich Della-Vos.* Washington, D. C.: Education Resources Information Center. (ERIC Document Reproduction Service No. ED297 137) Retrieved May 3, 2007, from http://eric.ed.gov/ERICWebPortal/custom/portlets/recordDetails/detailmini.jsp?_nfpb=true&_&ERICExtSearch_SearchValue_0=ED297137&ERICExtSearch_SearchType_0=eric_accno&accno=ED297137

School to Work. (1994). *School to work opportunities act of 1994.* Retrieved December 22, 2006, from http://www.ncrel.org/sdrs/areas/issues/envrnmnt/stw/sw3s-wopp.htm

Snedden, D. (1920). *Vocational education.* New York: The Macmillan Company.

U.S. Department of Education. (2003). *Carl D. Perkins Vocational and Technical Education Act of 1998.* Retrieved December 24, 2006, from http://www.ed.gov/offices/OVAE/CTE/legis.html

U.S. Department of Labor. (2006). *Workforce Investment Act of 1998: Its Application to People with Disabilities.* Retrieved December 22, 2006, from http://www.dol.gov/odep/pubs/ek01/act.htm

Weizenbaum, J. (1986). *Technology and structural unemployment: Reemploying displaced adults.* Washington, DC: Diane.

Workforce Investment. (2001). *History: Job Training Partnership Act, 1982–2000.* Retrieved December 28, 2006, from http://www.picsf.org/about/jtpa.htm

CHAPTER 3

HISTORICAL PERSPECTIVES OF THE DIFFERENT COMPONENTS OF VOCATIONAL EDUCATION

Victor C. X. Wang
California State University, Long Beach

Kathleen P. King
Fordham University

INTRODUCTION

This chapter contains a description and discussion of the historical perspectives of the different components within career and technical education (CTE). When one considers career and technical education, readers may just think of manual training, manual arts, industrial arts or just trade and industrial education. In fact, career and technical education encompasses agriculture education, business education, health occupations education, family and consumer science (formerly known as home economics), vocational-industrial education, technology education, technical education and

Building Workforce Competencies in Career and Technical Education, pages 43–60
Copyright © 2009 by Information Age Publishing
43

vocational guidance. Each component of career and technical education was developed in response to the needs of people in a given society.

It is well known that the last quarter of the nineteenth century saw an educational program known as manual training. It quickly spread into the secondary schools of the United States. Proponents of the manual training movement wanted to use manual training as a vehicle of achieving educational and intellectual values in vocational education and training. Since its early inception, manual training has fostered much debate concerning its values in the field. Some educators promoted the value of manual training while others opposed it bitterly. Manual training did not gain strength and acceptability until the waning years of the 1880s. Bitter opposition of manual training resulted from the lack of understanding of the history of manual training movement. Over the years, manual training has evolved. In the early 1900s, it was once called manual arts and later called industrial arts. Then in 1905, it was formally called vocational education. While vocational educators, students, and many in business and industry know the value of vocational education, it did not seem to have achieved the same status with liberal arts education. Therefore, leaders in the field suggested that career and technical education be used to replace the name vocational education.

Regardless of the name change and bitter opposition, career and technical education has been and will continue to be a vehicle by which millions of students will obtain and upgrade occupational competencies. Working around the world is not a dream but a reality as globalization brings different cultures together. As America changed from a mixture of peoples from many countries often described as a melting pot to a tossed salad, it is imperative that vocational educators help students develop workforce competencies by using strategic approaches so that our students can remain competitive in the global economy. Nowadays, competition comes not only from within the US but also from other industrialized and developing nations. Indeed, career and technical education has come a long way. The study of historical perspectives of different components of career and technical education perhaps can help us understand the plight of vocational education and defend its value in the field. What is more, the study of historical perspectives of different components of CTE can help us look to the future when intense competition is sure to arise given the nature of our global economy.

WHY THE HISTORICAL PERSPECTIVE?

Understanding the context and history of the different components of vocational education and how the field has developed over time is important to scholars, practitioners, and students. By learning the historical perspective of the field, we are in a position to know the changes that have taken place, what led to the changes and how the professionals in the field responded to these changes. This vantage point provides an opportunity to improve on current practices and to develop the relevant material such as this book required to advance the field.

Scholars and practitioners with limited history of how their disciplines have developed over time are at a disadvantage since they do not know where they are coming from, nor can they adequately anticipate trends for the future (Nafukho, Amutabi, & Otunga, 2005). The history of vocational educational education and training in the United States of America is important since the U.S. model has been adapted in many regions of the world. Knowledge of history also helps in the development of the principles that extend beyond mere impressions of current facts. This knowledge also improves practice by suggesting what has worked or not worked in practice before, why it did or did not work, and options or alternatives for consideration (Long, 1990; Nafukho, 2007).

The importance of the historical perspective of any discipline is noted as follows:

> ...history is to a people what memory is to the individual. People with no knowledge of their past would suffer from collective amnesia, groping blindly into the future without guide-posts of precedence to shape their course.... (Fafunwa, 1974, p. 13)

Since the vocational education field has changed from various names such as manual training, manual arts, industrial arts, vocational education, and now career and technical education, we feel that this chapter fills an important gap by providing the historical perspective of the field that we now refer to as career and technical education.

DEVELOPMENTS IN AGRICULTURE EDUCATION

In 1887, Congress passed an act providing for financial support for agricultural experiment stations. The provisions for the scientific study of agriculture were carried out in the land grant colleges having departments organized as experiment stations and in separate institutions organized for that purpose (Barlow, 1976). The 1862 Morrill Act provided for additional federal aid to the land grant colleges. In the next 18 years, agreement was difficult to reach regarding how much federal support would be provided. Finally in 1890, the second Morrill Bill provided further support for the land grant colleges. Evidenced in just these few examples is how federal funding has played a major role in the development of agriculture education.

Agriculture is not only one of the oldest vocations but one of the most significant in the development of civilized life. As primitive people began to settle and rise from the level of wandering hunters to that of homebuilders, agriculture became an important aspect of self-preservation. As agriculture developed in effectiveness, as a means of food supply, our society progressed (Bellwood, 2004). Hence, from an early period in man's history, agriculture has been of very great importance in the climb toward civilization; and it is today as basic as ever to the maintenance and progress of human life. Farmers, from the beginning of time, have encountered many troublesome problems. In early times, farmers worked long hours with inadequate equipment. They endured physical discomforts and frequently were subject to attack from unfriendly people.

Farm life has undergone many changes over a period of time. New farming equipment has made the work less of a drudgery. However, the following are problems, which are currently encountered in farming careers: (a) Weather and Climate—floods, hail storms, windstorms, temperature and adequate rainfall; (b) Erosion and Urban Expansion—Floods and winds remove good soil and highway and airports, housing developments, and sports complexes displace good farmland; (c) Insects and wild animals—insects eat crops, deer, rabbits, raccoons, squirrels, damage crops and coyotes eat animals; (d) People—in early days rustlers were a problem. The farmer still has to contend with rustlers, hunters and drug dealers. Many farmers lose cattle and other farm animals to careless hunters. Hunters also drive over land where crops have not been harvested and destroy the crops. Many also drive over fields when they are wet and produce ruts from 4-wheel drive vehicles; (e) Increased Mechanization—this is both an advantage and a disadvantage. The disadvantage being that the farmer must be able to maintain the farm equipment. The farm equipment is becoming more and more technical; therefore it is necessary to try to purchase farm equipment on which service can be obtained. (See for example Cochrane (1993) and University of California (2003).)

An agriculture revolution has been taking place as a result of the changes in mechanization. Farming dramatically changed from animal power to tractor power in the 1930s. The increase in use of hydraulics and combines occurred in the 1950s and 1960s and still greater use of minimum till machinery and herbicides occurred in the 1970s (Cochrane, 1993). New farm combines are utilizing many high tech options to control the harvesting units. These changes have resulted in fewer farmers, larger farms, higher farm incomes and greater capital investments. Success in farming currently requires knowledge and skill far beyond the requirement of those needed in the 1950s or earlier.

BUSINESS EDUCATION

Vocational business education had its origin in apprenticeship programs (Barlow, 1976). The early scribes, for example, were trained under an apprenticeship program. When the apprenticeship agencies failed to meet the need for bookkeepers and clerical workers, training programs were organized in academies and proprietary schools. However, commercial subjects reappeared in high schools at the turn of the 20th century. The courses become more vocational as a result of the stimulation of federal funds under federal legislation, especially the 1963 Vocational Education Act (VEA). The English grammar schools and academies of the United States offered courses in arithmetic, handwriting, and bookkeeping in the 18th and 19th centuries. These courses were said to prepare students for "life" as well as college entrance. Bookkeeping was included in the curriculum of the English high school of Boston in 1823 (Graham, 1933) Massachusetts enacted a law in 1827 in which instruction in bookkeeping among other subjects was specified for certain high schools.

Business education received less emphasis in public schools during the latter part of the 19th century because of the rise of private business colleges. These private commercial schools or colleges flourished in the United States between the years 1852–1893. Commercial courses were introduced into public high schools about 1890 through popular demand. The curriculums were borrowed from the private business colleges and the principle courses were bookkeeping, shorthand and typewriting.

> The public schools were slow to accept these subjects and frequently the commercial courses were used for the placement of slow learners. Because of this fact, the public schools were unable to compete with the private business colleges, especially in the quality of output. However, the popular demand for this type of program increased and by 1893 it was estimated that 15,000 students were enrolled in commercial education courses in the public high schools in the nation. (Roberts, 1965, p. 111)

Renewed interest in business education in the public schools occurred in the 20th century. Committees of the National Education Association in 1903 and again in 1919 pointed to the need for business education not only for vocational usage but also for mental discipline and general education. Business education was introduced into the junior high school curriculum at this time for general knowledge, exploratory values, and as means of reducing school dropouts. Specialized courses were used at first but later unified courses in business education were introduced (Roberts, 1965).

HEALTH OCCUPATIONS EDUCATION

Humans have required health care since the beginning of time. The early Egyptians accumulated some knowledge of healing from witchcraft and magic. In time, they learned to recognize and treat many diseases. Hippocrates of ancient Greece, usually referred to as the "Father of Medicine," changed the magic of medicine into the science of medicine and wrote many treatises on medicine. During the Dark Ages and Early Middle Ages, the Catholics founded some hospitals in the Western World, and the Moslems, utilizing the knowledge of the early Greeks, erected many hospitals for the care of the sick. During the Middle Ages, medicine in Europe was influenced by the Roman traditions remaining after the Dark Ages and the ecclesiastical medicine that existed in the monasteries. The Moslem ideas about hospital construction were accepted throughout Europe. The renaissance in medicine came during the 16th century when William Harvey treated medicine as a science rather than a tradition. Practical nursing became regarded as a profession rather than a charitable act or an unskilled service occupation. See Ackerknecht (1982) and Clendening (1960) as general examples of the history of medicine.)

Florence Nightingale became the dominant figure in nursing and nursing education as a result of her work in health care during the Crimean War (1854–1856). She established a school of nursing at St. Thomas Hospital in London about 1860. This school became the worldwide pattern for schools of nursing. Ms. Nightingale believed that nurses should live in homes or dormitories where moral responsibility and discipline could be developed (Clendening, 1960).

Early Schools of Nursing in the United States included one at Bellevue Hospital in 1873, and the University of Minnesota in 1909 as part of the university. Table 3.1 shows a detailed chronology of early hospitals. However, many of the hospitals of the 19th century were simply a place of sojourn for the sick and incidentally a convenient place for practical training of physicians (Williams, 2000).

Hospital improvement began in the United States in 1910 as a result of a study of the nation's medical schools by Dr. Abraham Flexner, which was funded by the Carnegie Foundation (Williams, 2000). The shortcoming of the medical profession, as revealed by this study led to state laws requiring high standards in the care of the sick. Many sub-standard hospitals were closed while others were improved. Patient care shifted from the home to the doctor's office and thence to the hospital. In 1935 one in every fifteen citizens was admitted to a hospital. By 1966 this became one in every seven persons; see Table 3.2 for a comparison of the number of hospital beds across these years. The increased use of hospitals was due to many factors

---

TABLE 3.1 History of Hospitals

- The Greeks first used hospitals to isolate the sick
- Moslems during the 8th and 9th century built well-planned hospitals
- Royal London Ophthalmic Hospital in 1804
- Charity Hospital—New Orleans 1737
- Massachusetts's General Hospital 1821
- St. Louis Hospital 1830
- Johns Hopkins Hospital 1889

Source: This information was gathered from several sources.

TABLE 3.2 Increase in Hospitals and Hospital Beds

Date	Hospitals	Beds
1910	4385	42,500
1935	6000	1,000,000+
1966	7127	1,700,000

---

including the introduction of new medicines and new techniques for the care of individuals and the prevention of disease.

FAMILY AND CONSUMER SCIENCE

Human survival throughout the ages has depended upon choice of food. During this time humans have selected the kind and quantity of food that has provided the proper nutrients for growth and development. Some people through the years have been less fortunate than others and have chosen or been forced to accept food that was lacking in some of the essential elements. These people have contracted dietary-deficiency diseases.

Some well-known examples of dietary-deficiency diseases are scurvy and beriberi, which have been cured by the use of proper diet. Human beings do not instinctively choose their food in accordance with the principles of good nutrition, but they must learn the kinds of foods that are needed, the methods of producing food, and the techniques of preparing the food for consumption.

Much progress has been made since the beginning of the 20th century in understanding the relationship between food and health. Scientists have discovered that more than 50 known nutrients found in food are necessary for the normal operation of the body. When any of these are lacking, some health problems may arise.

Early Vocational Home Economics Programs required that Home Experience become a part of the home economics program. This home experience is actually a home project where the student planned and carried out a project in relation to the home. Many of these were projects sanctioned by the parents and supervised by the home economics teacher and could be carried out during the summer months. Early in the 1880's, a plan for teaching the household arts to children in the form of play was originated and became known as the Kitchen Garden Movement (Barlow, 1976). According to Barlow (1976), the Industrial Education Association of New York in 1884 developed from the Kitchen Garden Association. This association endeavored to teach the poor of the city how to sew. Finally, this association established the New York College for training teachers in 1888. This college has become what is known as Teachers College of Columbia University. The Lake Placid, New York conferences contributed much to the development of home economics. During the summer of 1898, Ellen Richards was a visitor at the summer home of Mr. and Mrs. Melvin Dewey at Lake Placid. Dewey was the secretary of the New York State Board of Regents. Based on Barlow's 1976 accounts, Mrs. Richards spoke to the members of the Lake Placid Club on domestic problems, and through a suggestion that arose at that meeting, invitations were sent to a selected group of individuals to attend a conference of the Dewey home during the summer of 1899. The purpose of this kind of organization was to discuss the economic and social problems of the home. Courses of study for all areas of education were considered in relation to the growing home economics movement.

Many changes have occurred in family and consumer sciences programs as a result of new legislation and studies that have been made by various groups. Since the passage of the 1963 VEA the classes have been titled Secondary, Post-secondary and Adult. With the passage of the 1984 and 1990 Carl Perkins Vocational Education Acts, there has been an emphasis on programs that assist the displaced homemaker and the single parent. As a result of the back-to-the-basics movement from the "Nation at Risk Report" in the early 1980's, family and consumer sciences programs have had to compete for students as well as work with less funding. All of these changes have made an impact on what is being offered in the various programs. The Consumer and Homemaking Programs must now serve the following students:

1. Male and Females
2. Disadvantaged
3. Handicapped
4. Single Parents
5. Economocally Depressed

VOCATIONAL-INDUSTRIAL EDUCATION

Apprenticeship is an old form of education, used generously by the ancient nations, the Greeks and Romans, and throughout the Middle Ages, and the Renaissance (Barlow, 1976a). According to Barlow (1976b), apprenticeship in Colonial America was one of the fundamental educational institutions of the time. It represented a pathway to literacy for the boy or girl who could not pay for an education. It is also worth pointing out that in the Colonial period, there were the abundance of land, the mobility and freedom of the people, the willingness of the frontiersman to "make do" with makeshift implements and furnishings, and the immigration of mechanics and crafts-men who had been trained in Europe, all working against the apprentice-ship system. The factory in the nineteenth century delivered the heaviest blow to the system. Rapid development of labor-saving machinery contrib-uted much to the decline of apprenticeship (Barlow, 1976c).

The early settlers came to colonial America for many reasons, but few came for educational purposes. With few exceptions these settlers were satisfied with the educational programs of the mother country, and as a consequence the first schools of the New World were similar to those of the country from which the settlers came. Four main types of educational activ-ity were conducted in the colonies during the seventeenth century. These were apprenticeship, religious schools for instruction in reading and writ-ing, Latin grammar schools, and practical schooling in mathematics.

The early training of craftsman and industrial workers was conducted through on-the-job training and/or apprenticeship training. Apprentice-ship came to the New World in the early Colonial period. This type of train-ing in the colonies resembled that of the mother countries, except that it developed directly under the laws of the towns and counties. The Eng-lish apprenticeship system was modified to suit conditions and became the most important educational agency during the period of colonization and settlement.

In 1803 there were four cotton mills in operation in the United States. By 1812 manufacturing had a good beginning. The expansion of trade brought about the invention of new machines and the improvement of others in the agricultural and manufacturing industries. The development of the power loom in 1814, the locomotive in 1829, the mechanical reaper and the tele-graph in 1835, the sewing machine in 1846, together with the development of coal and iron mines and the growth of the railroads, brought about rapid changes in the nations economy. All of these changes put a strain on the apprenticeship programs.

The Mechanics' Institute originated in England during the early years of the nineteenth century (Barlow, 1976). It attempted to regain the educational values lost with the coming of the factory system. These same institutes soon spread to the United States.

Mechanical Institutes were first organized in New York City in 1820 by the General Society of Mechanics and Tradesmen. The Society established a library for apprentices and a school for children of mechanics. The school was organized to meet the need for elementary education for the children of indigent members. The New York public school system assumed responsibility for the Society's day school instruction in 1858. The second and most noted of the mechanics schools was the Franklin Institute of Philadelphia, which was established in 1824 for the purpose of extending the knowledge of mechanical science to its members (Barlow, 1976). Two other representative institutes are the Maryland Institute for the Promotion of the Mechanics Art, founded in Baltimore in 1826, and the Ohio Mechanics' Institute of the Cincinnati, founded in 1828. In keeping with the westward movement, the San Francisco Mechanics Institute was founded in 1854 (Barlow, 1976a).

About the time Mechanical Institutes were being organized in cities to provide adult education for city workers, the American Lyceum was organized for adult education in small towns and in the country. Josiah Holbrook, a teacher and founder of an agricultural and manual labor school, published a handbook in 1826 providing for a comprehensive plan for popular education. The plan consisted of the organization of local lyceums, to be affiliated with state lyceums and these in turn with a national lyceum (Holbrook, 1826). This movement began in about 1830 and by 1833 there were about 1000 lyceums in the United States. The lyceum movement which lasted until near the middle of the 19th century, served as a means of building up useful knowledge in the natural sciences among people of the smaller towns of the United States.

Technical Schools came into prominence during the first quarter of the 19th century. These schools had objectives somewhat similar to those of the mechanics institutes and lyceums. They were designed to provide education in the practical applications of science and mathematics. The first of these was the Gardiner Lyceum established in Gardiner, Maine in 1821. The second and most important of the technical institutes was the Rensselaer School established in Troy, New York in 1824. Many more of these institutes were established through 1895. These schools played an important part in the development of vocational education in the United States. While the mechanics' institute was interested primarily interested in the vocational needs of the population, the lyceum planned for the educational and cultural needs as well. The artist, the farmer, and the mechanic were supposed to find in the lyceum areas of interest and value (Barlow, 1976).

Many trade schools for employed and prospective workers in industrial vocations were organized during the last quarter of the 19th century. Beatty

(1918) chronicles the history of these schools as they included corporation, proprietary, and endowed schools. Among the first corporation school in the United States was the one developed in 1875 by the R. Hoe Printing Press Company of New York City. Other corporation schools that were organized were: Baltimore and Ohio Railroad in 1855, Westinghouse Machine Company in 1888, and General Electric Company in 1901 (Beatty, 1918). These schools also provided a much-needed service for developing industrial workers in the U.S. A number of states were interested in developing vocational schools at the beginning of the 20th century. Massachusetts, Wisconsin, New York, Connecticut, New Jersey, Indiana, Pennsylvania, and Rhode Island all had some vocational schools in operation before 1915.

TECHNOLOGY EDUCATION

Apprenticeships were conducted by the people of ancient times; however, like other forms of education, apprenticeships reached a low ebb over time. During the Middle Ages, a formalized apprenticeship system became the mode of instruction for the working class. This revival of interest was due in part to the programs of apprenticeship training organized by the guilds of this age. The guilds recognized early the importance of taking apprentices and requiring then to go through a course of training before being admitted to the trade as a journeyman or master craftsman. Records indicate that apprenticeships were practiced in England as early as the thirteenth century.

Apprenticeships established in the early colonial period resembled those that were practiced in England. However, since there were no guilds or similar craft organizations, the apprenticeship system was set up under the laws of the towns and counties. Hands-on training was learned while studying under a Master Craftsman of the trade. After a required period of training the individual became a journeyman. Then after a required length of time as a journeyman, an individual could become a Master Craftsman.

Significant American beginnings in industrial training took place at the Philadelphia Centennial Exposition in 1876, at which Victor Della Vos of Moscow's Russian Imperial Technical School displayed a series of student exercises in wood and metal (Barlow, 1967b; Bawden, 1950). This exhibit introduced to American educators an organized, systematic method of teaching hand skills. One of the visitors at the Centennial, who familiarized himself with the Russian exhibit, was John D. Runkle, president of the Massachusetts Institute of Technology. Realizing the value of tool instruction in general education, Runkle recommended that instruction shops be introduced at MIT. His recommendations were accepted and became a reality the following year (Barlow, 1976). John Runkle adapted the system to create the School of Mechanical Arts at the Massachusetts Institute of Technology in 1877, and Calvin Woodward opened a Manual Training High School at St. Louis' Washington University in 1879 (Coates, 1923; Miller, & Smalley, 1963). Both promoted training as necessary to the education of all youth. According to Gerbracht and Babcock (1969, p. 8), manual training's threefold purpose in the late nineteenth century was to keep boys in school, provide vocational skills and develop leisure-time interests which did not deviate too far from Locke's philosophy in vocational education covered in chapter one of the book.

As a result of this movement, a widespread establishment of secondary-level courses in mechanical drawing, woodworking, patternmaking, foundry, forging and machine shop soon followed. Publicly funded manual-training schools, and high schools bearing the labels; "technical," "polytechnic," and "mechanic arts", opened in the mid 1880s. "Shop" became an accepted subject in general high schools shortly after the turn of the century.

In 1888, Gustaf Larsson, a leader in the Scandinavian Sloyd Movement, came to Boston to educate teachers. His work at Boston's Sloyd Training School, which educated teachers from across the nation, did much to spread manual training, especially at the elementary level. The Sloyd approach for the first time had students construct well-designed and useful projects as a part of skill training. At this time, a secondary-level trade and industrial vocational education movement was also emerging. Trade and Industrial (T&I) Education schools tended to follow the Russian approach to skills training, while the manual arts movement grew from the Sloyd system and England's arts and crafts movement.

John Dewey's publication of "The School and Society" (1907) placed industrial occupations at the very center of the elementary school curriculum. In "The place of manual training in the elementary course of study" (1901) Dewey again expressed the use of the occupations as a vehicle of instruction. Professor Charles R. Richards (Bawden, 1950) in an editorial in the "Manual Training Magazine" (1904) suggested that the term "Industrial Arts" be used in place of "Manual Training." This gave rise to the Industrial Arts (IA) movement. Trade and Industrial (T&I) vocational education emerged as a major education program with the passage of the Smith-Hughes Act of 1917.

Since both T&I and IA were implemented about the same time, there was competition between the two in regard to the consistency of each. Some in IA wanted to make it prevocational while others wanted to keep its conception broad and make it an essential part of general education.

The period after World War II was a time of much curriculum study and recommendation. William Warner and his graduate students at Ohio State University published the first IA curriculum proposal in 1946–47 (Herschbach, 1997). It established the use of personnel management structures in the laboratory and concentrated on five areas of study: communications, construction, power, transportation, and manufacturing.

Curricular refinements that followed promoted content based on the technology of industry, inclusion of mass-production procedures, and further use of business structures. Donald Maley of the University of Maryland proposed student activities organized around investigation, exploration, analysis, testing, and the use of tools and materials to solve problems. Many states, including California, developed their own plans for industrial arts education. These plans may be found at the websites of the several state departments of education (ERIC Education Resources Information Center, n.d.).

TECHNICAL EDUCATION

For many years, higher education institutions have educated engineers, doctors lawyers, veterinarians, home economists and other professional workers. The public vocational schools have provided workers for industry, farming, wholesale, and retail selling, homemaking, and other occupations since about 1920. During the 1960s a need surfaced for workers that required both technical knowledge and skills of a different nature than those needed by tradesman, engineers, scientists, and other professional workers. This area of training was that known as technical education, which is a level of education that trains technicians and technologists.

Many factors have been responsible for the development of technical education. Among these are technological developments in industry, impacts of war, increases in the initial employment age, the mushrooming of technical information, larger high school enrollment and an increased interest in adult education.

With the Information and Digital Ages, technological development has increased even more rapidly since the 1990s. Scientists, engineers, technicians and skilled workers have been developing new materials, processes, and products during the years. These discoveries and inventions have improved levels of living and reduced, by mechanization, much of the drudgery of handwork. The roboticization of industry has replaced the worker in hot, heavy and hazardous occupations. The manufacture and use of many new processes and products have demanded workers and operators with new knowledge and skills different from those obtained heretofore in either trade or professional courses. These new knowledge and skills have been in the area of technical education.

More and more adults are becoming interested in educational programs. This increased interest is partly due to changes in the requirements of occupations in which adults are employed. New technological developments require new skills. Ordinarily these must be acquired by employed workers, especially if the new content is not so extensive as to make training on the job impractical. The rising trend in the educational level of all citizens, especially noticeable in recent years, has made adults more conscious of the need for both general and career and technical courses. In addition, continued developments and changes in technology underscores the need for continuing education across the lifespan.

The need for technicians, laboratory assistants, testers, supervisors, inspectors, and other technical workers is evident in many occupational fields. The more important areas of need at this time appear to be in agriculture, business, health, family and consumer sciences, industry, and public service (U.S. Department of Labor, 2005).

VOCATIONAL GUIDANCE

The vocational guidance movement developed almost simultaneously with the vocational education movement (Barlow, 1976, p. 52). John M. Brewer, a Harvard University Professor, considered vocational guidance as both the vestibule and the back porch for vocational education.

Vocational guidance is concerned with the problems and techniques involved in choosing an occupation and in becoming adjusted in it. Vocational guidance, like vocational education, had its origins in the changing nature of work and has developed concurrently with, but independently of, vocational education. The development of vocational guidance has been due to the efforts of individuals and organizations interested in the problems of workers and prospective workers who were struggling with occupational choices or were dissatisfied with choices previously made (Technical & Vocational Education & Training (TVET), n.d.). Vocational educators learned early in the history of vocational education that the choice of an occupation and the adjustment thereto were important factors in the efficient production of the worker.

The relationship of vocational guidance to the efficiency of work stimulated vocational educators to acquire some proficiency in vocational guidance to enable them to counsel more intelligently with vocational students. The need for more extensive knowledge and skill in vocational guidance led vocational educators to seek an expansion of guidance services and, as a result, federal funds were made available as a reimbursement for certain vocational guidance services. The use of federal funds and the parallel development of vocational education and vocational guidance have led to some difference in points of view in the relationship between the two. Some changes have occurred in the administration of the public school guidance program as result of the National Defense Education Act of 1958, which

TABLE 3.3   Early Philosopher's Views on Occupations

- Plato (427 BC–347 BC) suggested that each worker should be assigned to the one occupation for which he was naturally fitted.
- Cicero (106 BC–43 BC) stated, "We must decide what manner of men we wish to be and what calling in life we would follow; and this is the most difficult problem in the world."
- Pascal (1623–1662) discussed the importance of a wise choice of an occupation in his writings.
- John Locke (1695) suggested that children's natures and aptitudes should be studied as a means of determining their capabilities for earning and the extent to which improvement might be secured.
- Charles Dickens (1853) published the Bleak House, which depicted a youth who was in need of vocational guidance to find out what his natural bent was.
- Samuel Smiles (1859) published a volume entitled Self Help, which was designed to assist an individual in developing habits of industry.

Source: This information was gathered from several sources.

authorized federal funds for guidance services. This lesson is concerned with various aspects of vocational guidance programs.

Human's choice of an occupation prior to the industrial revolution was influenced by such factors as heredity, tradition, and superstition. The usual procedure during this time was for the son to learn the trade or profession of his father. Little consideration was given to such factors as aptitude, interest, and personal preference.

Early beginning: as illustrated in Table 3.3, the writing of the philosophers of ancient times indicates that some of them were concerned about occupational choices:

Work of Frank Parsons

Present-day programs in vocational guidance developed as a result of the work of Dr. Frank Parsons. Parsons was instrumental in founding the Vocational Bureau of Boston, which was organized to deal with occupational adjustment problems of both youth and adults (Barlow, 1976, p. 53). He found that people were greatly interested in seeking advice about occupations. In time, individual counseling gave way to vocational guidance. Parson's work in this area is represented in a timeline in Table 3.4.

In his book Dr. Parsons suggested the method of the vocational counselor involved the following consideration:

(a) Personal data, (b) Self-analysis, (c) The person's own choice and decision, (d) Counselors analysis, (e) Outlook in the vocational field, (f) Induction and advice, (g) General helpfulness in fitting into the chosen work.

TABLE 3.4   Dr. Parson and Vocational Choice Milestones

- He developed the Vocation Bureau, which formally opened in January 1908, in the Boston Civic Service House.
- The Vocational Bureau served individuals for ages 15–72.
- The bureau furnished information so that individuals could choose an occupation or career.
- Dr. Parsons established a vocation department at the Boston YMCA in 1908. A school for training counselors was initiated in the department.
- Dr. Parsons' book Choosing a Vocation was published in May 1909. He had died in September 1908.

The counselee was expected to record on paper his personal data and self-analysis. The counselor was instructed to test the counselee's choice of an occupation and to provide him with occupational information. Parsons is said to have been the first person to use the term vocational guidance in his first report on the work of the Vocational Bureau (Barlow, 1976, p. 53), and he paved the way for organizing vocational guidance programs in public schools by suggesting the educational institution should undertake this responsibility. However, according to Hershenson (2006), Pauline Agassiz Shaw, Meyer Bloomfield, and Ralph Albertson should be credited with initiating vocational guidance in the field. Parsons organized the work of the Vocation Bureau for the collection and study of information about occupations and workers. He recognized the importance of publicity and enlisted the assistance of friends and co-workers to carry on the work.

CONCLUSION

The origins of the different components of career and technical education and historical considerations reveal clear pathways regarding when and where vocational education came into being. Knowledge of the history of career and technical education will assist readers and learners in better understanding the current concept of vocational education. Without this knowledge of the history of career and technical education, readers or learners may find it hard to relate to current issues of career and technical education. As Kincheloe (1999, p. 93) noted:

> Without historical insight, vocational educational policy makers fail to gain insights into the relationship between schooling and work that the past may provide. As a result, vocational educational leaders may devote great energy to reinventing a pedagogy incapable of addressing the demands of democracy and the needs of an evolving economy....Historical consciousness can

help vocational educators recognize the inherent problems in particular assumptions or particular ways of operating and facilitate the development of pragmatic alternatives.

Rather than trying to convince anyone, vocational education reflects the concept that education is life, not just the preparation for life. It is built upon the ideal of individual differences among people; individual differences created and emphasized through the interaction of biological inheritance, the specific environment which surrounds the individual and the unique characteristics of each person. As you read this chapter, you have probably developed some common themes such as "survival," "progress" and "civilization." Indeed, such connections are quite accurate as vocational education has its roots in pragmatism (Evans & Herr, 1978).

REFERENCES

Ackerknecht, E. H. (1982). *A short history of medicine.* Baltimore: John Hopkins University.

Bawden, W. (1950). *Leaders in industrial education.* Milwaukee, WI: Bruce.

Barlow, M. L. (1967). *History of industrial education in the United States.* Peoria, IL: Charles A. Bennett.

Barlow, M. L. (1976a). 200 years of vocational education, 1776–1976: The awakening, 1776–1826. *American Vocational Journal, 51*(5), 23–28.

Barlow, M. L. (1976b). 200 years of vocational education, 1776–1976: Independent action, 1826–1876. *American Vocational Journal, 51*(5), 31–40.

Barlow, M. L. (1976c). 200 years of vocational education, 1776–1976: The vocational education age emerges, 1876–1926. *American Vocational Journal, 51*(5), 45–58.

Beatty, A. J. (1918). *Corporation schools.* Bloomington, IL: Public School. Retrieved April 25, 2007, from http://books.google.com/books/pdf/Corporation_Schools.pdf

Bellwood, P. (2004). *First farmers: The origins of agricultural societies.* Ames, IA: Blackwell.

Clendening, L. (1960). *Sourcebook of medical history.* Mineola, NY: Courier Dover.

Coates, C. P. (1923). *History of the manual training school of Washington University.* Dept. of the Interior, Bureau of Education Bulletin, 1923, No. 3. Washington, D. C.: U.S. Government Printing Office.

Cochrane, W. W. (1993). *The development of American agriculture: An historical analysis* (2nd ed.). Minneapolis: University of Minnesota Press.

Dewey, J. (1901, February). The place of manual training in the elementary course of study. *Manual Training Magazine,* 193–199.

Dewey, J. (1907). *The school and society: Being three lectures by John Dewey supplemented by a statement of the University Elementary School.* University of Chicago Press.

ERIC Education Resources Information Center. (n.d.). *Suggested master plan for industrial arts programs in North Dakota schools final report research series number 22.* Washington, D. C.: Education Resources Information Center. (ERIC Document Reproduction Service No. ED 115 979). Retrieved April 26, 2007, from

http://eric.ed.gov/ERICWebPortal/Home.portal?_nfpb=true&_pageLabel
=RecordDetails&ERICExtSearch_SearchValue_0=ED115979&ERICExtSear
ch_SearchType_0=eric_accno&objectId=0900000b800ec8bf

Evans, R. N., & Herr, E. L. (1978). *Foundations of vocational education.* New York: Macmillan Publishing Company.

Fafunwa, A. B. (1974). *History of education in Nigeria.* Ibadan: NPS Educational.

Gerbracht, C., & Babcock, R. (1969). *Elementary school industrial arts.* New York: Bruce.

Graham, J. (1933). *The evolution of business education in the United States and its implications for business.* Berkeley: University of Southern California Press.

Herschbach, D. R. (1997). From industrial arts to technology education: The search for direction. *Journal of Technology Studies 23*(1), 24–32 Retrieved April 25, 2007, from http://140.126.32.4/NTNU/read-TEES02/JTS-IATE-Haerschbach.pdf.

Hershenson, D. B. (2006). Frank Parsons's enablers: Pauline Agassiz Shaw, Meyer Bloomfield, and Ralph Albertson. *Career Development Quarterly, 55*(1), 77–84.

Holbrook, J. (1826). *American Lyceum, or Society for the Improvement of Schools, and Diffusion of Useful Knowledge.* Boston: Perkins & Martin. Retrieved April 25, 2007, from http://books.google.com/books/pdf/American_Lyceum__Or_Society_for_the_Impr.pdf

Kincheloe, J. L. (1999). *How do we tell the workers?* Boulder, CO: Westview Press.

Long, H. B. (1990). Psychological control in self-controlled learning. *International Journal of Lifelong Education, 9*(4), 331–338.

Miller, R., & Smalley, L. (1963). *Selected readings in industrial arts.* Bloomington: McKnight & McKnight.

Nafukho, F. M. (2007). Ubuntuism: An African social philosophy relevant to adult and workplace learning. In K. P. King & V. C. X. Wang (Eds.), *Comparative adult education around the globe* (pp. 59–67). Hangzhou: Zhejiang University Press.

Nafukho, F. M., Amutabi, M. N., & Otunga, R. N. (2005). *Foundations of adult education in Africa.* Cape Town, South Africa: Pearson/UNESCO.

Roberts, R. W. (1965). *Vocational and practical arts education: History, development, and principles.* New York: Harper & Row.

Technical & Vocational Education & Training (TVET). (n.d.). *Introduction.* Retrieved December 25, 2006, from http://www.tvet-pal.org/counseling/intro.html

University of California, Santa Cruz. (2003). *Teaching organic framing and gardening: Resources for instructors.* Santa Cruz: UC Santa Cruz Center for Agroecology and Sustainable Food Systems.

U.S. Department of Labor. (2005). *Tomorrow's jobs.* Retrieved April 26, 2007, from http://www.bls.gov/oco/oco2003.htm

Williams, S. J. (2000). *Essentials of health services.* Florence, KY: Thomas Delmar Learning.

CHAPTER 4

CURRENT INSTRUCTIONAL PROGRAMS IN CAREER AND TECHNICAL EDUCATION

Kathleen P. King
Fordham University

Victor C. X. Wang
California State University, Long Beach

Career and technical education (CTE) is a massive enterprise in the United States. Thousands of comprehensive high schools, vocational and technical high schools, area vocational centers, and community colleges offer career and technical education programs (U.S. Department of Education, 2006). On the importance of career and technical education, it is noted, "CTE is about providing knowledge and skills to individuals of all ages, allowing them to have choices in their future and to reach full earning potential. It is about learning for life, citizenship and career success" (Bray, 2007, p. 6). Virtually every high school student takes at least one career and technical education course, and one in four students takes three or more courses in a single program area. One-third of college students are involved in career and technical programs, and as many as 40 million adults engage in short-

Building Workforce Competencies in Career and Technical Education, pages 61–88

term postsecondary occupational training (U.S. Department of Education, 2006). This figure provides a compelling demonstration of the importance of career and technical education in the nation.

Instructional programs vary from current business education to vocational guidance within career and technical education. They have been offered largely in response to the "Nation At Risk" report (National Commission on Excellence in Education, 1983), which was released in the early 1980s. According to this report, many of our high school students were dropping out of schools and they did not compete with students from other industrialized nations. It may be true that U.S. students do not even compete with students from developing countries such as India and China. Educators in the field of career and technical education felt a strong need to offer interesting and relevant courses to high school students in order for them to complete high school. However, since many school districts have raised graduation requirements for the non-practical courses, math, science, reading and English and many schools have added exit exams in recent years, it has become more difficult for secondary school students to enroll in vocational education courses (Rothrock & Walker, 2007; Stone, Kowske, & Alfeld, 2004).

In fact the *No Child Left Behind* (NCLB) initiatives have placed such a great emphasis on outcomes rather than curricula that at this time educators and public constituencies see that the legislation may be leaving many students of different socioeconomic and/or racial strata and different learning or vocational interests behind. The most recent trend to counteract these trends in decreasing emphasis and/or interest in CTE is to integrate technology and general education content into vocational education courses (John Hopkins University, 2004; King, 2007a). In this chapter, readers have the opportunity to compare and contrast all of the courses offered in the different components of career and technical education program and help determine whether they are adequate enough given the nature of the Information Age within which we live.

CONTEMPORARY BUSINESS EDUCATION

Business Education has come a long way since 1980. It has taken most of that time to fully accept the idea that keyboarding should be taught on a computer keyboard or electronic typewriter. Some typewriting teachers resisted this inexorable change, clinging instead to teaching obsolete skills like mechanical centering and other formatting details. Some of the newer areas that are covered in business programs besides keyboarding skills include:

- Word Processing
- Desktop Publishing
- Electronic Mail
- Development of Human Capital

For example, the Development of Human Capital in a Technological Environment is important if a business is going to be competitive in the local and global market and survive. Some of the topics that should be covered are:

Globalization: Students should be aware of the social values and mores, cultures, politics, business protocols, religions, and general working habits of other countries in order to be better prepared to communicate with people worldwide.

Technological Integration: People must be educated to accept the fact that products, services, equipment, and working environment capitalize on integration and connectivity. In many cases people must decide on what combination of components to use to get a job completed efficiently. Beyond mastering the basics in technology, employees must understand how an information system relies on the interrelationship among many components. They must develop alternative ways of approaching a task, because the familiar way of doing something might not mesh with the work of other employees who are contributing to the product.

Knowledge Specialists: The demand for information specialists and knowledge engineers will increase as knowledge continues to grow at exponential rates. Workers need not memorize vast amounts of information. Instead they must find efficient ways to retrieve information from databases. Skills for searching and sorting information are extremely valuable. These skills will become even more vital as information database services proliferate.

Business Competitiveness: The importance of understanding business ethics and politics cannot be over emphasized. As greater amounts of information become available to consumers, business will be forced to become more accountable for their products and services. Future workers must learn that competitiveness does not mean unwillingness to share, especially as more and more large businesses enter into joint ventures.

The Work Ethic: It appears that our nation has come full circle in our personal values and ideals of work. Most people no longer work because of job satisfaction, but because monetary gains can upgrade their standards of living. It is important to develop attitude and skills that stress dependability, punctuality, loyalty, and the willingness to give an honest day's work.

Change: Change is a constant in our world today. It must not only be accepted but also sought. With the computerization of nearly every facet of life, individuals can become comfortable with technology; however, the technology is constantly changing so the business educator must continually pursue cutting-edge techniques and procedures lest their skills and knowledge become obsolete. In addition they need to pass along the vital perspectives of changing knowledge and lifelong learning to their students.

Diversity: It is a reality that we live, learn and work in a diverse world. Diversity refers to "any dimension that can be used to differentiate groups and people from one another" (Giovannini, 2004, p. 22). Within business education, diversity of learners and educators can be categorized into three dimensions, internal (age, gender, ethnicity, race, physical traits), external (geographic location, social economic status, personal habits, appearance), and organizational (work experiences, work location, work and learning content and environment). For business education programs to develop workforce competencies among learners, there is an urgent and compelling need to teach diversity (Adams, Sewell, & Hall, 2003).

These issues directly influence the development of Human Capital and affect society's ability to meet future challenges. Career and technical educators and especially business educators have a vast array of resources with which to address these issues (Darling, Greenwood, & Hansen-Gandy, 1998; Foxman & Easterling, 1995; Gay & Howard, 2000; Sabo, 2000). Addressing these issues is part of educating for life as well as training a better work force (Hill, 2006; King & Biro, 2006).

COURSES USUALLY COVERED IN BUSINESS EDUCATION

As mentioned earlier, the business education curriculum has more or less evolved as the public and industry made demands for more and more commercial or business education (Schmidt, 1990). For a number of years the secondary and post secondary offerings remained somewhat static. The following are generally accepted as indicative of the various offerings at secondary and post secondary levels:

Secondary offerings:

- Bookkeeping
- Shorthand
- Keyboarding
- Penmanship

- Economics
- Merchandising
- Salesmanship
- Entrepreneurship
- Marketing

Post-secondary offerings: In the case of graduate level programs which are mainly offered in business colleges or in colleges of education, Gaytan (2006) identified the following courses as forming the core curriculum of business education programs:

- Accounting
- Secretarial Science
- Computer Programming
- Web Page Design
- Legal Environment of Business
- Fundamentals of Computer Application
- Methods of Teaching Business Education
- Professional Writing in Business
- Instructional Strategies for Technology
- Managerial Communications
- Advanced Keyboarding
- Technology Support Systems
- Document Processing
- Managerial Reporting

Post-secondary programs are usually integrated or combined so that some of the course work covered in high school evolves as a combination course. Post-secondary programs are also more fortunate to have more sophisticated machines, so higher technological instruction can be provided at this level.

INSTRUCTIONAL PROGRAMS IN AGRICULTURE

Agriculture education is defined as resources for agriculture education programs, including classroom instruction, leadership, and supervised agricultural experience programs that prepare students for college or entrance into agricultural careers (California Department of Education, 2006). Since 1917, with the passage of the Smith-Hughes Act, federal and state legislation has provided leadership for the implementation and improvement of agricultural education programs. A successful agriculture education program must be based on three components: classroom instruction, Future

Farmers of America (FFA) leadership activities, and Supervised Occupational Experience Projects. Two major federal and state programs provide support for agricultural education programs: the Carl D. Perkins Vocational and Technical Education Act of 1998 (20 U.S.C. 2301 *et seq.*, as amended by Public Law 105-332), and the Agricultural Education Vocational Incentive Grant Program. The programs seek to accomplish four major purposes (California Department of Education, 2006) which stated:

- Enable local education agencies to improve the curriculum for students enrolled in agricultural education programs through the development and implementation of (a) an integrated academic and vocational curriculum, (b) curriculum that reflects workplace needs and instruction, and (c) support services for special populations.
- Increase the competence of future and current high school, middle grades, and regional occupational centers and programs agricultural education instructors in developing and implementing a new integrated curriculum, student and program certification systems, technical preparation strategies, and effective instructional methodologies.
- Promote the development and use of curriculum, instructional materials, and instructional strategies that prepare students in all aspects of the agricultural industry and foster critical thinking, problem solving, leadership, and academic and technical skill attainment.
- Increase linkages between secondary and postsecondary institutions offering agricultural education programs; between academic and agricultural educators; and among agricultural educators, the agricultural industry, professional associations, and local communities.

According to the literature, many benefits of agricultural education programs have been identified. Such benefits include:

- Collaboration, articulation, and networking with all levels of delivery systems (elementary through postsecondary) for instructors.
- Supervised entrepreneurial and workplace learning experiences for students.
- Linkages and partnerships with business and industry for instructors and students.
- Professional development opportunities for teachers, administrators, and counselors.
- Curriculum development based on performance and content standards for instructors

- On-site technical assistance in programs for instructors and students.
- A foundation for students in the academic and technical skills necessary for career and personal success.
- Student leadership and interpersonal skills.
- An authentic assessment of knowledge, skills, and abilities through on-demand demonstrations and portfolios. (California Department of Education, 2006)

Agriculture education programs consist of classroom work, shop work, organized youth activities, and in some cases supervised agricultural experiences. This kind of instruction requires that the instructors have college instruction and work experience to be able to manage agricultural educational program.

- Responsibilities of the Teachers include: Classroom teaching, supervising the farming and other experiences of students; engaging in community service; developing satisfactory public relations; maintaining adequate teaching facilities, materials, and equipment; organizing, supervising and conducting student club work; and making records and reports.
- Qualifications of the Teacher: Professional qualification dictates that the teacher graduates from an approved four-year agriculture education program from a land grant college. The teacher should have a minimum of two years of farm experience after the age of fourteen, preference is usually given to those that are farm reared. The teacher should have experiences with agriculture student organization and should have experience as a student in high school vocational agriculture. The teacher must have knowledge in teaching methods for both classroom and shop activities. The teacher must possess leadership abilities, resourcefulness, industriousness, open-mindedness, and dependability.
- Teaching Methods: The agriculture teacher must use a number of teaching techniques including: lecture, demonstration, group discussion, field trips, contests, group projects and student club activities.
- Teaching Materials: Such materials depend upon what course is being taught. However, textbooks, extension bulletins, shop manuals, handout materials, homework, slides, videos, and computers can be used to teach the classes.
- Related Class Instruction: In some cases an agriculture instructor may utilize other high school classes to supplement agriculture

classes. These may be salesmanship from the distributive education program, or typing from the business program.

- Building Utilized: An agriculture program should have a classroom, shop or laboratory tool room, washroom and an office/conference room.
- Equipment: These should include all kinds of farm mechanics, metalworking, woodworking, sheet metal and welding equipment. A good set of hand tools are also needed to be able to show the students how to use them in maintaining farm equipment and facilities.

COURSES TAUGHT IN AGRICULTURE PROGRAMS

For most agriculture programs, courses in animal care and production, plant care and production, farm mechanics, building construction, hydraulics, electricity, welding, lathe work, sheet metal work, masonry work, fence building and business management are included. (See for example Arizona Department of Education (2006); Georgia Agricultural Education (2006).) Certainly local geography, climate and industry indicators may have originally influenced local agricultural programs. However contemporary agricultural education programs cast a wider net of knowledge and skills for learners in order for them to realize the broad expanse of this innovative and essential field of study.

HEALTH OCCUPATIONS EDUCATION

Health Science Occupations Education (HSOE) prepares students for careers related to medicine, nursing, dentistry, and allied health programs. Students preparing for health careers or for teaching careers in health occupations can gain valuable career information and network with other professionals by participating in the HSOE program. This program provides students technical skills, health care competencies, and opportunities to obtain the knowledge necessary to satisfy the requirements for entry-level health care jobs. HSOE is dedicated to educating today's students for tomorrow's health-care community (Wisconsin Department of Public Instruction, 2006).

These programs are planned to prepare individuals below the professional level to provide patient care in health related settings. These settings may be long-term facilities (rest homes), clinics, hospitals, doctor's offices, hospitals, etc. This means that training is below the registered nurse as well as the medical doctor. The following areas could be included in this continuum at a Vocational School (ROP in California) or a Community College:

Regional Occupational Program

Practical Nurse
Dental Assistant
Medical Laboratory Assistant
Occupational Therapist Assistant
Medical Office Assistant
Medication Aide
Geriatric Aide
Home Health Care Worker

Community College

Dental Laboratory Technician
Radiological Technologist
Medical Records Technician
Respiratory Therapist

For further examples of occupations and related resources, HSOE programs may include the following helpful resources: North Carolina Public Schools (2006), Illinois State Board of Education (n.d.), and Health Occupations Students of America (HSOA) (2007).

These programs all use classroom instruction along with clinical instruction in a health care facility so that students spend 50 percent or more of their instructional time on-the-job under the supervision of a clinical instructor. The programs are under strict guidelines furnished by the appropriate State Boards in regard to:

- What is taught?
- When it is taught?
- Where it is taught?
- The maximum size of class for classroom instruction
- The maximum size of class for clinical instruction

All graduates of these programs must pass State Board Examinations after completing the program and before they are certified.

HEALTH OCCUPATIONS INSTRUCTION

A number of states have promoted the use of Competency Profiles as a system of planning the content of the various Health Occupations Programs

(Illinois State Board of Education, n.d.; North Carolina Public Schools; 2006). The use of these Competency Profiles assists the instructor and the student in evaluating whether or not the instructor or student has covered the items, which are listed on the profile.

Another use of the Competency Profiles is that of assisting the instructor in using competency-based education as a technique for guiding instruction. This Competency Based instruction can be modularized and it can also be individualized so that the students can progress at their own pace and in many cases be able to understand the material better (Illinois State Board of Education, n.d.; North Carolina Public Schools; 2006). If the Health Occupations curriculum is modularized, a number of the modules may be used in various health areas so that a sharing of materials such as multimedia can be used by the institution.

A good example of a module that could be produced that all health care programs could use would be one on how one should handle a patient with Acquired Immune Deficiency Syndrome (AIDS). This is one of the major problem areas that health care workers must face. Other areas that may be modularized so that all health care students may cover would be one on dealing with an aging population, and one on some new technological developments that all may need instruction on in relation to their program. Competency Profiles could be used to determine some common core curriculum materials that could be modularized and individualized. Some areas that may be examined are:

Medical Terminology
Anatomy
Physiology
Microbiology
First Aid
Taking Vital Signs
Observation Skills
Microscope use
Nutrition
Aseptic Techniques
Computer skills
The Metric System
Cardiopulmonary Resuscitation (CPR)
Moving and transferring patients
Simple Lab Tests
Blood Pressure Measurement

With the use of video enhanced instruction, students can view the videos over and over to be able to master any of the procedures, terms, etc. that need to be covered in a course. Only when the course is individualized and mediated, can the course be set up for the individual learner and individual differences.

Health Occupations Educators should take advantage of all the new technologies that are available to assist the instructor in providing good instructional material for their students. Carl Perkins Vocational Education funds are available to upgrade instruction through the use of video, computer assisted learning, etc. Increasingly more institutions will be able to use more DVDS, CDS, online video, streaming video and laser disks for instructional material since more of those are available.

Some writers are indicating that Health Occupations Educators should be considering offering a program, which would allow a student to become a multi-skilled practitioner (Hoberty, 1996). This would indicate that individuals should cross train in order to practice in more than one health related job. The student would obtain the required competencies to qualify for more than one job title. For example, a student may be qualified as a medical laboratory technician, radiographer, and respiratory therapist.

This movement has emerged as an effort to relieve workforce shortages in rural hospitals. Alabama and Illinois pioneered the development of programs to cross-train health care workers in the early 1970's and were widely adopted in the late 1980's (Bamberg & Blayney, 1989). Some hospitals and systems in California have also tried cross-training with limited successes.

If Health Occupation Educators utilize Competency Profiles as mentioned earlier, it should be fairly easy to decide on the core competencies and then have options that the student would follow for specific areas. If the student then decides to follow three or more options, cross training would be quite simple. Perhaps the greatest challenges are in obtaining agreement from the various governing boards as new health occupations continue to emerge.

CLINICAL INSTRUCTION

The Clinical Instruction for Health Occupations varies from program to program. For a number of the programs, such as Licensed Vocational Nursing (LVN), an instructor from the school also instructs at the clinical site. However, in some instances with other kinds of health programs the on-site instructor may be an employee of the facility in which the clinical is held (North Carolina Public Schools, 2006). In the case of LVN Programs, the instructor who teaches the classes in the institution also teaches on the clinical site. However, in some cases the institution employs persons who are strictly clinical instructors. This occurs because most instructors at a clinical site are limited to a maximum of ten (10) students when they may have 30 enrolled in the program. This would either require the instructor to have two (2) clinical assignments with fifteen (15) students each or an extra clinical instructor is employed to assist in the clinical setting. These numbers vary by type of program.

Students in the clinical setting are required to perform the various tasks required of the health worker in the particular occupation for which they are training. Since this is a requirement for the training, no reimbursement is required from the participating clinical institution. However, in some cases a small stipend may be given by the clinic institution while the student is training in the clinical setting.

HIGH TECHNOLOGY TRENDS IN VOCATIONAL-INDUSTRIAL EDUCATION

The fundamental problem that has faced vocational industrial education in recent years has been the rapid change from person-to-machines (Freeman, 1996; National Clearinghouse for Educational Facilities (NCEF), 2006). Economic and technological advancement have lead leading manufacturers to use more robots and computer controlled manufacturing centers and to employ fewer people in the skill area (El Camino College, 2006). The thought of robots and the computer-controlled machines doing work for us is fascinating, but it raises several important questions for career and technical education and society in general.

The fundamental problems facing industry in the United States are the cost of productivity and the maintenance of quality products. Economic planners promote reindustrialization with the use of robots and computer controlled manufacturing wherever possible in order to decrease costs of production and to increase the quality of the product being produced.

The manufacturing sector is feeling the influence of technology far more than most persons realize. The work force employed at the turn of the 21st century was drastically different than that employed only 15 years earlier. The widespread use of computer-aided design (CAD) and computer-aided manufacturing (CAM) has, for example, brought machine shops and engineering departments closer together (Connecticut State Department of Education, 2006). This affects the jobs of assembly-line workers dramatically. Workers will not assemble the products but rather direct the robots to do the work. Some of the contemporary terms being utilized in manufacturing are flexible manufacturing and just-in-time delivery. Flexible manufacturing simply means that a computer controlled manufacturing system is used. Just-in-time delivery means that parts and sub-assemblies are made just in time to be shipped and/or assembled. This dynamic decreases the stocking and warehousing of parts. These two concepts have greatly affected how manufacturing industries conduct their business.

Workers in factories will need to be better educated, especially in the field of computers. As technology advances, workers will need retraining on a continual basis in order to keep abreast of changes in the technology being used. Vocational Industrial Education programs need to keep up as well if competent, up-to-date workers are to be effectively prepared or retrained (Connecticut State Department of Education, 2006; El Camino College, 2006; National Clearinghouse for Educational Facilities (NCEF), 2006; Smith, 2000).Craft areas are also experiencing some new methods of conducting their tasks. For example, computers are used for material purchases and to track costs for projects. Designing and estimating of costs are also conducted with computers and software designed for those purposes. Building trades programs will need to incorporate computer instruction into their classrooms. If the vocational industrial education programs do not include instruction in these areas for future carpenters, contractors, and builders they will not be prepared to enter the labor market.

Service areas such as auto mechanics are also experiencing drastic changes as the automobile is being controlled more and more by computers. Automotive students will need to be trained on the newest computer based diagnostic equipment if they are to enter the automotive technology area and be able to service the modern automobile or truck (Connecticut State Department of Education, 2006).

The image of the skilled trades person does not appeal to a number of high school students. The number of persons who are counseled into these programs seems to be diminishing. Also the increased need for persons who have a good grasp of mathematics and science will limit the number of persons who can profit from some of the "High Tech" training needed for the manufacturing, craft and service sectors. Unless these deficiencies are corrected, the United States could face a serious shortage of properly trained persons for a technological society (Friedman, 2005; King, 2007b). There is a definite need to develop programs with government, industry, and education all working together in an effort to establish, once again, a high level of quality productivity in the United States.

Perhaps one of the ways that vocational industrial education can produce quality persons will be to work cooperatively with industry, the crafts and the service sector. Basic competencies in cognate, psychomotor and the affective domain can be addressed in the classroom at schools but the more in-depth cognate and psychomotor competencies can best be accomplished through cooperative programs or apprenticeships where the student works on-the-job with up-to-date equipment to be current with the industry, craft or service area. This would alleviate the cost to schools in obtaining the expensive machines being used in the crafts, industry or service areas.

CURRENT FAMILY AND CONSUMER SCIENCES PROGRAMS

Originating from the domain of "home economics" and expanding to a more comprehensive and problem-solving orientation, family and consumer sciences, human sciences, human ecology or home economics, is an academic discipline which combines aspects of consumer science, nutrition, cooking, parenting and human development, interior decoration, textiles, family economics, housing, apparel design and resource management as well as other related subjects. Today, family and consumer sciences combine social science, including its emphasis on the well-being of families, individuals, and communities, and natural science with its emphasis on nutrition and textile science. The discipline as it originated from home economics in the U.S. was first established at Iowa State University in 1875 and spread to other land grant universities (Schneider, 2000; Stage & Vincenti, 1997) The field appealed to women to have their own niche while men studied subjects such as agriculture or shop courses of study. For many years it was traditional for junior high and high school girls to study "Home Economics" (primarily cooking and sewing) while boys of the same studied "Shop" (carpentry, drafting, auto repair, etc.). Students of either gender were excluded, strongly discouraged or outright banned from taking the other subjects (Stage & Vincenti, 1997). Courses that are related to the traditional Home Economics and Shop designations now are recognized subject areas in Secondary education and have become universal subjects, in that students of both genders may participate in them.

Home Economics developed in the last 100 years to a broader cluster of studies which is termed Family and Consumer Sciences. Family and Consumer Sciences has gained great prominence in high schools and CTE schools across the USA and evolved as a field itself overtime. Originally Family and Consumer Sciences placed major emphasis upon the following due to societal needs:

1. Consumer Educations and Management
2. Nutrition and Food Management
3. Human Developments and Family Living
4. Housing and Living Environment
5. Clothing/Apparel and Textile Products

However, in the 1990s and 2000s, we experienced further development in the understanding of this field, especially through the continuing efforts of the national association, American Association of Family and Consumer Sciences as it continued to labor to keep the field relevant to societal needs.

The Body of Knowledge for the discipline and profession was identified more than twenty years ago to facilitate several evolving developments. Evolutions within the profession continue and include renewal of the certification examination and the standards for Accreditation of FCS programs. During this past year, several members of the Association have provided leadership in the revision of the CIP codes. Finally, dialogue during the FCS Higher Education Summit, held in February 1999 and a session at the 1999 Annual Meeting addressing a comprehensive vision for the future contributed to the decision to invite the elected leaders of professional organizations and societies of the family and consumer sciences profession to discuss the Body of Knowledge for the future...

A continuing trend in the field is the need for Family and Consumer Sciences professionals to function as specialists, requiring both considerable depth in one subject area specialization and the ability to integrate concepts from other areas of the family and consumer sciences knowledge base. The proposed conceptual framework addresses this need.

Basic Human Needs is one of the key elements. Basic Human Needs may be operationalized to include subject area specializations. Basic Human Needs may be conceptualized broadly to allow flexibility for programs and professionals to articulate in unique and varied ways the role of the specialist in Family and Consumer Sciences. New specializations and programs may emerge to focus on the interaction between the common body of knowledge, cross-cutting themes, and basic human needs. Basic Human Needs, as an organizing principle, include traditional specializations and make possible the emergence of new specializations. The dynamic nature of the framework provides a mechanism for continual reflection, enhancement, and development of programs and specializations in the field. (Baugher, Anderson, Green, Shane, Jolly, Miles & Nickols, 2003, p. 4)

Indeed, the reader may also see how Family and Consumer Science understanding of critical thinking skills and interaction among the specializations of the field one with the other is seen in the following quote,

During the past two decades, the curriculum in family and consumer sciences (FACS) education has undergone many changes. These changes are partly due to such events as the series of publications by Marjorie Brown and those she coauthored with Beatrice Paolucci (1978, 1979, and 1980) and The Carl D. Perkins Vocational and Applied Technology Education Act Amendments. The effects of these two phenomena are recognizable in the FACS education curriculum through both program and course offerings. In fact, secondary FACS education programs are moving toward career preparation and an interdisciplinary curriculum, and many programs deliver the content using a critical science perspective (Smith, 1998). (Smith & Hall, 1999)

This development is a significant leap forward from the original domain of Home Economics of the nineteenth century. It also critically demonstrates the continued insight and innovation of CTE educators and the capability of CTE careers to keep pace with hi-tech innovations, societal, and economic developments.

CURRENT OCCUPATIONAL PROGRAMS

Programs which are offered to assist individuals in developing competencies to become employable in occupations related to family and consumer sciences are offered at high schools, regional occupational programs, area vocational technical schools, and community colleges. Since all of these programs have an on-the-job or work-experience component, the instructors are required to become certified as instructor/coordinators so that they will have the competencies needed to coordinate the on-the-job experiences.

U.S. State Departments of Education (SDE) have specific guidelines under which these family and consumer science programs are to be operated. These are usually published on the SDE website. Two of these are described here.

> *Occupational Home Economics (OHE):* This is an institution based program that prepares students with attitudes and entry level skills for employment in home economics and related occupations through a combination of classroom instruction, simulation, and supervised work experience.
>
> *Home Economics Cooperative Education (HECE):* This is a cooperative instructional program where the student obtains skills through classroom and on-the-job training. Students receive direct related and indirect related instruction in the institution through regular classroom instruction. The psychomotor skills are obtained on-the-job through a training agreement with the training station in regard to what the student is going to be taught at the work place.

In addition to state standards, national standards have been developed for the field of Family and Consumer Sciences (Indiana Department of Education, 2006). These include Comprehensive Standards and Content Standards with the following major headings that are further subdivided and delineated in detail:

1. Career, Community, and Family Connections
   1.0 Integrate multiple life roles and responsibilities in family, career, and community roles and responsibilities.
2. Consumer and Family Resources
   2.0 Evaluate management practices related to the human, economic, and environmental recourses.
3. Consumer Services
   3.0 Integrate knowledge, skills, and practices required for careers in consumer services.
4. Early Childhood, Education, and Services
   4.0 Integrate knowledge, skills, and practices required for careers in early childhood, education, and services.
5. Facilities Management and Maintenance
   5.0 Integrate knowledge, skills, and practices required for careers in facilities management and maintenance.
6. Family
   6.0 Evaluate the significance of family and its impact on the well-being of individuals and society.
7. Family and Community Services
   7.0 Integrate knowledge, skills, and practices required for careers in family and community services.
8. Food Production and Services
   8.0 Integrate knowledge, skills, and practices required for careers in food production and services.
9. Food Science, Dietetics, And Nutrition
   9.0 Integrate knowledge, skills, and practices required for careers in food science, dietetics, and nutrition.
10. Hospitality, Tourism, and Recreation
    10.0 Integrate knowledge, skills, and practices required for careers in hospitality, tourism, and recreation.
11. Housing, Interiors and Furnishings
    11.0 Integrate knowledge, skills, and practices required for careers in housing, interiors, and furnishings.
12. Human Development
    12.0 Analyze factors that impact human growth and development.
13. Interpersonal Relationships
    13.0 Demonstrate respectful and caring relationships in the family, workplace, and community.
14. Nutrition and Wellness
    14.0 Demonstrate nutrition and wellness practices that enhance individual and family well-being.

15. Parenting
    15.0 Evaluate the impact of parenting roles and responsibilities on strengthening the well-being of individuals and families.
16. Textiles And Apparel
    16.0 Integrate knowledge, skills, and practices required for careers in textiles and apparel (Indiana Department of Education, 2006).

TECHNOLOGY EDUCATION—NEW PURPOSES— NEW STUDENTS

The nation has been besieged with reports on how U.S. students do not compare with students from other industrialized nations in terms of scores on mathematics and science (Baker, 2006; Friedman, 2005; Nussbaum, 2006). The solution most school districts have taken has been to add more mathematics and science courses for high school graduation. Many times students will only obtain more of the same instruction. If this did not work the first time, why should *more of the same* indicate better results? Education should mirror life. Given the complexities of life in our society, it would seem unwise to suggest that learning can effectively take place in isolated disciplines with the expectation that the students can effectively acquire and synthesize knowledge from the different areas.

Perhaps the leaders in our school systems should consider fundamental changes in regard to how these competencies are being taught. If the students are going to apply or use mathematics and science in business and industry, it would seem that it would be best to study these concepts in an integrated system as in Technology Education. With Technology Education at the core of schools offerings, they would be preparing students for our technological world. This preparation would be helpful to those that are going to follow the professions such as engineering or medicine as well as those that plan on pursuing technology as a career. Technology Education is returning to the system that John Dewey supported years ago when he stated that we should use the occupations as the vehicle of instruction. At this time Technology Education can be the vehicle for all instruction especially for mathematics and science, which is crucial.

Some universities are requiring that Liberal Arts majors study technology education as a requirement for graduation. The University of Illinois at Champaign-Urbana, for example, suggests that study in "technologies" is equivalent to study in the sciences, as they propose major reforms of undergraduate education. The University of Illinois considers technological literacy a requisite for any person considered "liberally educated" at the bachelor's degree level.

Technology Education instructors will have a full agenda if they are to serve higher-ability, college-bound students. The future is very positive but also very demanding. The study of technology forces thinking and interaction across disciplines. The integration of math and science with technology education as the core will facilitate student understanding of mathematical, scientific and technological principles. A multidisciplinary approach toward technology education is desirable and inevitable if higher-ability college-bound students are going to be taught. (John Hopkins University, 2004; King, 2007a). Instructors also need to satisfy a number of learning styles and recognize that students can be different. Lessons will need to be directed toward capitalizing on individual differences. Meaningful learning activities that integrate math, science and technology will need to include more problem solving and analytical skills. With technology rapidly changing, technology instructors will be required to remain flexible, adaptable, and open-minded in order to stay current. (Bray, 2007; Connecticut State Department of Education, 2006).

With Technology Education as a core subject, college-bound students can apply mathematical and scientific concepts in an experiential, hands-on environment. Current literature suggests that hands-on experiences increase knowledge by as much as a factor of two or more. Beyond increased knowledge, retention is increased with the application of newly acquired knowledge (Connecticut State Department of Education, 2006; King, 2007a). Technology Education is about applying knowledge and we have learned that active learning is critical for preparing students for college. Technology education must go beyond only hands-on experiences—it must become hands-on/minds-on education if it is to be effective.

In addition, the school is a melting pot of diverse backgrounds. And in the midst of this diversity, the educational system must retain and provide students with worthwhile, relevant experiences. Technology education as a core subject can provide these worthwhile experiences with a hands-on application approach.

As a core subject in the college preparatory program, technology education can educate high-ability students in schools (Nussbaum, 2006) as well as those that originally were scheduled in industrial arts. This "new" student population will require new approaches to instruction, approaches that are rigorous and that are based on design, critical thinking, problem solving, and application (Friedman, 2005; Gura & King, 2007).

{1}Characteristics of Technical Education

A technical education program is a terminal program not preparatory to a college degree but geared to meet the needs of agriculture, business health occupations, family and consumer sciences, and industry types of careers. Technical education programs vary in length from a single unit course of a few weeks to an integrated program operating on a part-time basis for several years.

Pre-employment programs in technical education are usually one to three years in length. These programs are available at community colleges, or at the 13th and 14th grade levels.

Technical education programs are especially effective for young adults, and most other technical education students who have a mature attitude. Most pre-employment programs require high school graduation or a GED as a prerequisite for entrance. However, they may have an open-enrollment policy which has no academic requirements beyond these.

TEACHING METHODS AND MATERIALS

Teaching methods for technical education emphasize shop and laboratory skill, fieldwork, and actual performance on the job as well as curriculum materials. Individualized instruction, home study, and small classes with extended opportunities for individual progress are important characteristics of the program (Bray, 2007). Modern curriculum materials are used with the computer, online learning, and continued workplace partnerships/internships facilitated through technology being core elements of instruction.

TECHNICAL PROGRAM INSTITUTIONS

A variety of institutions provide education for technical occupations, but the range of courses and the number of students enrolled frequently fall short of the demand for these trained persons. Technical courses are offered in community colleges, technical institutes, engineering schools, area vocational-technical schools (AVTS), technical high schools, and regional occupational programs (ROP). Some of these institutions, together with other special schools, offer correspondence courses in technical education. Technical education courses are also offered through trade associations and in industry. These courses are offered in both public and private institutions.

Area Vocational-Technical School Offerings: Many Area Vocational-Technical Schools and ROP's are offering a great number of technical courses as a result of the new "High-Tech" industry explosion. Career and technical schools may serve both secondary and post-secondary students in areas throughout most states. Many of the former vocational areas have become so specialized that a technical approach is required so that graduates are able to enter the technical field areas. For example, auto mechanics and auto body repair were formerly considered vocational areas of instruction, however, with the new emphasis on computers in auto mechanics and the uses of new construction and materials in auto body repair, persons entering the labor market in these two areas are required to have a more "in-depth" technical training.

Career and technical schools usually offer certificates of attendance, and many of the community colleges accept the training from the AVTS as a portion of an associate degree. There has been a movement to 2+2 agreements where AVTS program hours can be converted to credit hours and used toward an associate degree at a community college and in some cases toward a BS degree in 4-year institutions.

Community College Offerings: Many types of curriculums are usually provided in community colleges, including:

- Curriculums that will coordinate with continuing study at a four-year liberal arts college or university program (transfer courses).
- General education curriculum of a terminal nature.
- Career and technical education of a terminal nature.
- Technical education of a terminal nature.
- Career and technical education that may be transferred.
- Community Service courses that could be career and technical in nature. This could be college credit, Continuing Education Units (CEU's), or non-credit.

Community Colleges issue Associate in Arts (AA) degrees, Associate in Science (AS), certificates of attendance, Continuing Education Units (CEU's) and a variety of other two-year degrees. Some community colleges are part of state systems, some may be branches of state colleges or universities, and many of them are single institutions with their own boards or are part of a larger community college district. Community colleges may be both public and private.

Technical High School Offerings: High Schools seldom offer more than one or two programs that may be considered technical education. Some of the high schools are highly selective in who may be enrolled in these programs, and are usually called "magnet schools." Selection may be based upon scholastic records, examinations, and recommendations from school officials. With the current emphasis on obtaining the basics, usually English, foreign language, mathematics, and science, for graduation requirements, competition exists for the student's time while attending high school. Normally high school students would not have the time to devote to courses which are technical in nature.

Technical Institute Offerings: Technical institutes are usually directed to offering technical education curricula. Technical Institutes are usually operated as a separate school, but sometimes they are administered through a board of control of a public school system. This may also include the Board of Regents for higher education systems. The technical institute is usually a post-secondary institution. The principal objective of a technical institute is to educate men and women for occupations that require specialized knowledge supplemented by a broad range of operational procedures. Technical institutes may operate both day and evening programs.

Technical institutes offer programs different from those of the community college. Many times they are more intensive and do not include the general education component required of community college programs. The admission practices are different from community colleges and the students who attend may be older. Instruction in a technical institute follows more closely that which may occur in industry rather than that which occurs in community colleges.

Extension and Correspondence Study: These offerings are organized to assist persons to prepare for or progress in technical occupations. They are offered by both public and private schools and colleges. Most universities have extension divisions that provide class instruction in various extension centers and public schools throughout a state. The extension centers are usually located in towns and cities some distance from the parent institution where the need for these courses is evident. The extension center facilities may include laboratories, a library, a dormitory, and conference and assembly rooms.

Technical education appears to be especially suited to home study because much of the technical content involves basic sciences and applied technology which may be acquired from home study courses. Many persons are unable because of economic and personal reasons to attend day school and extension classes. They are willing to engage in home study, and the wide variety of home study courses enables these persons to select a course or series of courses in which they are interested. Correspondence courses of a technical nature are available for agriculturists, businessmen, health workers, homemakers, industrial workers, and social workers. Course offering include a wide range of subject matter similar to the course offerings of day schools. The maintenance of high standards of achievement is an especially important consideration in home study programs. The National Home Study Council, which was organized to promote high standards and ethical practices in this field, has been instrumental in improving home study programs.

TECHNICAL PROGRAM CURRICULA

The curriculum in technical education includes both technical and general activities, and these activities are arranged or grouped into subjects or other categories for instructional purposes. The general education content, such as English, psychology, social science, and speech, is usually included in pre-employment technical education curriculums and frequently omitted in in-service programs. The technical content of the curriculum is designed to provide occupational competency. This content is usually determined by means of an occupational analysis. For example, see Connecticut State Department of Education (2006).

As a general rule a technical curriculum will consist of:

1. 50% Specific Technical Studies (Information necessary for the technical area)
2. 25% Direct Related Studies (Math and Sciences)
3. 25% Indirect Related Studies (English, Speech, Psychology)

CURRENT CONCEPTS OF VOCATIONAL GUIDANCE

Vocational Guidance: is the process of helping a person to develop and accept an integrated and adequate picture of himself and of his role in the world of work. It has a specific goal; it assists individuals to find satisfying, interesting and realistic roles in the environment. Vocational guidance is the process of helping individuals know themselves, their interests and abilities and the world of work and its needs to be able to reach a mature career decision (Technical & Vocational Education & Training (TVET, n.d.). Vocational guidance refers to the services that may assist individuals of any age and at any point throughout their lives, to make educational, training and occupational choices and to manage their careers. It includes services provided to those who have not entered the labor forces services to job seekers and services to those who are employed (Organisation for Economic Co-operation and Development, n.d.).

Concept and Content

The concept of Counseling and Vocational Guidance refers to expert (science based) assistance and support with the aim to help individuals (EKEP-National Resource Centre for Vocational Guidance (EKEP-NRCVG), 2003):

- Explore, analyze and develop the factors constituting their self-concept (interests, personal qualities and characteristics, values, skills, etc.),
- Explore, evaluate, process and classify information and alternative education and vocation pathways with respect both to their needs and choices and to labor market requirements,
- Integrate information about education and vocation/career with information derived from self-observation so that they develop to decision-making capabilities both with respect to their orientation in education and choices in occupation(s) befitting their particular psychosocial make up,
- Create and implement their own education and vocation plans.

Ultimately, the individuals will be able to make the correct choices with respect to their future occupation/vocation and thus be (re)included into active life.

Counseling and Vocational Guidance activities target individuals who are:

- About to make a choice with respect to their education and vocation,
- In search of new fields of study/training,
- Already employed but dissatisfied with their current occupation, hence in search of new areas of training and professional development,
- Unemployed or have lost their jobs for whatever reason and wish to resume employment, and
- Threatened with social exclusion owing to personal circumstances or misfortune. (EKEP-NRCVG, 2003)

Vocational Guidance is not a device for finding the one job an individual can do best. Experience has shown that almost every person can achieve success in a number of occupations. These concepts recognize the fact that individuals may have occasion to make a number of occupational choices and adjustments throughout their life-span, and therefore vocational guidance becomes a continuous process of assisting individuals understand themselves better as a basis for making decisions concerning their careers. Perhaps the 1966 definition developed by the American Vocational Association (AVA) states this fairly clearly: "Vocational Guidance is the process of assisting individuals to understand their capabilities and interests, to choose a suitable vocation, and to prepare for, enter, and make successful progress in it."

CONCLUSION

Eighty-five years after the passage of the first piece of federal vocational education legislation, career and technical education is evolving from its original and sole focus on preparing students for work immediately following high school (U.S. Department of Education, 2006). Today's career and technical education programs increasingly incorporate rigorous and challenging academic content standards and provide a non-duplicative sequence of courses leading to an industry-recognized credential or certificate, or an associate or baccalaureate degree (U.S. Department of Education, 2006).

For the most part, content of the curricula within career and technical education is designed to provide occupational competency and it is quite scientific according to principles of learning and principles of teaching. Educators in the field take great care to group together both technical content and general education content. The most recent move is to integrate technology into vocational education curricula. All of these efforts are geared towards raising the competitiveness of our students in this so termed globalization. As Rojewski (2002) noted:

> Overall, a number of consistent themes emerge from the myriad educational reform reports and initiatives advanced over the past several decades. Prominent themes include the integration of academic and vocational education: emphasis on developing general (transferable) work skills rather than focusing on narrow, job-specific work skills; articulation between secondary and post secondary vocational programs; adjustments in programs to accommodate changing workforce demographics; preparation for a changing workplace that requires fairly high-level academic skills; familiarity and use of high technology; higher order thinking skills including decision-making and problem-solving; and interpersonal skills that facilitate working in teams. (p. 7)

However, whether instructional objectives can be reached largely depends on qualifications and certification of instructors in the field. In many states in the United States, a number of uncredentialed instructors teach various subjects in the field of career and technical education. Some of them have no knowledge of instructional theories. If this practice continues, the quality of instruction will be negatively affected in the long run. Unless this problem is fixed, regardless of how scientific the content of the curricula is, our students will not achieve the required learning objectives in career and technical education.

In addition, career and technical education programs should seek to offer innovative programs that aim at developing workforce competencies. Such programs should include in their content important topics such collaboration, adaptability, lifelong learning, cultural sensitivity, inclusion and globalization, reflective thinking, entrepreneurial and entrepreneurial thinking, critical thinking skills, problem solving skills, proactive teaching and learning, decision making, management skills, and leadership.

REFERENCES

Arizona Department of Education (2006). *Current CTE program and curriculum frameworks.* Retrieved April 17, 2007, from http://www.ade.az.gov/cte/CurriculmFramework/

Baker, S. (2006, January 23). Math will rock your world. *Business Week* Retrieved February 1, 2006, from http://www.businessweek.com/magazine/content/06_04/b3968001.htm

Bamberg, R. R., & Blayney, K. D. (1989). The education of multiskilled health practitioners: Results of a national survey. *Journal of Health Occupations Education, 4* (2), 72–93.

Baugher, S. L., Anderson, C. L., Green, K. B., Shane, J., Jolly, L., Miles, J., & Nickols, S. Y. (2003). *'Body of Knowledge' for family and consumer sciences.* Retrieved April 17, 2007, from http://www.aafcs.org/about/knowledge.html

Bray, A. (2007). Leading edge: The beginning of 2007 is an exciting time for career and technical education. *Techniques: Connecting education and careers, 82* (1), 6.

California Department of Education. (2006). *Agriculture education.* Retrieved December 21, 2006, from http://www.cde.ca.gov/ci/ct/ae/

Connecticut State Department of Education. (2006). *Connecticut technical high school system curricula.* Retrieved April 21, 2007, from http://www.cttech.org/central/curriculum/main-menu.htm

Darling, C. A., Greenwood, B. B., & Hansen-Gandy, S. (1998). Multicultural education in collegiate family and consumer sciences programs: Developing cultural competence. *Journal of Family and Consumer Sciences, 90*(1), 42–48.

EKEP-National Resource Centre for Vocational Guidance (EKEP- NRCVG). (2003). *Concept & content.* Retrieved December 22, 2006, from, http://www.ekep.gr/english/Guidance/main.asp

El Camino College. (2006). *Robotics academy.* Retrieved April 17, 2007, from http://www.elcamino.edu/academics/cte/robotics.asp

Freeman, L. (1996). Vo-Tech goes hi-tech. *School Planning and Management 35*(3), 3–8.

Friedman, T. (2005). *The world is flat: A brief history of the Twenty-First century.* New York: Farrar, Straus and Giroux.

Foxman, E., & Easterling, D. (1995). Diversity issues and business education. *Journal of Education for Business, 71*(1), 22–29.

Gay, G., & Howard, T. C. (2000). Multicultural teacher education for the 21st century. *The Teacher Educator, 36*(1), 1–16.

Gaytan, J. (2006). Focusing on accountability in business teacher education. In S. D. Lewis, M. Balachandran, & R. B. Blair (Eds.), *Meeting the challenges of business education through innovative programs* (87–98). Reston, VA: NBEA.

Georgia Agricultural Education (2006). *Georgia agricultural curriculum resource and reference.* Retrieved April 17, 2007, from http://aged.ces.uga.edu/Browseable_Folders/Curriculum/curriculum.htm

Giovannini, M. (2004). What gets measured gets done: Achieving results through diversity and inclusion. *The Journal for Quality and Participation*, 21–27.

Gura, M., & King, K. P. (2007). *Classroom robotics: Case studies of 21st century instruction for the millennial student.* Charlotte, NC: Information Age.

Health Occupations Students of America (HSOA) (2007). *HSOA homepage.* Retrieved April 17, 2007, from http://www.hosa.org.

Hill, R. (Ed.). (2006, Winter). *New Directions in Adult and Continuing Education* Issue 112.

Hoberty, P. (1996). The extent of multi-skilling education in respiratory care educational programs. *Respiratory Abstracts* No. OF-96-122. Retrieved April 17, 2007, from http://www.cardinal.com/mps/focus/respiratory/abstracts/abstracts/ab1996/A00001282.asp

Illinois State Board of Education. (n.d.). *Health occupations (CTE occupational programs area).* Retrieved April 17, 2007, from http://206.166.105.35/career/html/cte_health.htm

Indiana Department of Education, (2006). *National standards for family and consumer education.* Retrieved April 17, 2007, from http://www.doe.state.in.us/octe/facs/natlstandards.htm#order

John Hopkins University (2004). *Why technology? A brief history of CTE history.* Retrieved April 17, 2007, from http://cte.jhu.edu/aboutus_history.html

King, K. P. (2007a). Bridging the gap in K–12 education with career and technical education: The view from adult learning. In V. Wang, & K. P. King (Eds.), *Innovations in career and technical education: Strategic approaches towards workforce competencies around the globe* (pp. 133–165) Charlotte, NC: Information Age.

King, K. P. (2007b). Robotics: Prime opportunities for careers and student learning. In M. Gura, & K. P. King. *Classroom robotics: Case studies of 21st century instruction for the millennial student* (pp. 133–144). Charlotte, NC: Information Age.

King, K. P., & Biro, S. (2006, Winter). A transformative learning perspective of continuing sexual identity development in the workplace. In R. Hill (Ed.), *New Directions in Adult and Continuing Education Issue 112* (pp. 17–27). San Francisco: Jossey-Bass.

National Clearinghouse for Educational Facilities (NCEF). (2006). *Career and technical education classrooms and facilities.* Retrieved April 17, 2007, from http://www.edfacilities.org/rl/tech_ed.cfm

National Commission on Excellence in Education. (1983). *A nation at risk: The imperative for reform.* Washington, D. C.: Author. (ERIC Document Reproduction Service No. ED 251 622)

North Carolina Public Schools (2006). *CTE- Health Occupations Education.* Retrieved April 17, 2007, from http://www.ncpublicschools.org/workforce_development/health_occupations/index.html

Nussbaum, B. (2006, January 23). Davos will be different, *Business Week*, 96.

Organisation for Economic Co-operation and Development. (n.d.). *Annex 6 glossary.* Retrieved April 20, 2007, from http://www.oecd.org/dataoecd/27/53/27573989.pdf

Rojewski, J. W. (2002). Preparing the workforce of tomorrow: A conceptual framework for career and technical education. *Journal of Vocational Education Research, 27*(1), 1–27.

Rothrock, D., & Walker, C. J. (2007). *Get R.E.A.L.: Aligning California's public education system with the 21st century economy.* Retrieved April 17, 2007, from http://www.lhc.ca.gov/lhcdir/CTE/RothrockWalkerMar07.pdf

Sabo, S. R. (2000). Diversity at work. *Techniques, 75*(2), 26–28.

Schmidt, J. (1990). *A chronology of business education in the United States.* Reston, VA: National Business Education Association.

Schneider, A. (2000, Oct. 13). It's not your mother's home economics. *The Chronicle of Higher Education 47*(7), p. A18. Retrieved April 21, 2007, from http://chronicle.com/weekly/v47/i07/07a01801.htm

Smith, B. P., & Hall, H. C. (1999). Explanatory style of Family and Consumer Sciences teachers in Georgia. *Journal of Family and Consumer Sciences 17*(1), 30–37. Retrieved April 21, 2007, from http://www.natefacs.org/JFCSE/v17no1/v17no1Smith.pdf

Smith, J. (2000). Rethinking school design. *Buildings 94* (8), 50, 56, 59.

Stage, S., & Vincenti, V. B., (Eds.). (1997). *Rethinking home economics: Women and the history of a profession.* Ithaca: Cornell University Press.

Stone, J. R., Kowske, B. J., & Alfeld, C. (2004). Career and technical education in the late 1990s: A descriptive study. *Journal of Vocational Education Research 29* (1) Retrieved April 21, 2007, from http://scholar.lib.vt.edu/ejournals/JVER/v29n3/stone.html

Technical & Vocational Education & Training (TVET). (n.d.). *Introduction.* Retrieved December 25, 2006, from, http://www.tvet-pal.org/counseling/intro.html

U.S. Department of Education. (2006). *Career and technical education.* Retrieved December 14, 2006, from http://www.ed.gov/about/offices/list/ovae/pi/cte/index.html

Wisconsin Department of Public Instruction. (2006). *Health science occupations education.* Retrieved December 21, 2006, from http://dpi.state.wi.us/cte/hoehome.html

CHAPTER 5

COMPARING THE RUSSIAN, THE SLOYD, AND THE ARTS AND CRAFTS MOVEMENT TRAINING SYSTEM

Victor C. X. Wang
California State University, Long Beach

Kathleen P. King
Fordham University

This chapter investigates vocational educators' preferences among 3 foreign systems that have been used frequently in vocational education in the United States: the Russian system, the Sloyd system, and the Arts and Crafts Movement. Thirty-two (64% of 50) in-service vocational educators enrolled in teacher credentialing programs in the Department of Occupational Studies at California State University, Long Beach during the fall of 2003 completed a 6-point Likert-type scale designed to measure teaching preferences relative to methods associated with each training system. Data were analyzed using descriptive statistics and analysis of variance. Results indicated a slight preference for the Sloyd system and the Arts and Crafts

Building Workforce Competencies in Career and Technical Education, pages 89–105

Movement over the Russian system, although differences were not significant ($p > .05$).

INTRODUCTION

At the beginning of the 20th century, the educational system of the United States had adopted methods from three foreign training systems: the Russian system, the Sloyd system, and the Arts and Crafts Movement (Bott, Slapar, & Wang, 2003; Brehony, 1998; Grubb, 1998; Roberts, 1965; Roche, 1995). These approaches were adopted primarily in response to the sharply increased need for skilled workers during the period of the industrial revolution. At the time of the Industrial Revolution, the expansion of capitalism, an increase in world trade, and a rapid shift from farm work and small business to large business enterprises, with a concurrent emphasis on increased manufacturing production, placed a burden on schools, including colleges and universities, to supply needed skilled manpower (Grubb, 1998; Roberts, 1965). Education was perceived as the solution to the related problems of increased job dissatisfaction associated with industrial labor, including factory sweatshops, unsafe working conditions, pollution, and a general decline in work satisfaction (*Oklahoma State University*, n.d.a.; Chen, 1999). Other problems in the late 1880's that eventually led to changes in U.S. education included a growing dissatisfaction with dull and impractical academic curricula, the lack of practical training available for architects and engineers, and the unavailability of alternative academic options for students who performed poorly in traditional academic subjects (*Oklahoma State University*, n.d.a.). At the same time, a movement to revamp the public education system according to a variety of philosophies began in the Scandinavian countries, England, France, Germany, and the United States, and other countries. These philosophies were influenced by religious beliefs, politics, and economics in a general social upheaval that eventually became global in scope (Brehony, 1998; Cumming, 2001; Roberts, 1965; Roche, 1995). The Russian System, the Sloyd System, and the Arts and Crafts Movement all contributed to the remodeling of the U.S. educational system, and the influence of these approaches can still be felt to this day (Grubb, 1998; Roberts, 1965).

We were interested in identifying vocational educators' teaching preferences relative to the Russian system, the Sloyd system, and the Arts and Crafts Movement, especially in light of the advantages and disadvantages of each system. We sought to determine if vocational educators preferred one of the foreign training methods over the remaining two methods. Specifically, we wanted to know what were the preferences of vocational educators relative to:

1. Emphasizing a logical procedure where students advance based on results from a series of graded exercises (Russian System).
2. Encouraging student self-direction and initiative (Sloyd System).
3. Emphasizing aesthetic and creative side of work (Arts and Crafts Movement).
4. Reaching large groups of students in the least possible time (Russian System).
5. Focusing on neatness and accuracy (Sloyd System).
6. Utilizing rotation of work (Arts and Crafts Movement).

According to Bott et al. (2003), an experiment conducted in Boston in the 1890s explored whether the Sloyd system or the Russian system better met the needs of American students. As a result of this experiment, the Boston schools began to use the Sloyd system almost exclusively.

Today's teachers face problems that are similar to those faced by teachers in the late 1880s. The present technological revolution can be compared to the Industrial Revolution because it has created the same needs for changes in curricula, teaching methods, and skills and knowledge of students (*Oklahoma State University,* n.d.a.). With technology advances increasing exponentially, employers need highly skilled workers as well as workers who are flexible, able to solve problems, self-initiating, and foresighted about their possible advancement in the workplace (Grubb, 1998). Instructional methods employed by instructors can have drastic effects on how well students learn. By examining foreign historical systems of education, answers to the problems of the present may be revealed.

HISTORICAL BACKGROUND

Since the inception of the Russian manual training method advanced by Victor Della Vos in 1876, vocational education instructors of the United States have adopted and adapted a series of foreign training methods. After the Russian training method was successfully introduced into America, the Sloyd System (which originated in Scandinavia) and the Arts and Crafts Movement (which originated in England as a protest against poor craftsmanship) were brought to the United States for the purpose of improving American vocational education instructors' training methods (Bott, Slapar, & Wang, 2003). Each of these teaching designs is different and distinct from one another, and all were explored by American educators. Victor Della Vos brought his ideas of rigidly formal instruction from Russia to an exhibit at the 1876 Centennial Exposition in Philadelphia. Swedish educators Lars Erickson and Gustaf Larsson started classes in the Sloyd system in Anoka, Minnesota in 1884 and in Boston in 1888. The Arts and Crafts Movement exerted its influence in the United States during the latter part of the 19th century. Whereas The Russian and Sloyd systems focused upon the skill of the student and worker, the Arts and Crafts Movement emphasized the creative and aesthetic side (Brehony, 1998; Crawford, 1997; Cumming, 2001; Fish, 1997; Roche, 1995). A description of each training system follows.

The Russian System

Victor Della Vos, who in 1868 became the director of the Moscow Imperial Technical School, developed the Russian System of competency-based instruction, which was partly influenced by Pavlov's research on conditioning (Grubb, 1998). His task analysis approach, developed in Moscow in the 1860s and brought to America at the 1876 Centennial Exposition in Philadelphia, was wholeheartedly accepted by John D. Runkle, who was the president of the Massachusetts Institute of Technology (MIT) where he introduced laboratories in his institution. The Russian system was also adopted by Professor Clavin M. Woodward, Dean of the Polytechnic faculty of Washington University in St. Louis, Missouri (*Oklahoma State University*, n.d.a.). Both of these men, for the first time, developed and introduced shop courses for their engineering students (*Oklahoma State University*, n.d.a.). At that time, engineers and architects did not receive a good educational foundation in theory and practice of construction techniques (*Oklahoma State University*, n.d.a.). Partly for this reason, the Russian System of industrial education, including the theory and principles behind it, was adopted throughout the United States and also in many parts of the world. The object of the Russian System during this global industrial revolution was to instruct as many students in as little time as possible in order to supply skilled manpower for the country's needs (Bott et al., 2003; Roberts, 1965).

Teachers of the Russian System of manual training utilized a systems approach in which a specific curriculum was devised by breaking training into its components, and each of those were taught as a separate entity. The system consisted of three stages: the first being the study of the materials and tools, the second was acquisition of the skills to use the materials and tools, and the third was actual construction of a part of a whole item (Bott, Slapar, & Wang, 2003; Roberts, 1965). For instance, students studied wood-working, then rotated to another discreet lesson such as blacksmithing, then joinery and so on; each module contained its own shop, tools, and curriculum (Roberts, 1965). Lessons began with drawings, and each student had his or her own tools and a place to work. After drawings were mastered, students progressed to an increasingly difficulty, but students did not graduate to another activity without complete mastery of the first (Grubb, 1998; Roberts,

1965). Teachers of the Russian System were expected to be expert models of knowledge and skill and to upgrade their skills continually.

Advantages of the Russian System

The logical, sequential aspects of the Russian System create a structured atmosphere of concentrated effort and focus where knowledge is built upon knowledge in a logical fashion. This system benefits students in that they are taught in a manner that allows for no confusion in the acquisition and application of knowledge and skills (Grubb, 1998). Students of this method graduate with a known body of knowledge, learned in the materials and tools as well as the uses of both. This method is especially beneficial to both the student and the employer because the students gain skills and the employers can trust that the graduates will be assets to the companies. This consistency of results translates into increased earnings for both the new employee and the company (Grubb, 1998). Another benefit of the method is that it produces a large number of skilled workers in a relatively short time, as was needed during the Industrial Revolution (Bott et al., 2003; Roberts, 1965).

Disadvantages of the Russian System

Although the Russian system produces students who are learned, they often do not have the freedom to create something on their own or to even to finish a project (Bott et al., 2003; Roberts,1965). Their learning is relegated to only small exercises, and when on the job after graduation, students may lack skills to be self-initiating or to solve problems, such as in engineering and other higher-order work, a limitation which fails students and employers (Grubb, 1998). Furthermore, although students graduate in the Russian System with a certain amount of skill, they may lose individual creativity in the training process. A secondary criticism of the Russian, skills-oriented method of teaching is that because teachers focus exclusively on skills, they may not keep abreast of new forms of problem-solving, which limits their ability to teach needed knowledge to their students, leads to an incomplete curriculum, thereby cheating the students of valuable information (Grubb, 1998).

The Sloyd System

The Sloyd System was adopted in schools in Boston and Albany, New York in the late 1880s and in Chicago in 1894 (Bott et al., 2003). This system emphasized individualized instruction instead of the assembly-line teaching of the Russian method. Sloyd, which means "handcrafts" in Scandinavia, began in Scandinavia in response to the increasing demand for new types of workers, such as clerks, technicians, and engineers. After much travel and study in Alaska, Uno Cygnaeus, a Finnish preacher and teacher, developed a system of folk education for the Finnish school system. He observed the differences between civilized and uncivilized peoples of the region. Melding the ideas of Johann Heinrich Pestalozzi, the father of manual training who espoused the use of objects and manual labor to teach and to help poor children improve their social conditions, and Friedrich Froebel, a student and co-worker of Pestalozzi, Cygnaeus devised his own system to teach manual studies based on hand-eye coordination (Brehony, 1998). These educators believed that children learn best by doing handwork because, among other reasons, they are naturally creative. Cygnaeus believed that handcrafts should be taught by the traditional teacher and not in a technical school, and that handcrafts should be a part of the regular curriculum. In 1866, his system was adopted in all Finnish schools.

During the 1880s, educator Otto Salomon of Sweden, through the influence of Cygnaeus, developed the Sloyd System, which is still used throughout the world today. Salomon took a more structured approach that comprised three key elements: (a) making useful objects; (b) analysis of processes, and (c) educational method. The Sloyd system, especially as espoused by Froebel, was based on a religious belief that children should be prepared for work at an early stage because of God's own model of hard work (Brehony, 1998). Some followers of the European Froebel Movement believed in race capitulation, the concept that former stages of evolution are evident, physically as well a culturally, as people pass from embryo to adulthood and that childhood is but one stage of an evolving series of hierarchical ordered stages with the inherently hierarchical notion of race (Brehony). They believed that manual dexterity was a stage of development that preceded the development of the brain; subsequently, they believed that use of the hands could train the mind (Brehony).

The Sloyd system became a fashion, a popular movement that expanded into England and the United States at about the same time as did the Russian System. This new idea spread in response to government demands for workers who were knowledgeable in areas of trade and finance, which quickly became highly competitive on a global scale (Brehony, 1998). Children in grammar schools were given cards on which to sew, do cardboard work, and woodwork because it was believed that the mind could be trained by the use of hands (Brehony). The movement evolved in the United States to encompass morality and respect for workmanship. Moreover, unlike book learning, the Sloyd system led to the creation of self-motivation among students and to students taking an interest in their studies; thus, it encouraged children to transfer learned skills to other activities. Children learned by doing, displayed initiative, and exhibited an understanding of the importance and the value of those who worked with their hands (Brehony).

Individualized instruction and the use of a good model were the key points of Sloyd system (Roberts, 1965). Classes began in a small way by Erickson and Larsson, and when an experiment was conducted in Boston in the 1890s to see whether the Russian or Sloyd System was the preferred method of teaching grammar grades, the Sloyd System won (Roberts, 1965). Consequently, the Sloyd system spread to other schools, and by 1893–1894, the Report of the U.S. Commissioner of Education stated that "25% of all schools offering manual training in grades 7 through 12" incorporated the Sloyd method, or eighteen schools altogether (as cited in Bott et al., 2003, p. 38). The Sloyd method, unlike the Russian System, encouraged the use of measuring tapes and other devices, freehand work and individualized expression, neatness and accuracy, pride in workmanship, and regular teachers were to be used rather than artisans (Bott et al.). Another distinction between the two teaching systems was that Sloyd students could make a whole item, while the students of the Russian System were limited to an exercise that produced nothing of value. By 1904, however, Sloyd, as a specialized approach, began to disappear, as the philosophy of John Dewey took precedence (Brehony, 1998). Dewey presented the case for combining academic instruction with manual training, and Sloyd ideas, with their emphasis on learning skills for work for work's sake, were set aside (Brehony, 1998). Dewey believed that children should be taught through a trade rather than be taught a trade for work's sake (*Oklahoma State University*, n.d.b.)

Advantages of the Sloyd System

Benefits to students of the Sloyd method of instruction include more freedom of artistic expression and the advantages of teaching from whole-to-part, which allows students to learn the concept of the whole project, thus enabling them to finish a product that can be later used or sold (Bott et al., 2003; Roberts, 1965). Students make a completed model rather than participate in a limited exercise, as in the Russian style. Because a variety of tools and materials and self-expression are involved, students are more motivated to learn with this method than with the others (Roberts). The Sloyd method brings out the whole individual more than the Russian because students can better relate work to the world and to themselves (Bott et al., 2003: Roberts, 1965).

Disadvantages of the Sloyd System

Educators have criticized the Sloyd method as being too formal and inflexible, a criticism also levied against the Russian System (Bott et al., 2003). Also, because of the increased flexibility and the decreased formality and rigidity associated with learning in the Sloyd system in comparison to the Russian system, there may be a loss in expertise compared to the Russian method. Educators employing the Sloyd system also have more responsibility for keeping up-to-date on technological developments in order to be effective teachers (Grubb, 1998). Faced with a difficult and time-consuming task instead of a purely structured approach, a teacher employing the Sloyd system must integrate skills as well as theory to teach students how to make a whole item and then be able to use it.

The Arts and Crafts Movement

The Industrial Revolution brought many changes to the world, including advances in machinery, medicines, a global economy, and large factories. Thousands of workers spent their days in mindless and often dangerous work on assembly lines. Reacting to the loss of fine craftsmanship, pride in workmanship, and freehand labor, the Arts and Crafts Movement began in England and spread to the United States (Bott et al., 2003; Cumming, 2001). The movement claimed many followers. The famous architect Frank Lloyd Wright and the prominent educator and philosopher John Dewey were influenced by this movement, with Dewey becoming its spokesperson. Other supporters of the movement emerged from discontent with conditions wrought by the Industrial Revolution. Social philosopher Thomas Carlyle expressed concern about the loss of personal freedom and expression, and John Ruskin vehemently attacked the value of objects created by an impersonal system rather than through a labor of love (Cumming). Another main leader of the movement in England was architect and writer William Morris. Morris spoke for the movement and built a showplace for art and design where ordinary men and women could peruse for ideas to use in their own homes and churches (Cumming, 2001; Roche, 1995).

This outpouring of protest gained strength and support as artisans and craftsmen of all types organized a movement against the poor craftsmanship promulgated by factory methods of mass production (Cumming, 2001; Roberts, 1965; Roche, 1995). The Arts and Crafts Movement was characterized by Roche as an ideology that could be interpreted as a sort of renaissance of the spirit of man, as a struggle against oppression of machines upon man, and as an overcoming and taking control of one's own life and destiny. The Arts and Crafts Movement stressed the importance of good craftsmanship and aesthetic quality. When incorporated into elementary schools, the movement utilized a method that rotated students among classes in drawing, designing, clay modeling, and woodcarving (Bott et al., 2003).

Three principles guided the Arts and Crafts Movement in England: (a) unity of art, which defined all forms of art as equal rather than in a hierarchy where one type of art was worth more than other types of arts and which opposed the superiority of professionalism; (b) joy in labor, which was the idea that people could use their imaginations to derive pleasure from the experience of work as opposed to working in stultifying factories; and (c) design reform, whereby the designs of objects used by ordinary people were changed to look as if they belonged in the place where they were used (e.g., a kettle looked like it belonged in a kitchen), but objects also were stylized, representing taste as opposed to wealth and refinement and craftsmanship as opposed to ostentation (Crawford, 1997). Factory-made items and late-Victorian ostentatiously styled pieces of jewelry were no longer valued, whereas finely crafted, artistic items were valued.

Advantages of the Arts and Crafts Movement

When the Arts and Crafts Movement was introduced, many educators turned to its ideas to counteract criticisms of the rigidity and inflexibility of the Russian and Sloyd systems. The movement invited students to create using good craftsman skills and brought new value to honest work. Students took pride in workmanship, and they experienced pleasure in work, which had been largely missing to that point (Brehony, 1998; Roberts, 1965). They were allowed to use improved models for their work, take field trips, use other types of materials, and enjoy the benefits of a large, less constrictive curriculum (Roberts). Drawing skills were related to other schoolwork, and students were allowed to make their own designs (Roberts). Students of the Arts and Crafts Movement, because of their lack of constriction, were better equipped than students of the Russian and Sloyd systems to solve problems and express initiative and creativity. Consequently, they were well suited for high-paying jobs that required cognitive thinking skills (Grub, 1998). Innovative study motivated students, creating an interesting learning environment (Roberts).

Disadvantages of the Arts and Crafts Movement

The Arts and Crafts Movement encouraged teachers and students to be creative and innovative, but this freedom may have cost students the in-depth skills and knowledge afforded by the more rigid curricula of the Russian or Sloyd systems. Although Arts and Crafts students were creative and self-initiating, they had less self-discipline in their learning habits than their counterparts in the Russian and Sloyd systems. The Arts and Crafts Movement was wrapped in social, religious, and political overtones, and some students may have lost sight of educational objectives in favor of the glamorous prospects of joining a movement for the movement's sake (Crawford, 1997). During the early days of the movement, philosophical discussions were an essential part of the process. Because it was difficult to separate the making of an object from the reason behind it, these discussions addressed questions of whether the item derived from practical necessity or politi-

TABLE 5.1   Advantages and Disadvantages of the Russian System, Sloyd System and Arts & Crafts Movement

Training Systems	Advantages	Disadvantages
Russian System	1. Emphasizes a logical procedure where students advance based on results from a series of graded exercises. 2. Reaches large groups of students in the least possible time.	1. Loses individual creativity in the training process. 2. Limits ability to teach needed knowledge.
Sloyd System	1. Encourages student self-direction and initiative. 2. Focuses on neatness and accuracy.	1. Loses expertise in comparison with the Russian method. 2. Lacks unity of theory and practice.
Arts & Crafts Movement	1. Emphasizes aesthetic and creative side of work. 2. Utilizes rotation of work.	1. Costs students the in-depth knowledge. 2. Become less self-disciplined in students' learning habits.

cal purposes. In this milieu, students may have become more interested in extra-curricular activities than in academic duties.

Summary

Vocational educators in the United States have adopted numerous training methods associated with the Russian system, the Sloyd system, and the Arts and Crafts Movement. Each of these training systems has its own set of advantages and disadvantages. Table 5.1 provides a summary of the advantages and disadvantages of the training methods associated with the Russian system, the Sloyd system, and the Arts and Crafts Movement.

INSTRUCTIONAL PREFERENCES OF VOCATIONAL EDUCATION INSTRUCTORS OF THE UNITED STATES

Although there are disadvantages associated with training methods from the Russian system, the Sloyd system, and the Arts and Crafts Movement, each training system's influence can still be felt to this day (Grubb, 1998; Roberts, 1965). The laboratory experiences that John Runkle started at MIT are in use in almost every vocational education classroom, whether it be welding, horticulture, cosmetology, or family and consumer sciences. In fact, it is probable that most or all vocational education teachers find a lab of some sort indispensable because students cannot learn enough to apply their trade of study successfully without hands-on experience. Competency-based education, which the Russian and Sloyd systems advocated, has been the basis of many curricula, including the Modules of Employable Skills developed by the International Labor Office, the Developing a Curriculum (DACUM) process initiated in Canada, and the *serie metodica ocupacionis* (i.e., shopwork methodological series) that developed in Brazil and then spread throughout South America. Many secondary schools in the United States have included competency-based curricula since the 1960s, as have schools in Australia and England (Grubb).

Teachers and curriculum designers of today can avail themselves of texts and other information developed over the years by the research and development of individuals and companies. Those who design a curriculum can use catalogs that list competencies for a particular curriculum. For instance, The Vocational and Technical Education Consortium of States (V-TECS) has produced extensive catalogs for many professions that delineate duties, tasks, and performance objectives in an employment-referenced data base that is used for curriculum development (Finch & Crunkilton, 1999). Other similar catalogues are used for exploratory programs and information for competency-based education is offered by texts such as, *Curriculum Development in Vocational and Technical Education: Planning, content, and implementation* by Finch and Crunkilton. Incorporating Russian and Sloyd ideals in content and purpose, this textbook is an example of the comprehensive nature of curriculum planning used in the United States today. Also, the Sloyd pedagogical library at Naas, Sweden contains thousands of books, periodicals, and other references in a large data base on Sloyd and is open to students and educators interested in the system.

Woodwork and shop have been included in many grammar schools and high schools as well as in tech-prep schools and other types of schools across the United States. Tasks taught in these classes use the methods delineated by Finch and Crunkilton (1999), such as the V-TECS task analysis approach in which all the tools used in various trades are listed and taught, as well as the tasks associated with them. This approach is in line with the Russian system. The DACUM approach also uses this method, listing all the tools needed and the curriculum for that class (Finch & Crunkilton). Each task relates to the next task, as in the Russian system, and then the whole is completed, as in the Sloyd system. This is an example of combining two systems so that students learn each individual tool and task and then complete a whole product in a logical and systematic manner. However, Grubb (1998) pointed out that most vocational instructors in Secondary schools in the United States use the skills-only method in which students work on needed skills with little attention to the overall picture (i.e., the Russian system). In community colleges observed by Grubb, students used the Russian approach in which they devoted a specified unit of time to learning a particular skill, or they learned on a whole-top art basis, as advocated by the Sloyd system, when a problem solving approach was necessary, such as in such trades as computers and automobile systems. Although type of class can dictate the type of teaching used, most teachers in secondary schools and community colleges, as observed by Grubb, used the skills-oriented Russian system, with a few teachers incorporating the systems-oriented Sloyd system. The practice of working at one's own pace while crafting an item of one's own design disintegrated during World War I when objects were mass-produced, and slowly crafted items became a luxury (Cumming, 2001). However, as Cumming reported, teachers maintained that students did not want to work in factory assembly lines producing cheaply designed objects; rather, they valued craftsmanship and the beauty of natural materials.

Methods

Sample

The Occupational Studies Department, California State University, Long Beach enrolled approximately 90 in-service instructors who were employed in the secondary, postsecondary schools and Regional Occupational Programs in the state of California. In the fall semester of 2003, 50 in-service instructors were enrolled in teacher credentialing programs in the department. Of the 50 in-service instructors, 32 (64%) participated in the study. These 32 instructors represented almost all of the secondary and postsecondary schools and regional occupational programs in California that were actively involved in vocational teacher credentialing programs. Participation in the study was voluntary, and responses were kept confidential.

Instrumentation

We designed the instrument used to collect data, modeling it after existing surveys used at two universities. We distributed a survey to each instructor. The survey included two sections: a demographics section and a six-point Likert-type scale designed to measure the instructors' preferences of the three foreign training systems. The demographics section asked for area of instruction and number of years in the occupation. On the second section, participants responded to six items, rating their teaching preferences relative to training methods associated with the Russian system, the Sloyd system, and the Arts and Crafts Movement. Designed to reflect the advantages of the training systems, the items were as follows:

1. I use a training method that emphasizes a logical procedure where students advance based on results from a series of graded exercises. (Russian system)

2. I use a training method that encourages student self-direction and initiative. (Sloyd system)
3. I use a training method that emphasizes the aesthetic and creative sides of work. (Arts and Crafts Movement)
4. I use a training method that reaches large groups of students in the least possible time. (Russian system)
5. I use a training method that focuses on neatness and accuracy. (Sloyd system)
6. I use a training method that utilizes rotation of work. (Arts and Crafts Movement)

Participants rated their teaching preferences relative to each item on a six-point Likert-type scale: 1 (always), 2 (almost always), 3 (often), 4 (seldom), 5 (almost never), and 6 (never). Three vocational educators in the Department of Occupational Studies at California State University, Long Beach, who were not included in the study sample, comprised the sample for a pilot study conducted to validate the instrument. Data gathered from the pilot study were used to determine where there was a need to revise the instrument. The pilot study also was used to test for understanding of items on the instrument. Results indicated that there was no need to revise the instrument. Thus, the questions were considered content valid. The alpha reliability coefficient for the instrument was .78.

Data Analysis
We calculated means and standard deviations for each of the six items on the instrument. Mean scores were used to determine instructors' teaching preferences. An analysis of variance was used to determine if there were significant differences among instructors' preferences for methods associated with the Russian system, the Sloyd system, and the Arts and Crafts Movement.

Findings

Responses on the demographics section of the instrument indicated that among the 32 respondents, 3 (9.4%) were trade instructors (e.g., welding, electronics, mechanics, automotive service, air conditioning and refrigeration, industrial maintenance, tool and die technology, industrial processing); 10 (31.3%) were literacy instructors; 5 (15.6%) were academic instructors; and 1 (3.1%) was a business instructor; 1 (3.1%) was a health instructor; and 12 (37.5%) were instructors who taught other occupational skills (e.g., cosmetology, food science, woodworking, hotel management).

TABLE 5.2 Means and Standard Deviations

Item	M	SD
Item 1 (Russian System)	3.00	1.24
Item 2 (Sloyd System)	2.41	1.16
Item 3 (Arts and Crafts Movement)	2.66	1.31
Item 4 (Russian System)	3.13	1.24
Item 5 (Sloyd System)	2.72	1.20
Item 6 (Arts and Crafts Movement)	2.41	1.32

Years of experience as an instructor ranged from 1 to 27 years, the average being 6 years.

Table 5.2 presents the means and standard deviations for the six items regarding respondents' preferences for each training method. The item numbers correspond with the numbers of the items as noted in the Instrumentation section; the training system measured by the item is indicated in parenthesis. Overall, the results demonstrated that the instructors preferred methods from the Sloyd system and the Arts and Crafts Movement to methods from the Russian system, although they also preferred some aspects of the Russian system, as indicated by the mean of the responses to item 1 (M = 3.00), which indicated that instructors almost always or often used methods associated with the Russian system in teaching. The mean for item 4 indicated that instructors in the sample seldom used methods associated with the Russian system in teaching. The means for items 2 and 5 showed that instructors almost always used methods associated with the Sloyd system in their teaching. The means for items 3 and 6 indicated that instructors often or almost always used methods from the Arts and Crafts Movement in their teaching.

Although there were differences in the mean scores for the items related to each system, results from the ANOVAs indicated that the differences were not significant ($p > .05$). Results from the ANOVAs are summarized in Table 5.3 and Table 5.4.

Discussion and Recommendations

The Russian system, the Sloyd system, and the Arts and Crafts Movement have long influenced the curricula that vocational educators use. Results from this study indicate that vocational educators prefer training methods associated with the Sloyd system and the Arts and Crafts Movement over methods associated with the Russian system, although differences are not statistically significant. These findings support results from the 1890s histor-

TABLE 5.3   Comparing Means for Training Methods: Items 2, 3, and 4 (One-Way ANOVA)

Item	F	p
Item 2 (Sloyd System)	1.30	0.31
Item 3 (Arts and Crafts Movement)	0.86	0.62
Item 4 (Russian System)	0.90	0.58

TABLE 5.4   Comparing Means for Training Methods: Items 1, 5, and 6 (One-Way ANOVA)

Item	F	p
Item 1 (Russian System)	1.91	0.11
Item 5 (Sloyd System)	2.13	0.07
Item 6 (Arts and Crafts Movement)	1.18	0.38

ical experiment conducted in Boston that indicated that the Sloyd system met students' needs better than the Russian system (Bott et al., 2003).

American society currently is characterized by rapid technological changes, innovation, and creativity. To meet these demands, vocational educators must emphasize student self-direction and the aesthetic and creative sides of work, which are the heart and soul of the Sloyd and Arts and Crafts Movement training systems. Associated with mass production, the Russian training system seems to be more in line with "the more, the better" syndrome that dominated the minds of vocational educators during the Industrial Revolution. Today, student self-direction and initiative, aesthetics, creativity, and rotation of work seem to be buzzwords in vocational education in the United States. Another reason why the Russian system is not preferred may be that the training method takes place in an instruction lab rather than a construction lab; this formal class method of instruction provides little opportunity for self-expression or for recognition of individual differences. Because the Russian system is based on results from a series of graded exercises, it does not enhance the concept of learning by doing that is well accepted by vocational educators in the United States.

This study was designed to bring together the historical facts relating to three important and influential foreign teaching methods in the United States and to determine which one of the foreign training methods vocational educators prefer. There is no significant difference in preferences among the three methods; rather, all three, in combination, are still used. It is surmised that because of the length of time the methods have existed in the United States (i.e., over 100 years) and because educators regularly share successful teaching methods, the three training systems have made their way into mainstream vocational education and that teachers select the method(s) that best suits their needs.

Further research should include a qualitative component to find out why certain methods are preferred, and observations and interviews should be conducted to obtain a comprehensive understanding of which teachers prefer methods from each system (i.e., who teaches what and why). Another recommendation is to examine the influence of vocational educators' own training backgrounds to determine personal instructional preferences. Also, it should be noted that institutional objectives might require vocational educators to use certain approaches regardless of personal preferences. Further research should focus on institutional objectives to determine instructional approaches. Curriculum developers, teachers, students and their families, and industry all can benefit from information about instructors' preferences. Eventually, findings may be generalized to the general population in order to predict and clarify classes needed in secondary schools, community colleges, trade schools, technical schools, colleges, universities, and state employment development departments. Vocational education programs can be developed to instruct students how to make a smooth transition from school to work or to retrain in employment.

An increased understanding of teaching methods within their historical context, the purpose of these methods, and their relationship to present educational needs assists vocational education instructors in making decisions about how to improve teaching effectiveness and how to provide the workforce with skilled and knowledgeable students. It is our hope that readers of this research will find the information useful and that further research will continue.

REFERENCES

Bott, P. A., Slapar, F. M., & Wang, V. (2003). *History and philosophy of career and technical education*. Boston: Pearson.

Brehony, K. J. (1998). 'Even far distant Japan is showing an interest': The English Froebel Movement's turn to Sloyd. *History of Education 27*, 279. Retrieved April 6, 2003, from EBSCOHost Academic Search Elite database.

Chen, X. (1999). *The Industrial Revolution: It's affects and consequences.* Retrieved April 15, 2003, from http://members.tripod.com/xuchen/indusrevolt/

Crawford, A. (1997). Ideas and objects: The Arts and Crafts Movement in Britain. *Design Issues, 13*(1), 1–7. Retrieved April 11, 2003, from EBSCOHost Academic Search Elite database.

Cumming, E. (2001). The Arts and Crafts Movement. *British Heritage, 22*(4), 1–5. Retrieved April 11, 2003, from EBSCOHost Academic Search Elite database.

Finch, C. R., & Crunkilton, J. R. (1999). *Curriculum development in vocational and technical education: Planning, content, and implementation* (5th ed.). Needham Heights, MA: Allyn & Bacon.

Fish, M. (1997). Assessing recent interpretations of the Arts and Crafts Movement. *Art Journal, 56*(3), 90. Retrieved April 11, 2003, from EBSCOHost Academic Search Elite database.

Grubb, W. N. (1998). *Preparing for the information-based workplace: Pedagogical issues and institutional linkages.* Retrieved April 11, 2003, from http://mitsloanMIT. edu/iwer/papers.html

Oklahoma State University. (n.d.a.). Progressive discourses: Revisiting the purpose of OCED. Retrieved April 12, 2003, from http://home.okstate.edu/homepages.nsf/ toc/oced5313_links!OpenDocument&ExpandSection=2#_Section2

Oklahoma State University. (n.d.b.). *Snedden & Prosser vs. Dewey: The great debate.* Retrieved April 12, 2003, from http://home.okstate.edu/homepages.nsf/toc/ oced5313_links!OpenDocument&ExpandSection=4#_Section4

Roberts, R. W. (1965). *Vocational and practical arts education: History, development, and principles* (2nd ed.). New York: Harper & Row.

Roche, J. F. (1995). The culture of pre-modernism: Whitman, Morris, & the American Arts and Crafts Movement. *The American Transcendental Quarterly, 9*(2), 1–12. Retrieved April 11, 2003, from EBSCOHost Academic Search Elite database.

CHAPTER 6

FUNDAMENTALS OF CURRICULUM DEVELOPMENT IN CAREER AND TECHNICAL EDUCATION

Victor C. X. Wang
California State University, Long Beach

INTRODUCTION

Career and technical education (CTE) is about preparing people, young and old, for the world of work. Those who seek a teaching credential in CTE plan to teach their own occupational skills to younger generations of learners. Naturally, learning to develop a sound and meaningful curriculum will be the very first step towards securing a teaching credential. A teaching credential will equip those aspiring instructors with skills and knowledge to teach others in the field. However, given their prior occupational experience, those with occupational knowledge, skills and attitudes may not be necessarily successful instructors in CTE. Mager (1997) reminds us that, "though it is a remarkable accomplishment to have developed the skills and knowledge needed to be considered competent in one's craft, those skills are not the same as those needed for teaching that craft" (p. vii).

Building Workforce Competencies in Career and Technical Education, pages 107–127
Copyright © 2009 by Information Age Publishing
All rights of reproduction in any form reserved.

He further argues that "just as an ability to make a tuba is not the same as an ability to play one, an ability to play one is not the same as an ability to teach someone else to do likewise" (p. vii).

In order to teach others (pedagogical mode of instruction) or to help others learn (andragogical mode of instruction) (Knowles, Holton, & Swanson, 2005), a critical success factor is to learn to develop a sound and meaningful curriculum. Without a curriculum, what would we expect those with teaching credentials in CTE to teach or to help others learn in the field? As a common Chinese proverb goes, without rice, even the cleverest housewife cannot cook (Yuan, 2007). Similarly, Westerners posited that knowledge of curriculum is, by definition, central to the professional teacher and an essential orientation for all professional responsible beginners (as cited in Print, 1993, p. 1). All the above scholars emphasize the importance of the knowledge and skills of curriculum development and how important it is for new instructors in CTE. To acquire knowledge and skills about CTE curriculum, new instructors are required to familiarize themselves with the characteristics of CTE curriculum. The following characteristics were provided by Curtis and Crunkilton (1999) and they are coupled with additional explanations:

Orientation: CTE curriculum is oriented toward process (experiences and activities within the school setting) and product (effects of these experiences and activities on former students). Process leads to product. Product may further reinforce process.

Justification: CTE curriculum justification extends beyond the school setting and into the community. Just as the curriculum is oriented toward the student, support for the curriculum is derived from employment opportunities that exist for the graduate. Employers can provide feedbacks to graduates regarding whether CTE curriculum has worked for them or not. Revisions on CTE curriculum may be based on employers' feedbacks.

Focus: CTE curriculum deals directly with helping the student to develop a broad range of knowledge, skills, attitudes, and values, each of which ultimately contributes in some manner to the graduate's employability. The CTE curriculum focus also includes the integration of academic studies such as mathematics, communication skills, and science with applied studies so that students are better able to link these academic content areas to applied CTE content. Developing CTE curriculum requires integration of other academic studies. Other academic skills enhance one's skills on CTE curriculum development. This also falls in line with one of the objectives of CTE as covered in the book.

In-School Success Standards: In-school success must be closely aligned with performance expected in the occupation, with criteria used by instructors often being standards of the occupation. Instructors of CTE always follow industry standards. To make CTE students perform on the required level, often times instructors teach occupational analysis in schools.

Out of School Success Standards: A CTE curriculum must be judged in terms of its former students' success. Thus, there is a major concern for the product or graduate of the curriculum, particularly with respect to employment-related success. This means learning objectives in a CTE curriculum must be achieved. Without achieving student learning objectives, we cannot say that a student is successful in an occupation or on a job. A successful curriculum must specify clearly written observable and measurable student learning outcomes.

School—Workplace—Community Relationship: Whatever relationship exists between the CTE curriculum and the community, it should be recognized that strong school-workplace-community partnerships may often be equated with curriculum quality and success. This indicates that one's workplace determines whether a school curriculum has worked or not. If not, this means poor quality on a school curriculum.

Federal involvement: The operation of CTE curricula have to meet certain federal requirements. Some requirements may place undue restrictions on curriculum flexibility, and thus hinder attempts at innovation or at meeting the needs of certain student groups. Once funded, schools are required to conform to the standards by the Federal Agencies. This may result in less curriculum flexibility.

Responsiveness: The contemporary CTE curriculum must be responsive to a constantly changing world of work. A well reasoned curriculum may work for some time for the workplace, but the nature of work often changes, hence requiring contemporary CTE curriculum to be changed.

Logistics: Bringing together the proper facilities, equipment, supplies, and instructional resources is a major concern to all persons involved in the implementation of CTE curriculum. This falls in line with one of the philosophies by Prosser covered in the book.

Expense: The dollars associated with operating certain CTE curricula are sometimes considerably more than for their academic counterparts. This is because CTE curricula require occupational analysis, which may require more time and money. This is not true all the time. The common saying goes like, "every fourteen dollars spent on higher education, one dollar is spent on CTE."

The special characteristics of CTE education require curriculum developers to follow as many models as possible to design sound and meaningful curricula. Whether a CTE curriculum works or not, this is determined by students' workplace such as one's occupations or jobs. Those curricula that have failed to equip CTE students with necessary skills, knowledge and attitudes are deemed as meaningless curricula. Therefore, they must be redesigned. Simply putting together instructional materials would violate instructional design that must be aimed at aiding the process of learning rather than the process of teaching (Gagne, Wager, Golas, & Keller, 2005). Indeed, a curriculum is aimed at "intentional" learning as opposed to "incidental" learning. The target goals and desired learning outcomes guide the design and selection of learning activities (Gagne et at., 2005). Gagne (1985) defines learning as a process that leads to a change in a learner's disposition and capabilities that can be reflected in behavior; curriculum development must aid this process so that students can acquire skills valued in the world of work by studying the sound and meaningful curricula created and taught by professional teachers with prior occupational skills and knowledge.

This chapter will strive to cover relevant information from curriculum history, curriculum theory, philosophies of curriculum development, curriculum processes to curriculum implementation and evaluation so that those who seek a teaching a teaching credential in CTE will have enough confidence to blend curriculum development with their prior occupational knowledge and skills. With adequate coverage of these essential aspects, teachers of CTE will be able to develop sound and meaningful curricula that will bear the basic characteristics as described by Curtis and Crunkilton (1999).

CURRICULUM HISTORY

As noted by Glatthorn, Boschee and Whitehead (2006, p. 33), "understanding the history of curriculum development is useful for both scholars and practitioners. It results in a deeper awareness of the extent to which curricular changes are often influenced by and are a manifestation of larger social forces." Glatthorn et al. (2006) further indicated that understanding the history of curriculum development offers a broader perspective from which to view so-called innovations and reforms, which often seem to reverberate with echoes of the past. Towards this end, Glatthorn et al. (2006) prepared a time line that reflects the major curriculum theory and practice of the past century plus a decade. The time line was translated into:

- 1890–1916 was termed as Academic Scientism
- 1917–1940 was termed as Progressive Functionalism
- 1941–1956 was termed as Developmental Conformism
- 1957–1967 was termed as Scholarly Structuralism
- 1968–1974 was termed as Romantic Radicalism
- 1975–1989 was termed as Privatistic Conservatism
- 1990–1999 was termed as Technological Constructionism
- 2000–present was termed as New Privatistic Conservatism

While it is beyond the scope of this chapter to cover all the theories and practice, two theories have greatly influenced and shaped curriculum development in CTE (Glatthorn et al., 2006). Progressive functionalism was characterized by the confluence of two seemingly disparate views: the progressive, child-centered orientation of the followers of John Dewey and the functional orientation of curriculum scientists. For Dewey (1944, pp. 318–319):

> An education which acknowledges the full intellectual and social meaning of a vocation would include instruction in the historic background of present conditions; training in science to give intelligence and initiative in dealing with material and agencies of production; and study of economics, civics, and politics, to bring the future worker into touch with the problems of the day and the various methods proposed for its improvement. Above all, it would train power of re-adaptation to changing conditions so that future workers would not become blindly subject to a fate imposed upon them.

Translated into curriculum development in CTE, Dewey called for not only technical aspects of curriculum development, but also social and cultural aspects (Wang & King, 2008). Progressive functionalism also argues that the curriculum should be derived from an analysis of the important functions or activities of adult life (Glatthorn et al., 2006). Taylor (1911) advocated that any task could be analyzed for optimal efficiency by observing skilled workers, studying the operations they carried out, determining the time required, and eliminating wasted motion. Taylor's theory later became what is now known as "scientific management" which is evident in curriculum development (Berman, Bowman, West, & Wart, 2006). Now to develop a curriculum for contemporary workers, task analysis and occupational analysis seem to be one of the first steps towards a successful curriculum.

The second theory that has influenced and shaped a curriculum in CTE seems to be developmental conformism with its chief leader as Ralph Tyler (1950). Currently, scholars and practitioners generally agree that curriculum development involves attention to four basic issues: identifying objectives, selecting the means for attaining those objectives, organizing those means, and evaluating the outcomes, Tyler's historic questions in the curriculum development really helped reinforce the four basic issues in CTE and these questions must be answered:

1. What educational purposes should the school seek attain?
2. How can learning experiences be selected that are likely to be useful in attaining these experiences?
3. How can learning experiences be organized for effective instruction?
4. How can the effectiveness of learning experiences be evaluated?
   (Tyler, 1949, as cited in Glatthorn et al., 2006, p. 43)

Of course, this section of curriculum history has not addressed early foundations of curriculum as other chapters in the book have addressed critical issues such as organized apprenticeship programs for scribes in Egypt and the Russian training system brought to North America by Victor Della Vos. The advantages and disadvantages of the Russian training system in relation to curriculum development as opposed to the Sloyd system and the Arts and Crafts movement have also been analyzed in Chapter 5 in greater detail. With a brief curriculum history in mind, now let's move on to curriculum theory.

CURRICULUM THEORY

While curriculum theory is usually esteemed by scholars in the field as an important component of curriculum studies, most practitioners dismiss it as completely unrelated to their day-to-day work. The truth is that sound theory can be of value to both scholars and practitioners in CTE. Glatthorn et al. (2006, p. 73) posited,

> Curriculum theory can provide a set of conceptual tools for analyzing curriculum proposals, for illuminating practice, and for guiding reform. Melding theory and the reality of school curriculum together is an important step in the educational planning process. Not all curriculum theories translate smoothly into real-world practice.

In addition, curriculum theory serves different functions in CTE. Curriculum theory can provide educators with a critical perspective on the society and its schools. This view falls squarely in line with John Dewey's call for inclusion of cultural and social aspects in curriculum development (Dewey, 1944). Another point of view shared by Ralph Tyler seems to be concerned with guiding practice. A curriculum theory encompasses a set of related educational concepts that affords a systematic and illuminating perspective of curricular phenomena (Ellis, 2004; Glatthorn et al., 2006; Wang, 2008) and it will help educators make more reasoned choices.

Based on maturity and complexity, curriculum theorists can be classified as traditionalists, conceptual empiricists, or reconceptualists. Ralph Tyler is considered one of the traditionalists who are concerned with the most efficient means of transmitting a fixed body of knowledge in order to impart the cultural heritage and keep the existing society functioning (Pinar, 1978). To traditionalists, curriculum can be viewed as notions of class, teacher, course, units, lessons and so forth. Those who are concerned with the development of a syllabus, transmittal of data and knowledge via lecture, formulation of goals and objectives, assessment, and a focus on an end product belong to Tyler's group, the traditionalists. In a sense, we are all traditionalists like Tyler in CTE as we are all committed to the concept of basic knowledge and cultural literacy in school curricula.

Conceptual empiricists derive their research methodologies from the physical sciences in attempting to produce generalizations that will enable educators to control and predict what happens in schools. Robert Gagne is one of these theorists who advocates intentional learning as opposed to incidental learning and emphasizes the use of target goals and desired learning outcomes to guide the design and selection of learning activities (Gagne et al., 2005; Glatthorn, et al., 2006).

The reconceptualists emphasize subjectivity, existential experience, and the art of interpretation in order to reveal the class conflict and the un-equal power relationships existing in the larger society (Glatthorn et al., 2006, p. 77). Curriculum theories can be further divided into four catego-ries based on their domains of inquiry (Glathorn et al., 2006, p. 78):

Structure-oriented theories are concerned primarily with analyzing the compo-nents of the curriculum and their interrelationships. Structure-oriented theo-ries tend to be descriptive and explanatory in intent.

Value-oriented theories are concerned primarily with analyzing the values and as-sumptions of curriculum makers and their products. Value-oriented theories tend to be critical in nature.

Content-oriented theories are concerned primarily with determining the content of the curriculum. Content-oriented theories tend to be prescriptive in nature.

Process-oriented theories are concerned primarily with describing how curricula are developed or recommending how they should be developed. Some pro-cess-oriented theories are descriptive in nature; others are more prescriptive.

Although all curriculum theories are useful to educators in CTE, curric-ulum tends to be emphasized as end product. In other words, curriculum theory should be concerned with achieving an end product. What goals and objectives are used to achieve product or result? This is the fundamen-tal question curriculum developers in CTE constantly ask themselves. In view of curriculum as end product, content-oriented theories seem to be more relevant to CTE educators.

Also, if we go beyond the content-oriented theories or the traditional approaches to curriculum development as emphasized by Tyler, we may tend to stress one more aspect of curriculum theory, that is, curriculum as a process. According to Smith (1996, 2000), viewing curriculum as process places emphasis on the interaction among teacher, student, parent, and knowledge rather than on a syllabus and/or on an end product. The focus is on what is actually taking place in the classroom as well as the learning process itself. According to Glatthorn et al. (2006), critical thinking, listen-ing, and communication are important components of process curriculum.

Often an emphasis is placed on thinking about planning, justifications of procedures, and actual interventions, as well as providing feedback and changes during the curriculum process (p. 93).

The use of curriculum theories can help predict what happens in the classroom and what actually happens in the classroom. Educators in CTE need relevant curriculum theories in developing strategies to transmit knowledge (prior occupational knowledge and skills) via a syllabus, focus on an end product, state and demonstrate a process of learning. Without the guidance of curriculum theories, curricula developed by educators in CTE would not be considered as sound or meaningful. Like curriculum theories, philosophies also guide the practice of curriculum development. The next section of the chapter addresses how one's philosophies guide curriculum development.

PHILOSOPHICAL OVERVIEW OF CURRICULUM DEVELOPMENT

Given the historical background of career and technical education, it has been associated with competency-based education (Elias & Merriam, 2005; Wang, 2005). One's competencies can be broken down into knowledge, skills and behaviors and they must be demonstrated by the learner. It is natural that in CTE, instructors require that learners do job analysis, task analysis, performance objectives and even occupational analysis (Wang, 2008). The purpose of these activities is to ensure that learners' or workers' roles or performance objectives are stated in behavioral terms. In other words, the learners' performance objectives must be observable and measurable. Towards this end, CTE instructors emphasize using Bloom's taxonomy to develop competency-based curriculum which will result in observable and measurable student learning outcomes (Wang & Farmer, 2008). To support this competency-based curriculum, Elias and Merriam (2005) write:

> The criteria to be used in assessing student competency are direct outgrowths of the competencies themselves, stated explicitly and in advance, including specified conditions for mastery. The assessment of a student's competency uses performance as the primary source of evidence, while at the same time taking into account evidences of a student's knowledge. Student progress is determined by demonstrated competency rather than in time periods or course completion. Finally, the individual's learning experience is guided by feedback. (p. 100)

Their in-depth analysis has influenced a number of curriculum developers in not just CTE, but also in other fields such as elementary education and higher education. In order to develop curricula that comply with industry standards, Bloom's taxonomy has been heavily used in CTE. Since the mid-1990s, "competency-based education" has been replaced by "standards-based" or "skill standards." Therefore, it is no great surprise that all accreditation agencies seek to find out whether educational establishments conform to their states' common standards and specific standards. There are many sources that adult vocational education instructors can use to develop a curriculum or course for skills-based vocational technical instruction. In most cases, instructors use *The Dictionary of Occupational Titles*. Job descriptions can be another valuable source. On the importance of job descriptions, Elias and Merriam (2005) emphasize the importance of job descriptions as they provide detailed task analysis. The literature defines such task analyses as deconstructing a job responsibility into detailed steps of procedures, usually sequential. Documents available in industry, career and technical education, military and business provide pre-developed task analyses for many existing job descriptions and responsibilities.

Educators may engage in competency based education practice by designing instructional objectives and materials abased on the outcomes, the task analysis for a given position (Elias & Merriam, 2005; Taylor, 1911; Tyler, 1949; Wang, 2008). Proceeding to the next stage of instructional design and assessment leads to developing learning assessment measures and strategies which will identify mastery of the content. The assessment used to evaluate such learning should be criterion referenced, performance and skills based (Elias & Merriam, 2005; Glatthorn et al, 2005)

It is evident that this integrative approach is consistent with the foundational arguments of traditionalists such as Tyler (1949) and Taylor's (1911) scientific management theory, which were covered in the chapter. According to Tyler and Taylor, we have to learn to conduct not only task analysis but also instructive objectives. Instructional objectives revolve around five categories of learning outcomes (Gagne, Wager, Golas, & Keller, 2005). Whether it is an adult basic education course, the military training course, HRD course, or vocational-technical training course, employers are anxious to return to "needs-driven education and training and away from providing a patchwork of unconnected training courses covering topics recognized as 'nice to know' but not immediately germane to the jobs at hand" (Carnevale, Gainer, & Villet, 1990, p. 31). Therefore, the five kinds of learned capabilities in a given course ensure that jobs can be successfully completed. Gagne et al. (2005) identified the following five kinds of learned capabilities that adult vocational education instructors can use to develop sound curricula for their courses. Based on the five learned capabilities, different examples of performance rather than those provided by Gagne et al. are as follows:

- Intellectual Skill: Demonstrating the use of different part of speech for a word.
- Cognitive Strategy: Using a picture to learn foreign word.
- Verbal Information: Listing immigration regulations.
- Attitude: Choosing to take a college class.
- Motor Skill: Drawing a picture.

Indeed, without developing the five learned capabilities as ensured by a successful and meaningful curriculum, we cannot successfully complete our jobs. Therefore, the issue of competency-based education becomes important. Why is standards-based education important to adult vocational education instructors and students? To answer this question, Elias and Merriam (2005, p. 100) went into details by noting:

> It allows for individual differences in terms of the starting point for instruction; the time it takes a student to master competencies is flexible and dependent upon individual ability; learning specified competencies may be done in a variety of ways from formal class activities to life or work experiences; criterion-referenced evaluation is non-threatening; it is an ideal vehicle for a self-directed individual learning experience.

What Elias and Merriam stressed really enhanced the concept of competency-based education. However, what appears to be difficult to curriculum developers in Career and Technical Education is the fact that there are thousands of tasks and occupations in the field. If they fail to write performance objectives to be performed accurately, learners will be confused and fail to meet the needs of employers. Towards this end, Gagne et al. (2005) suggest that we write objectives that communicate:

1. Situation (context in which the learned outcome will be performed)
2. The type of learning being performed (a "learned capability" verb classifying the type of learning)
3. The content or object of the performance
4. The observable part of the behavior (action verb)
5. The tools, constraints or special conditions applied to the performance (acceptable performance)

A classical example Gagne et al. (2005) provided contains all five components and this example can used across curricula in adult vocational education. In addition, this example conforms to Tyler's (1949) model in that he emphasized the importance of writing observable and measurable performance objectives:

In a computer laboratory situation, given a simple set of specifications for a data table [situation], the student will demonstrate [learned capability verb] the construction of a database table in Microsoft Access [object] by typing it into the computer [action verbs], using the appropriate data types, and selecting an appropriate key [tools, constraints and/or special conditions]. (p. 134)

Because career and technical education prepares people to enter a job or occupation, developing standards-based education has become the norm in the field. CTE in business or industry is needed to enhance employees' on the job performance. The same thing can be said about military training or Human Resource Development in companies. Employee education and training are needed to carry out company goals. From the above writing, it is not hard to conclude that there is a strong relationship between behaviorism and curriculum design and program development in adult vocational education. If education is a process of changing the behavior patterns of people (Tyler, 1949), standards-based education should be used to guide learning experiences.

However, standards-based education is not all rosy. Critics of this mode of education argue that not all competencies desirable for certain occupations can be specified. If they can be identified, they can be difficult to perform. This is true. They also argue that standards-based education predetermines the end product of a learning experience. What if other learning occurs during the process or shifting to different outcomes as a result of formative evaluations? Then the changes are not easily accommodated in the behaviorist framework? Considering the above criticisms, critics claim that standards-based education lacks in concern for the student and inhibits creativity (Elias & Merriam, 2005). It may work well with the Russian training method or the Sloyd system (Wang & King, 2008), but it works less well in other systems. Relying solely on standards-based education, makes one fail to recognize the differences between a behaviorist and humanistic orientation.

The goal of humanistic education is the development of persons—persons who are open to change and continued learning, persons who strive for self-actualization, and persons who can live together as fully functioning individuals (Maslow, 1970; Elias & Merriam, 2005, p. 124). This goal of education is in striking contrast with that of standards-based education. The goal in curriculum development and design is no longer writing observable and measurable performance objectives. Instead, the field has moved to a broader goal which is more learner-centered. According to many leaders in the field, there has been a decided shift to focusing on assisting learners grow and develop in accordance with their needs and interests (Elias & Merriam, 2005; King, 2005; Knowles, Holton, & Swanson, 2005).

The wider affiliation with humanistic education philosophy is at the root of this shift of educators' and programmatic educational goal setting. Because it is rooted in this educational philosophy, it also has a more individualized focus in which respect of learners, and learner motivation become central tenets (King, 2005). In this orientation the curriculum is a means to an end, not the goal (Elias & Merriam, 2005).

Indeed, teaching a prescribed curriculum is not the goal of humanistic educators. Since curriculum functions as a vehicle that can promote the real goal of humanistic education—the development of self-actualizing individuals, one of the ways that humanistic educators strive for is to help learners improve interpersonal relationships in a cooperative, often times group learning experience. By creating such learning experience, learners can work together to analyze their prior experience and needs and interests and develop meaningful curricula with their course instructors. Such is the so termed humanistic mode of curriculum development, which seems to have worked well with adult learners in career and technical education. Having addressed the curriculum history, the curriculum theory and the curriculum philosophies, the next issue that needs to be addressed is curriculum processes.

CURRICULUM PROCESSES

Curriculum processes have to do with curriculum planning. Successful curriculum is concerned with a goal-based model of curriculum planning that provides organizing strategies to determine the locus of control in decision making and what organizational structures are needed. In terms of finding available planning models (Caffarella, 2002) to educators, there are a plethora of existing models in the literature. But the one that stands out and proves to be effective is the goal-based model popularized by Glatthorn et al. (2006).

No doubt that this goal-based curriculum model provides a big picture of the curriculum planning processes. However, if we examine this model more carefully, we can find out that this model does not go beyond the traditional approach of curriculum development as emphasized by Tyler (1949) and the behavioral philosophy as a guiding practice as emphasized by Elias and Merriam (2005). After all, the curriculum is the plans made for guiding learning in the schools, usually represented in retrievable documents of several levels of generality, and the actualization of those plans in the classroom, as experienced by the learners and as recorded by an observer; those experiences take place in a learning environment that also influences what is learned. Given such a premise, Tyler (1957, p. 79) defines the curriculum as all the learning experiences planned and directed by the school to attain its educational goals. To support Tyler's definition of the curriculum, Schiro (1978, p. 28) offers this explanation, "the word curriculum means output of the curriculum-development process that is intended for use in planning instruction."

To have a big picture of the planning processes is not enough. Educators especially in CTE are required to acquire specific skills in needs assessment, task analysis, and student performance objectives. These skills will support the goal-based curriculum planning model and above all, they will provide educators with what "ought" to happen, and they more often than not take the form of a plan, an intended program, or some kind of expert opinion about what needs to take place in the course of study (Ellis, 2004, p. 4). These skills will help translate our occupational skills and knowledge into a sound and meaningful curriculum that help us see what should happen in a learning environment.

Kaufman (1982) defines a needs assessment as a process of identifying gaps between what is and what should be. Through the use of a needs assessment, educators can examine curriculum goals and objectives in order to best identify instructional opportunities. Mager (1997, p. 2) noted, "the only justification for instruction is that one or more people cannot yet do something they need or want to be able to do. Unless these two conditions exist, there is no valid reason to instruct." Glatthorn et al. (2006, pp. 144–145) further justify the use of a needs assessment in curriculum planning by saying:

> Information derived from a quality needs assessment program can be used to infuse change directly into the classroom. The result is a major improvement in the teaching and learning process and a major improvement in the learning environment. Effective curriculum planning, therefore, should always include some type of needs assessment. It is through the development of quality needs assessment programs that administrators, curriculum leaders, and teachers can best facilitate systemic educational change and reform in our schools and in our classrooms.

According to Gagne et al. (2005), there are two major types of task analysis. The first is generally known as a procedural task analysis which is not unfamiliar to educators in CTE. Educators in this area normally take a course titled "occupational analysis" which covers procedural task analysis. A procedure task analysis describes the steps for performing a task, for example, the steps to change a tire. Procedural task analysis involves breaking the task down into steps the learner must perform to complete the task. For almost every occupation, procedural task analysis can be found from the "dictionary of occupational titles." The second is the learning-task analysis which involves with identifying prerequisite competencies or enabling skills that can be performed. This analysis must be done after the target objectives have been specified.

Please note that performance objectives can be used interchangeably with behavioral objectives or learning objectives. In other educational arenas, performance objectives are referred to as student learning outcomes. As noted by Gagne et al. (2005, p. 133), "one purpose of performance objectives is to communicate the aims of instruction (to students, administrators, other teachers, and parents) and provide a foundation for the development of instructional activities and assessment of learning." When writing performance objectives, educators should keep in mind what the learner should know, do, or feel. Gagne reminds us that an objective is useful when it communicates to the learner what they should be able to do after instruction. Gagne enumerates essential elements of objectives which can guide the objective writing process; he lists situation, type of learning, content, the observable part of behavior and tools (Gagne, 2005).

One concern with writing performance objectives is that no active verb is related to evidence. See the following examples:

1. Graduates will be historically grounded practitioners.
2. Knowledge of learners and learning.
3. Develop as a professional educator.
4. Be a multifaceted professional.

Another concern is that novice educators tend to use "squish" or "vague" words when writing performance objectives. See the following examples:

1. Understand…
2. Knows…
3. Demonstrate understanding of…
4. Demonstrate knowledge of…
5. Demonstrate an awareness of…
6. Be familiar with…
7. Recognize…

These squish or vague words are not observable or measurable in behavioral terms. Of course, there are other models that educators can follow when writing good and meaningful performance objectives. For example, Bloom's Taxonomy (1956) provides action verbs that reflect six levels ranging from students' lower order thinking skills to higher order thinking skills. Once curriculum processes are completed, the next item to be addressed will be curriculum implementation and evaluation.

CURRICULUM IMPLEMENTATION AND EVALUATION

Curriculum implementation can be most challenging if there is not buy in from all sides such as students, school administrators, and school districts. Educators in CTE who wish to implement a new curriculum need to take into consideration the following factors that characterize successful implementation:

1. Teachers perceive the need for the new curriculum. Without successfully identifying the gap between the current need of the new curriculum and the desired need of the new curriculum, the new curriculum cannot be implemented.
2. The curriculum changes are not unduly complex and are clearly explained to teachers. Without knowing any new changes, other teachers cannot help implement the new curriculum.
3. Quality materials supporting the new curriculum are made available to teachers. Teachers must have access to the qualify materials in CTE.
4. Previous attempts to change curricula have been successful. If those attempts have failed before, this means the new curriculum cannot be implemented.
5. Administrators are strongly encouraged to take responsibility for implementing the new curriculum in their schools and are given the necessary training. Administrators are expected to be leaders in curriculum implementation. If they are not experts, how can they be expected to help teachers in CTE?
6. Teachers have had substantial input into the new curriculum and are provided with the necessary staff development. Teachers must be bone fide experts in curriculum in CTE. They must have the required academic backgrounds in CTE.
7. There is strong school-board and community support. Community can provide feedbacks regarding what curriculum has worked and what has not. Then, school-board needs to provide these feedbacks to teachers in CTE.
8. There is a carefully developed implementation plan that makes specific provisions for monitoring implementation. The whole thing about curriculum implementation is that it is carefully planned and directed. Specific provisions must be followed for successful curriculum implementation.
9. Administrators take the necessary steps to prevent and respond to the problem of "overload"—when teachers feel overwhelmed and overworked in implementing the new curriculum. A good idea here is to offer teachers release time to implement the new curriculum.

10. Administrators play an active role in advocating and supporting the new curriculum. If leaders do not support the new curriculum, there won't be buy in on the part of teachers, let alone students.
11. Teachers have an opportunity to share ideas and problems with each other and receive support from supervisors and administrators. This process will help curriculum developers improve the new curriculum for future implementation. This process should be an ongoing process. (Ellis, 2004; Fullan & Park, 1981, as cited in Glatthorn et al., 2006, p. 256; Wang, 2008)

Only when the above factors are properly addressed, can a high level of curriculum implementation be expected. Once curriculum implementation is completed, the next issue to be addressed will be curriculum evaluation. Evaluation in CTE is to help the educational process better relate to individual learners so that learners can successfully perform their jobs, using their acquired workforce competencies obtained from studying the sound and meaningful curriculum developed by their educators. Two concepts come to mind when evaluating a curriculum in CTE: merit and worth. Merit refers to the intrinsic value of a CTE curriculum (Mathis & Jackson, 2008). Merit is established without reference to a context. Worth refers to the value of a curriculum in CTE in reference to a particular context or a specific application. For example, an adult basic education course may have a great deal of merit in the eyes of expert: It may reflect sound theory, be built upon current research, and embody content experts deem desirable. However, the same course may have relatively little value for a teacher instructing unmotivated working class youth: It may require teaching skills that the teacher has not mastered and learning materials that the students cannot read. In this situation, curriculum evaluation should be concerned with assessing both merit and worth.

There are many ways and models to evaluate a given curriculum. Since career and technical education has been shaped by the behavioral philosophy and it is competency-based education, Tyler's objectives-centered model has proved to be more effective for CTE educators. According to Glatthorn et al. (2006, p. 303), his model is relatively easy to understand and apply. It is rational and systematic and focuses attention on curricular strengths and weaknesses, rather than being concerned solely with the performance of individual students. In addition, Tyler's model emphasizes the importance of a continuing cycle of assessment, analysis, and improvement. However, Tyler's model is not without deficiencies. According to Guba and Lincoln (1981),

Tyler's model does not suggest how the objectives themselves should be evaluated. It does not provide standards or suggest how standards should be developed. Its emphasis on the prior statement of objectives may restrict creativity in curriculum development, and it seems to place undue emphasis on the pre-assessment and post-assessment, ignoring completely the need for formative assessment. These deficiencies may be true especially when we consider the fact that learning is not only shaped by behavioral philosophy, but also by humanism. According to humanism, learning is considered an internal process. Thus, it cannot be measured in behavioral terms. This is true when we think about our student population in CTE. The majority of our students are adult learners who may embrace humanism in learning. Regardless of this philosophical orientation, behavioral philosophy and competency-based education have dominated career and technical education for years. Therefore, Tyler's (1949) model continues to influence many assessment projects in CTE. To give our readers an opportunity to appreciate and apply Tyler's model critically, his model can be used rationally and systematically through several related steps.

The first step is to start with previously determined behavioral objectives. These objectives need to specify both the content of learning and the student behavior expected. The second step involves instructors in identifying the situations that will give the student the opportunity to express the behavior embodied in the objectives, which may evoke or encourage this behavior. For example, if you wish to assess oral language use, you need to identify situations that evoke oral language. The third step is to select, modify, or construct suitable evaluation instruments, and check that instruments for objectivity, reliability, and validity. The fourth step is to make sure that the instruments are used to obtain summarized or appraised results. The fifth step is to compare the results obtained from several instruments before and after given periods in order to estimate the amount of change taking place. The seventh step is the analyze the results in order to determine strengths and weaknesses of the curriculum and to identify possible explanations about the reason for this particular pattern of strengths and weaknesses. The last step is the use the results to make the necessary modifications in the curriculum (Tyler, 1950, as cited in Glatthorn et al., 2006.)

Because of the weaknesses in the Tyler model and the overemphasis of behavioral philosophy and competency-based education in CTE, alternative models were developed in the 1960s and 1970s. These alternative models are Stufflebeam's (1971) Context-Input-Process-Product Model, Scriven's (1972) Goal-Free Model, Stake's (1975) Responsive Model and Eisner's (1979) Connoisseurship Model. It is beyond the scope of this chapter to discuss the strengths and weaknesses of these alternative models. Although these models prove to be useful in other educational fields, the Tyler model still remains a dominant model in CTE. There is nothing wrong in focusing curriculum evaluation on student performance in CTE. After all, a performance-based assessment program is to evoke more stimulating, intellectually challenging tasks for students (Guskey, 1994).

CONCLUSION

While innovations have been sought to develop a sound and meaningful curriculum for today's workforce in the United States, competency-based education has remained the driving force in the field of career and technical education. Recently, with the passing of the *No Child Left Behind legislation*, standards (state and national) have driven curriculum to look first at the standards, and then mold curriculum decisions around those standards (Glatthorn et al., 2006, p. 325).

The behavioral philosophy has stood out as a guiding philosophy among all other philosophies such as humanistic, progressive, radical, analytic, liberal and post modern philosophies. Indeed, a competency-based curriculum relates closely to a behavioral philosophy. The *No Child Left Behind legislation* has confirmed the traditional approach to curriculum development. Although history shows that scholars and practitioners in the United States have been striving to decentralize its curriculum in all subject areas, curriculum development in CTE has never deviated too much from the traditional use of curriculum models such as the Tyler Model which emphasizes examining learning objectives in behavioral terms. This is not to say that other approaches are not useful to curricular reform. Rather, the key to curricular reform is finding a multitiered approach involving high-quality classroom instruction combined with targeted, small-group interventions enhancing learning. All across the United States, skills training has become a high priority.

With the onset of a new millennium, public attention has been sharply focused on curricular innovations and instruction. Policymakers and parents see direct evidence that our country's future depends upon the education of the workforce, and they worry that schools are not as effective as they need to be (Glatthorn et al., 2006, p. 326). With the global economy increasingly demanding high levels of skills, knowledge and attitudes from both workers and managers, scholars and practitioners in CTE are required once again to take a closer look at curriculum history, curriculum theory, curriculum philosophies, curriculum processes and curriculum implementation and evaluation to ensure that sound and meaningful curriculums can be developed in the field. Without such sound and meaningful curriculums, our country's workforce cannot remain competitive in this curricular reform movement of the post-Sputnik era. Some other questions should enter our national conversation: What are the trends and issues involved in CTE? How is technology impacting the delivery and implementation of curriculum in this field?

Finally, Darling-Hammond (1996) seems to have set a direction for America's educators not only in CTE but also in all educational arenas.

Her provocative explanations should set us all thinking about America's future:

> In this knowledge-based society, the United States urgently needs to reaffirm a consensus about the role and purposes of public education in a democracy—and the prime importance of learning in meeting those purposes. The challenge extends far beyond preparing students for the world of work. It includes building an American future that is just and humane as well as productive, that is as socially vibrant and civil in its pluralism as it is competitive. (Darling-Hammond, 1996, p. 11)

As CTE is defined as preparing people, young and old, to enter the world of work, learning to design sound and meaningful curricula should be the prerequisite for CTE educators in training. Without the basic skills, knowledge and attitudes needed to thrive in CTE, America' future envisioned by Darling-Hammond will be a dream that cannot come true.

REFERENCES

Berman, E. M., Bowman, J. S., West, J. P., & Wart, M. V. (2006). *Human resource management in public service: Paradoxes, processes, and problems* (2nd ed.). Thousand Oaks, CA: Sage.

Bloom, B. S. (Ed.). (1956). *Taxonomy of educational objectives.* London: Longman.

Caffarella, R. S. (2002). *Planning programs for adult learners: A practical guide for educators, trainers, and staff developers* (2nd ed.). San Francisco: Jossey-Bass.

Carnavale, A. P., Gainer, L. J., & Villet, J. (1990). *Training in America: The organization and strategic role of training.* San Francisco: Jossey-Bass.

Curtis, R. F., & Crunkilton, J. R. (1999). *Curriculum development in vocational and technical education: Planning, content, and implementation* (5th ed.). Boston: Allyn & Bacon.

Darling-Hammond, L. (1996). *What matters most: Teaching for America's future.* New York: National Commission on Teaching and America's Future.

Dewey, J. (1944). *Democracy and education: An introduction to the philosophy of education.* New York: Macmillan.

Eisner, E. W. (1979). *The educational imagination: On the design and evaluation of school programs.* New York: Macmillan.

Elias, J. L., & Merriam, S. B. (2005). *Philosophical foundations of adult education* (3rd ed.). Malabar, FL: Krieger.

Ellis, A. K. (2004). *Exemplars of curriculum theory.* Larchmont, NY: Eye on Education.

Fullan, M., & Park. P. (1981). *Curriculum implementation: A resource booklet.* Toronto: Ontario Institute for Studies in Education.

Gagne, R. M. (1985). *The conditions of learning* (4th ed.). New York: Holt, Rinehart & Winston.

Gagne, R. M., Wager, W. W., Golas, K. C., & Keller, J. M. (2005). *Principles of instructional design* (5th ed.). Belmont, CA: Wadsworth/Thomson Learning.

Glatthorn, A. A., Boschee, F., & Whitehead, B. M. (2006). *Curriculum leadership: Development and implementation.* Thousand Oaks, CA: SAGE.

Guba, E., & Lincoln, Y. (1981). *Effective evaluation.* San Francisco: Jossey-Bass.

Guskey, T. (1994). *What you assess may not be what you get. North Central Association: Commission on Accreditation and School Improvement.* Retrieved June 19, 2008, from http://www.ncacasi.org/documents/other/what_you_assess

Kaufman, R. A. (1982). Needs assessment. In F. W. English (Ed.), *Fundamental curriculum decisions* (pp. 53–67). Alexandria, VA: Association for Supervision and Curriculum Development.

King, K. P. (2005). *Bringing transformative learning to life.* Malabar, FL: Krieger.

Knowles, M. S., Holton, E., & Swanson, A. (2005). *The adult learner* (6th ed.). Boston, MA: Elsevier Butterworth Heinemann.

Mager, R. F. (1997). *Making instruction work or skillbloomers: A step-by-step guide to designing and developing instruction that works* (2nd ed.). Altanta, GA: CEP Press.

Maslow, A. H. (1970). *Motivation and personality* (2nd ed.). New York: Harper & Row.

Mathis R. L., & Jackson, J. H. (2008). *Human resource management* (12th ed.). Mason, OH: Thomson South-Western.

Pinar, W. F. (1978). The reconceptualization of curriculum studies. *Journal of Curriculum Studies, 10*, 205–214.

Print, M. (1993). *Curriculum development and design.* Australia: Allen & Unwin.

Schiro, M. (1978). *Curriculum for better schools: The great ideological debate.* Englewood Cliffs, NJ: Educational Technology.

Scriven, M. (1972). Pros and cons about goal-free evaluation. *Evaluation Comment, 3*(4), 1–4.

Smith, M. K. (1996, 2000). *Curriculum theory and practice. The encyclopedia of informal education.* Retrieved June 18, 2008, from http://www.infed.org/biblio/b-curric.htm

Stake, R. E. (Ed.). (1975). *Evaluating the arts in education: A responsive approach.* Columbus, OH: Bobbs Merrill.

Stufflebeam, D. L. (1971). *Educational evaluation and decision-making.* Itasca, IL: Peacock.

Taylor, F. W. (1911). *The principles of scientific management.* New York: Harper & Bros.

Tyler, R. (1949). *Basic principles of curriculum and instruction.* University of Chicago Press.

Tyler, R. W. (1950). *Basic principles of curriculum and instruction.* University of Chicago Press.

Tyler, R. W. (1957). *The curriculum then and now. In Proceedings of the 1956 Invitational Conference on Testing Problems.* Princeton, NJ: Educational Testing Service.

Wang, V. C. X. (2005). Teaching philosophies of Chinese vocational education instructors. *International Journal of Vocational Education and Training, 13*(1), 7–21.

Wang, V. C. X. (Ed.) (2008). *Curriculum development for adult learners in the global community Volume I: Strategic approaches.* Malabar, FL: Krieger.

Wang, V. C. X., & Farmer, S. J. (2008). Adult teaching methods in China and Bloom's taxonomy. *International Journal for the Scholarship of Teaching and Learning, 2*(2), 1–15.

Wang, V. C. X., & King, K. P. (Eds.) (2008). *Innovations in career and technical education: Strategic approaches towards workforce competencies around the globe.* Charlotte, NC: Information Age.

Yuan, H. W. (2007). *Chinese proverbs.* Retrieved August 30, 2007, from http://www.wku.edu/~yuanh/China/proverbs/q.html

CHAPTER 7

FRAMING STRATEGIC PARTNERSHIPS GUIDED BY ADULT LEARNING

Bridging the Education Gap with CTE

Kathleen P. King
Fordham University

This case study research examines the use of several adult learning principles in career and technical education for the purpose of extending them to secondary and other career and technical programs to help bridge the compulsory education vs. higher education (K–16) educational gap. The focus is on the NCCTE exemplary and promising award program standards and a sampling of programs that have received this designation. Findings include the frequency of use of identified adult learning principles, trends in their use, and examples. Additionally, a related emphasis on softskills and recommendations for applying these experiences and findings to secondary education are offered.

Building Workforce Competencies in Career and Technical Education, pages 129–158
Copyright © 2009 by Information Age Publishing

INTRODUCTION

In the midst of the Post-Information Age, vocational education now includes high schools, postsecondary education, trade and technical schools, and other career-to work programs. While high schools are often dominated by concerns related to competition for admissions to the best higher education institutions, this field has developed over the years to be a valuable option for both college and non-college bound students. The rising costs and extended timeline of pursuing a college education is not always available to young adults and they may need to move into the workforce more rapidly thereby making career-to-work programs indispensable (Delci & Stern, 1997; Scott & Bernhardt, 1999). These conditions, and others, have contributed to a gap that vocational, or more recently named "career and technical education" has been attempting to bridge (Kerka, 2000; Levesque, Lauen, Teitelbaum, Alt, & Librera, 2000).

With career and technical preparation including a post-high school time frame, the characteristics and needs of students as adults become more urgent as adults of all ages attend such programs (Brown, 1999; Castellano, Stringfield, & Stone, 2002; Wonacott, 2002). To facilitate a smooth, effective transition from high school to the workplace or postsecondary education, administrators, educators, trainers, and career counselors can then examine the field of adult learning to support both our CTE efforts in high schools in our adult education, vocational and technical programs further. One strategy to do this is to not just refer to theories and principles of adult learning, but also examine best practices among career and technical education to see how they already use adult learning to bridge the gap.

This chapter addresses questions that also emerge from educational and socioeconomic trends including: What teaching and learning issues need to be addressed among learners as they continue in their adult years? What theory, research, and best practices in adult and vocational education can allow us to address this trend? And, how can program and curricular planning in career and technical education on both ends of the continuum—secondary and postsecondary—benefit from or incorporate this knowledge base? Specifically, the chapter explores how adult learning principles (e.g., active learning, immediate application of knowledge, and building on the experience of learners) are and can be used further to guide and shape programs in career and technical education in secondary and postsecondary settings.

Building upon a review of the literature, this research analyzes the National Center for Career and Technical Education's (NCCTE) Exemplary and Promising Program standards of outstanding practice and several member programs. This analysis is an extended case study that includes both a national scope and individual specificity (Creswell, 1998; Yin, 2003). The

NCCTE standards, and multiple examples within the case, are examined across selected programs. The results are presented based on the theoretical propositions of the study rather than as a case study descriptive narrative to articulate more fully the findings and their meaning based on our framework of examining the compulsory education vs. higher education (K–16) gap (Yin, 2003).

This research entailed five major research questions. First, through a survey of the literature, how is career and technical education addressing the compulsory education vs. higher education (K–16) gap within our current economic, political, and educational settings? Second, what insights does the adult learning literature provide into salient characteristics of adult learners relevant to career and technical education settings? Third, how do the NCCTE standards for exemplary programs demonstrate these adult learner principles, or not? Fourth, what do four sample programs from the NCCTE awards program reveal as they are analyzed for their possible illustration, operationalization, and maximization of adult learning principles? Finally, what recommendations for secondary, postsecondary, and career and technical education research and practice can be made based on the application to and further development of adult learning in this context?

CAREER AND TECHNICAL EDUCATION FILLING THE COMPULSORY VS. HIGHER EDUCATION (K–16) GAP

As I surveyed the literature of the CTE field regarding theory, research, practice and program planning, specific trends became and some emerged as standing out more than others. Over the past 30 years this educational movement has transitioned from a remedial and vocational school often less highly valued, but duly provided service to school systems to become a clearly recognized valuable alternative for preparing young adults for trade, technological, and professional careers with or without postsecondary study as part of their future. No longer solely serving a marginalized population, career and technical education is providing valuable preparation and career alternatives for a wide-range of students (Bragg & Reger, 2002; Kerka, 2000; Wonacott, 2002). During a time when the costs of higher education have skyrocketed, many adults cannot pursue that pathway, or if they do, they pursue it over an extended period of time. These economic factors have increased the value of career and technical education that prepares secondary and postsecondary learners in shorter, work-oriented, hands-on programs of study.

Very often these programs are also based on local occupational needs and federal or independent occupational forecasts such as the U.S. Department of Labor's *Occupational Outlook Handbook (2006)* (Kerka 2000; U. S.

Department of Labor, 2006). The field of career and technical education has similarities and differences across its many applications. From computer-aided graphics to welding, from culinary arts to agriculture, and from early childhood education to emergency medical technicians, one is impressed by a sampling of the vast expanse of programs and careers included in this field (Bragg & Reger, 2002). Certainly different content areas, but also different expectations, philosophies, and requirements compose the constellation of programs included in career and technical education.

However throughout its history vocational education, and now career and technical education, (CTE) has consistently addressed the needs of young and older adults who are examining their formal education and attempting to match it immediately to their careers.

Based on interview with program leaders, which we will describe shortly, frequent questions and concerns of these learners include,

• How can my education build upon my interests and abilities to prepare me for a valuable occupation?
• How does what I am learning in the classroom apply to real life?
• What is the value of what I am learning?
• How can this area become not only a job, but also a career for me?
• How can I prepare to continue my learning into the future?
• And how can I learn the many things I need to know to succeed in the workplace?

Rather than stopping at a credential, career and technical education has increasingly become a platform from which to explore and build perspectives and skills in understanding learners' ongoing educational and professional needs (Brown, 2002; Wonacott, 2002).

Today career and technical education is more prominently providing a bridge from requisite secondary education to a lifelong opportunity for education and development. The research reported in this paper begins to explore how we can learn from successful career and technical education programs and bring these approaches into secondary and postsecondary education so that our learners and curriculum might benefit from a stronger bridge and smoother transition of purpose and practice.

THE VIEW FROM ADULT LEARNING

As educators and trainers consider career and technical education, we are examining it from the perspective of adult learning principles. In this light, the literature of adult education provides insight into salient characteristics of adult learners relevant to career and technical education settings. While the adult learning field is vast and diverse, over the years many common principles have consistently emerged (Caffarella, 2002; Cooper & Henschke, 2007; Imel, 1998; Lawler & King, 2000). While I recognize that different learning theories have and continue to emerge, the focus here is on overarching learning principles that have been identified in the literature including, involving learners in planning, cultivating self-directed learning, involving learners in active learning, learning for application, building on learner's experience, building a climate of respect, and cultivating collaborative skills (Lawler & King, 2000).

The principle of *involving adult learners in planning* is one that closely links to cultivating self-directed learning. As we work with learners to include them in needs assessment, content selection, assignment selection, and/or evaluation decisions, we are providing opportunities for them to learn how learning can be planned. Whether the learners are college students, employees, or literacy students, participating in planning learning builds ownership of, motivation for, and relevance of educational initiatives (Caffarella, 2002; Lawler & King, 2000). As recommended by Caffarella (2002), "A second strategy for building learner support [of adult learning programs] is to actively involve current and potential learners in planning and conducting the programs" (p. 86). This principle has never been an easy one to integrate into traditional organizations or curricula and distinctly challenges a teacher-centered and authoritarian model. However, when learners are involved in the planning of learning it promotes powerful results to support and extend learning experiences and qualitatively change learners' and teachers' perspectives.

These experiences in planning can also be a basis for building patterns and skills for *self-directed learning*. By educators not keeping the planning process exclusive or invisible, learners who engage in planning begin to see themselves increasingly as able to make decisions about learning (Caffarella, 2002; Vella, 2002). Programs can demonstrate their involvement in cultivating self-directed learning when learners determine needs, set goals, and evaluate their own performance, among other tasks. Rather than depending on an outside authority/teacher to lead the way, learners experience the freedom, autonomy, and power of leading the way for themselves. The locus of power in educational decisions shifts from the outside, to the learner. Merriam and Caffarella (1999) state that this structure much more closely resembles how learners face many learning opportunities in their adult years, "...this form of learning can take place both inside and outside institutionally based learning programs. For the most part, however, being self-directed in one's learning is a natural part of adult life" (p. 293). Shifting the control and direction of learning from teacher to learner in the formal classroom opens the door to a natural transition when the learner encounters formal and informal lifelong learning opportunities.

Such involvement in self-directed learning sets the stage for *involving learners in active learning*. These learners cannot be passive recipients of knowledge that comes from an authority. Learners must be engaged in seeking and experiencing learning as recognized by Lawler (1991), "Adults learn more effectively and efficiently when they actively participate in the educational activity" (p. 39). Hands-on activities, small groups, and project-based learning are examples of how learners can become active participants (Caffarella, 2002; King, 2005; Lawler & King, 2000). Demonstration techniques are examples of how hands-on experience can be clearly illustrated in the area of technology learning. When a course in word processing consists of lectures about how the program works and then transitions to working through lessons in the program in the computer laboratory, new information is more fully and vividly understood through active learning and experience. Adult learners overwhelmingly respond positively to experiences that enable them to interact with, critically examine, and experience new information, skills, and ideas (Caffarella, 2002; Merriam & Caffarella, 1999; Vella, 2002). Active learning techniques can transform a once quiet classroom to one humming with activity, inquiry, and learning.

This active learning can be easily meshed with *learning for application* among learners as project-based learning, case studies, and group projects are used. Rather than memorizing content, when adult learners engage in using the information for a specific application, it takes on new meaning and urgency. Indeed from the beginning, adult learners continually ask why material is being taught and how they will use it (Vella, 2002). As we build on this need and interest in our educational programs, we capture intrinsic needs and motivation (Caffarella, 2002; Cochran, 2007; King, 2005; King & Wright, 2007; Lawler & King, 2000). An example from faculty development reveals that faculty, as adult learners, exemplify the need to see application, "If there is a prevailing attitude that this new learning will not enhance their professional life or that there is little support, affirmation, or reward, the faculty [adult learners] may see little or no need to attend or learn" (Lawler & King, 2000, p.11).

In formal educational settings this emphasis on motivation is often seen as an optional approach; however in informal educational settings, such as independent and avocational learning, application often becomes the purpose of learning. Without the need to use the learning, many informal educational pursuits would not even be started. In their busy and complex lives, adults need to see the usefulness, and the application, of any learning within which they might invest themselves. Cultivating a vision for application of learning introduces adult learners to valuable strategies for lifelong learning.

Adult learners do not learn in a vacuum. Instead their learning is scaffolded on prior, and many times extensive, experience. When educators unleash many opportunities for understanding, application, and extension they *build on learners' experience* (King, 2005; Lawler & King, 2000). Caffarella (2002) succinctly states this point, "Adults have a rich background of knowledge and experience and learn best when this experience is acknowledged and new information builds on their past knowledge and experience" (p. 29). Rather than teaching content in isolated fragments, if we can bring learning into learners' webs of experience, we know they will more quickly understand and more successfully retain the learning (Vella, 2002).

Building on learners' experiences includes assessing prior learning and experiences. Providing opportunities for class discussions, small group activities, and reflective practice all cultivate the activity of drawing out past experiences that apply to new learning. As learners wrestle with how new learning fits together with prior understanding, they open the door to not just learning subject matter, but also to integrating learning into their understanding and perspective in fundamental ways. Much like the old lesson plan mnemonic—"Hook–Took–Look"—prior experience can be an invaluable "hook" into learners' understanding, validation, motivation, and context for learning.

Within a learning environment that builds on experience, *a climate of respect*, encouragement, and support is necessary to ensure learners' personal, professional, social, and emotional safety. Vella (2002) describes this vividly as she relates;

> Safety is a principle that guides a teacher's hand throughout planning, during the learning needs and resources assessment, in the first moments of the course. The principle of safety enables the teacher to create an inviting setting for adult learners. People have shown that they are not only willing but also ready and eager to learn when they feel safe in the learning environment. (p. 8)

If learners feel their prior experience is open to harmful criticism by others, or if they sense that their experience may be devalued, then they cannot take the risks involved in investing themselves genuinely into the learning experience. Educators therefore need to consider how to communicate and cultivate respect, encouragement, and support in their relationships with the students, their classrooms, and their programs. Such an environment is often explicitly identified by ground rules for communication, appreciation for diverse opinions and experiences, and confidentiality (Caffarella, 2002; Merriam & Caffarella, 1999; Vella 2002). However, other adult learning principles also integrate with this positive climate. For instance, students quickly recognize respect, encouragement, and support when they participate in planning their learning and valuing their experience.

Finally, *cultivating collaborative skills* through small groups is an adult learning principle that prepares learners for the workplace and personal life as it builds teamwork, leadership, communication skills, and interpersonal understanding (King, 2005; Scribner & Donaldson, 2001). Much of our experience as adults involves working with other people; and developing collaborative skills will help learners to succeed in these circumstances. Collaborative skills may be developed in adult learning settings through many forms including working in small groups, on team projects, group presentations, and role-playing (Caffarella, 2002; King, 2005; Vella, 2002). Vella effectively illustrates benefits of collaborative learning as she discusses teamwork:

> In a team, learning is enhanced by peers. We know that peers hold significant authority with adults, even more authority than teachers. Peers often have similar experiences. They can challenge one another in ways a teacher cannot. Peers create safety for the learner who is struggling with complex concepts, skills, or attitudes. I have seen significant mentoring go on in teams: peers helping one another, often with surprising clarity, tenderness, and skills. (p. 23)

As adults explore relationships with others, they gain new strategies for learning that include communication, appreciation, cooperation, negotiation, and conflict resolution. Such activities can release the power of collaborative skills for lifelong learning and ongoing professional development that are encountered through living and learning in adulthood.

This overview of adult learning principles from the literature provides a context for determining if and how the principles are implemented in NCCTE standards and the related exemplary and promising career and technical education programs.

CASE STUDY—NCCTE PROGRAM—PHASE ONE

NCCTE Program Background

The National Centers for Career and Technical Education (NCCTE) is a non-profit organization that represents leaders of some of the nation's premier providers of career and technical education and their instructors, administrators, and counselors. Additionally, the consortium includes a national advisory council of leading experts, internationally recognized consultants, and other collaborating institutions, agencies, and organizations. The vision of the NCCTE's National Research and Dissemination Centers states, "as primary sources of research-based information, [the Centers] will significantly affect the quality of knowledge and understanding necessary to advance career and technical education in the United States" (NCCTE, 2003, para. 1).

Method and Analysis

Method. This research was pursued as a qualitative case study. It examines the prevalence of specific categories, or principles, within the NCCTE program. The method of document review and interview of a lead administrator was selected in order to provide a baseline and context of data for the alter study in which several exemplar CTE programs would be studied. Rather than just study the schools, the research deemed it important to gain fuller background about the values, mission, goals and perspectives of the organization.

Procedures. The NCCTE documents and interview of the co-director of the organization were used to collect data about the NCCTE program. The documents were obtained via mail after the interview and while others were available on the Internet and were reviewed and analyzed prior to the interview. These documents described the NCCTE organizational program's mission, purpose, reports, publications, and history were obtained from NCCTE to examine the awards program in general, and most specifically the standards, or outstanding practices, upon which prospective career and technical education program applications are assessed.

The interview with one of the co-directors of the program was arranged in advance, and most of the questions were sent in advance with the opportunity to ask follow-up questions. The interview was conducted by phone. Purposes of the interview included: (a) to gather more first hand perspectives in-depth background about NCCTE, (b) to determine the basic educational orientation of the NCCTE program, (c) to gain an overview of the awarded programs and (d) Check the categories of adult learning principles, which the researcher had identified from the literature with the interviewee. Results of this interview would guide the final development of categories to be used in the school CTE program leader interview protocol and coding protocol for school CTE program documents.

Analysis. The researcher gathered, examined, categorized, coded, and tabulated the data using these protocols (Yin, 2003). In these ways the coding was created through a process grounded in both the literature of adult learning and the context of NCCTE Exemplary and Promising Programs initiative. This process provided a focused, or bounded, approach to examining the vast possibilities of data collection and analysis for the stated research questions (Creswell, 1998; Yin, 2003).

Findings: Standards and Adult Learning

The NCCTE's outstanding standards for exemplary and promising status in career and technical education include 15 categories: access and inclusiveness, align with standards, certification and credentialing, curriculum reform, evaluation and continuous improvement, placement and retention, partnerships, professional development, program and instructional delivery, program and institutional leadership, technology enhancements, transition options, student development and leadership, sustainability and finances, and systematic and whole school reform (NCCTE, 2002). While nearly half of these standards are organizationally oriented, many also address the planning and delivery of teaching and learning. It is from among these guidelines that the linkages with adult learning principles become evident.

The adult learning principles were not present in every one of the NCCTE practices. This finding confirms expectations that the NCCTE program review has additional purposes while also exemplifying adult learning principles. Table 7.1 provides a matrix of the principles and practices determined in this analysis and this section describes how the NCCTE program demonstrates each principle within the 15 NCCTE categories.

Learning for Application. Direct linkages from the following NCCTE practices to learning for application are evident. *Alignment with standards* by the NCCTE's definition is based on what is effective in the workplace.

TABLE 7.1 Principles and Practices Identified among NCCTE Exemplary and Promising Programs Outstanding Practices Standards[a]

Learning Principles[b]	NCCTE Outstanding Practices Standards[a]
Learning for application	• Align with standards • Certification and credentialing • Curriculum reform • Placement and retention • Technology enhancements
Involving learners in active learning	• Curriculum reform
Building on learners' experience	• Program and instructional delivery
Cultivating self-directed learning	• Curriculum reform • Student development and leadership
Cultivating collaborative skills	• Partnerships
Building a climate of respect, encouragement, and/or support	• Partnerships
Involving learners in planning	• Student development and leadership

[a] Selected from, the 15 NCCTE practice standards categories are: access and inclusiveness, align with standards, certification and credentialing, curriculum reform, evaluation and continuous improvement, placement and retention, partnerships, professional development, program and instructional delivery, program and institutional leadership, technology enhancements, transition options, student development and leadership, sustainability and finances, and systematic and whole school reform (NCCTE, 2002)

[b] Adult learning principle identified as parallel CTE principle-based on interview with NCTE interview and Dr. King's expertise of adult education learning (King, 2005).

Certification and credentialing make concrete the purposes of career and technology programs to develop skills that are directed to application in the designated area. *Curriculum reform* specifically encourages problem-based learning that is one example of learning for application. *Placement and retention* makes explicit the close coordination of curriculum and student learning for preparation for the workplace. And finally *technology enhancements* demonstrate learning for application as it ensures that students can experience and gain proficiency in using current technologies.

Involving learners in active learning. The emphasis of *curriculum reform* supports problem-based learning. Such activities can incorporate several modes of active learning as learners engage in problem-solving, critical thinking, collaborative learning, research, and planning. Rather than an archetype, authoritarian, teacher-centered classroom, students should participate actively in discovering, interacting, analyzing, and applying their learning.

Building on learners' experience. This principle is evident in developing *program delivery, instructional delivery,* and *transition options* when learners' experience, knowledge, and skill are assessed to plan their learning. This emphasis is seen not only in current programs of study, but also for the purpose of effectively moving among educational programs and institutions where applicable. Building on learners' experience reduces redundant learning experiences, wasted time and resources, and validates and further progresses learners on continuous pathways towards their educational and vocational goals.

Cultivating self-directed learning. The standard for *student development and leadership* articulates the goal of learners developing experience and confidence as leaders of their own learning and among their peers. *Curriculum reform* also supports this principle as learners engage in problem solving much like they will in the workplace and further cultivate self-directed learning perspectives and experience. The independence and confidence the learners gain within their learning, organization, and field lay the practical groundwork for taking charge of their own learning as they continue to grow within their professional and personal skills in the future.

Cultivating collaborative skills. *Organizational partnerships* provide the opportunity to demonstrate collaboration within professional settings to the learners. Such collaboration can demonstrate effective and appropriate communication, collegial support, negotiation, and problem solving within and among groups.

Building a climate of respect. *Partnerships* also provide learners experience with prospective employers in real-life environments. Professional respect may be demonstrated in the classroom and reinforced with peers and superiors in work placement assignments. These experiences can have important results in guiding learners in how to recognize and facilitate respect and support.

Involving learners in planning. Opportunities for *student development and leadership* engage learners in planning their education and careers. Even when learners do not have much choice among courses in a closely specified program, these development and leadership experiences can afford participation in other aspects of their educational planning for a class, the organization, and/or themselves. Gaining experience in planning one's career and including ongoing professional development in it are important gains from participating in such programs.

In addition to these principles being evident in many of the specific NCCTE standards, standard number nine, *program and instructional delivery,* is a major guideline that supports "program and instructional approaches that have been proven to work" (NCCTE, 2002). Certainly the adult learning literature can provide a valuable, rigorous, and reputable resource of educational philosophy, curriculum theory, learning theory, program planning, and assessment and evaluation to build program, classroom, and student learning experiences. This standard can provide an overarching rationale for using adult learning principles in career and technical education.

Standard number twelve, *transition options,* articulates the need to build "linkages between secondary and postsecondary education" so that barriers will not arise and remediation will not be needed (NCCTE, 2002). This standard explicitly states the thesis of this research and demonstrates that high standards for career and technical education represent the need and benefits of bridging the compulsory education vs. higher education (K–16) gap. Indeed, the twelfth standard indicates that programs should plan to bridge this gap directly through organizational and curricular planning.

Based on how the adult learning principles are represented in the NCCTE standards, a perspective of "bridging the compulsory education vs. higher education (K–16) gap" is evident in this program. Looking to career and technical programs for examples and recommendations in pursuing both of these points is consistent with their purposes. In these ways the fundamental framework of the research problem and questions are confirmed in these data.

CASE STUDY—INDIVIDUAL NCCTE PROGRAMS PHASE TWO

Individual Programs Background Now Being Studied

As stated, this study also examined career and technical programs that had been cited by NCCTE as *exemplary* or *promising* based on the NCCTE's stated standards. Programs submitted applications to apply for this status and NC-

CTE examiners made site visits to the finalist programs. Such programs included both secondary and postsecondary programs. They are representative of programs across the United States and include awardees for the years 2000 and 2001. Materials about the programs were gathered via NC-CTE documents and their Web site.

CTE School Program Participants

Participants in the study included both individuals who were interviewed and programs that were studied. Four interviews were conducted. All of these participants were instructors in their programs, while two were also directors. Three of the programs represented in the interviews were from the exemplary category and one was from the promising category. The programs were located in Virginia, Phoenix, and two were in Oklahoma. These programs ranged in the number of students from 23 to 2500 and faculty numbering from 1 to 49. All of the programs had postsecondary learners, while two also had secondary learners enrolled. Three specific programs of study were identified: certified network administrator (CNA), database management, and graphic design. The remaining program had many career and technical areas including: autobody, banking/retail, computer technology programs, computerized office programs, facilities and maintenance, food preparation, medical assistant, machine trades, meat cutting, nursing, printing trades, and welding.

Data regarding 30 programs were reviewed via program documents, with 23 programs for the year 2000 and 7 for 2001. Additionally, among these programs 7 had been awarded exemplary status and 23 awarded promising. Several of these programs served more than one constituency of learners so that the distribution was secondary learners, 20 (66.7%), adult learners, 10 (33.3%), and postsecondary learners, 10 (33.3%). Occupational areas of these 30 programs were many and represent the following categories: automotive, business and marketing, construction, culinary arts, education, finance, health services (e.g., nursing, EMT, surgical technician), hospitality and tourism, industrial maintenance, interior design, technical computer-related, manufacturing, office technologies, and transportation.

Method

Selection for Phase Two. The programs included in the initial review included for this study were all of those receiving awards in 2000 and 2001 for which sufficient data were available. Regarding the phone interviews these were conducted with one of the co-directors of the NCCTE program to confirm and extend the initial assessment and analysis of the award program and purposes. These interviews also provided further insight into programs that had both secondary and postsecondary programs. Recommendation by the co-director concurred with the preliminary findings to indicate four programs to be interviewed in-depth in the **second phase of the study**. Purposely the selection of interviewees was not random, as the aim was to determine best practice from which to build recommendations.

Data Collection Phase Two. Data was gathered through published documents, questionnaires, and interviews. Following preliminary evaluation of these NCCTE published documents, the interview with the NCCTE program co-director was conducted, and semi-structured interviews were conducted with each of the four career and technical education programs. All interviews were transcribed.

These interviews and questionnaires not only address whether programs used adult learning principles, they also asked for examples of how they are used. In addition, realizing that these programs represented valuable experience in the field of secondary and postsecondary education, the interviewees were asked directly what they perceived as similarities and differences among such learners. Additionally, rather than solely relying on the "outside" researcher to determine recommendations, building upon best practice and educational expertise, those questioned were also asked for recommendations. In this way the case study included self-analysis and reflective practice and could be substantially rooted in not only adult learning theory, but also grounded in career and technical education experience.

Data Analysis Phase Two. Qualitative analysis of this case study included coding by themes of adult learner characteristics and principles developed from the literature (Creswell, 1998). Additionally, the limited quantitative data were evaluated for frequencies, and other basic descriptive statistics. As with many case studies this research included examining, categorizing, tabulating, and recombining the qualitative and quantitative data (Yin, 2003) to build an understanding of both the NCCTE program and a selective sample of program awardees.

Findings and Discussion–Interviews–Phase Two

Through the interviews it was again evident that the adult learning principles that had been identified in the literature and recognized in the NCCTE standards were also evident within the individual programs. Four basic trends were recognized in the interviews and program documents. First, in-depth discussions revealed that these four programs used the learning principles frequently. Second, the postsecondary programs indicated use of more of the learning principles than the secondary. Third, programs with classes where secondary and postsecondary learners worked together demonstrated the viability of using the adult learning principles with secondary students in this context. Finally, the emphasis in career and technical education programs on softskills was recognized and found to be consistent with the use of adult learning principles. Each of these observations will be discussed in this section.

Use of adult learning principles. The interviews offered the opportunity to learn whether program leaders recognized the same principles in their programs and if so, how these principles were operationalized. Table 7.2 presents these findings with the mean rating and standard deviation on a 1–5 Likert scale in which 1 is "Never" and 5 is "Always."

Application. The interviews revealed that all of the programs, 100%, used "learning for application" as a major theme of their learning experiences and rated it as "5/Always." Indeed, adult, vocational, and career education has been grounded in this principle in the literature and many initiatives have emerged from the need to have such application explicitly integrated into the curriculum. However, it was confirmation and validation to see that these programs incorporated learning for application through simulated environments, true-to-life projects, and actual commerce through either program/school-based services or work in conjunction with local businesses.

Several quotes demonstrate the primary role of application in these programs:

> I use a lot of project based [activities] that's how I test my students' project based tests. For example, you may have noticed on the Web site, we are dealing with web design. We actually take on Web sites that need to be developed as community service for non-profits or some businesses and they pay or donate money to the student organization. But the students actually develop a real project as their test project, instead of taking a written test, and they do take online certification tests for certification in the software. But I use projects to assess them and to help them build their portfolios at the same time.

> Several of our programs also are used for trade. That is, you see people coming in here to pick up their meat orders. In our meat-cutting program they actually work on taking and filling orders. So the students get to see what it is really like.

> I think one [recommendation] is that at least having someone in the faculty who has come from that industry, rather than just from the academic [realm]. Simulate the business environment as closely as possible. This is applied learning, so everything needs to be tied back [to application].

> In this program they might be sent by their employer or a government agency to obtain certain skills and proficiencies. So what we do in the classroom has to be directly connected to application…All the training is hands-on, from making posters in printing to simulations of other work assignments.

TABLE 7.2 Frequency of Learning Principles Used Based on Interviews

Learning principles	M	SD	Examples
Learning for application	5.00	.00	• Build network from donated computers • Do work for companies • Project-based assignments • Simulate the work environment and culture • Real-life case study examples to apply their learning
Involving learners in active learning	4.875	.25	• Hands-on • Simulations • Create projects • Field trips • Case studies
Building on learners' experience	4.75	.50	• Build on previous courses • Assess technology skills upon entrance • Evaluate skills. Determine what learners need
Cultivating self-directed learning	4.75	.50	• Self-paced program • Monthly progress reports by the students • Critical thinking skills used to solve problems • Self-paced with parameters as guides
Cultivating collaborative skills	4.50	1.00	• Team projects • Critique and help one another constantly • Teams solve case studies • Some communication workshops
Building a climate of respect, encouragement, and/or support	4.50	.58	• Emphasize respect in the classroom and workplace • Collaboration and work as peers-colleagues • Taking into consideration interests and needs of learners throughout courses • Monthly presentations by students in which they support and encourage one another • Celebration of certification awards
Involving learners in planning	4.25	.50	• Students set target dates • Students review course objectives and suggest assignments, special speakers, and content • Student suggestions regarding the curriculum • Students identify their progress and needs

Note: (N = 4 individuals each representing a program of more than 15, therefore the group characteristics are indicative of approximately n = 60)

Active Learning. Regarding "involving learners in active learning," the programs again scored this very high on the scale (M = 4.875) and with little variation in scores (SD = .25). Examples of active learning illustrate that some of the common teaching methods used in career and technical settings include several of these learning principles simultaneously as in the following quotes, respondents cited hands-on projects, simulations, project development, case studies, and field trips as opportunities for active learning. For example:

> One of the things that the students here just finished [demonstrates active learning.] We had 30 donated computers and what the students did was based upon previous things that they had learned and throughout the last year and a half. They had to build the network from the computers, make the computers work, create the network cables, you know, make the whole thing come together.

> I try to do questioning and elaboration type of things as we're kind of exploring. Again, I have the luxury of having a small enough class I only have 16 students in a session, I can have a personal rapport, it's hard to do that if you have 200 students. I can question them as to their understanding, but also take it a step farther with elaboration and say, "How would you apply this?" So those are two active learning techniques. Obviously they do hands-on and practice and things. We have a guest speaker or a take a tour and they get to see the application of the technology toward particular business objectives.

Learner Experience. Regarding "building on learners' experience" three out of the four interviewees rated this item "5/Always" and found it to be an integral part of their program. Programs were consistent in evaluating the students' skills when coming into the programs and at least one program allowed students to "place out" of requirements or take course substitutions if learners demonstrated knowledge and proficiency. As illustrated in the following quotes, these program directors did not mention the use of techniques to draw out experience from the learners as some adult education techniques employ, but instead mostly mentioned course placement:

> And so I try [to] employ different learning strategies that are appropriate for them and one of the things that I try to use the most in that respect is the use of analogies. [Based on] what kind of background that they have, if their background is business, then I might try to use a different analogy than if their background is science or engineering. As much I can, because some of the time I can't help them with an analogy....I also try to give them case studies where the technology would be used. If they're coming from a different discipline then I will try to think of case studies or examples where the technology that they're learning would be applied to the profession that they came from. I've had everything from retired teachers to school counselors, to new college graduates with degrees in mathematics and physics to engineering, and I've had kind of a wide variety of students, so I try to relate it in that respect to maybe the discipline they are coming from.

> Primarily what I just try to use is that I sit down with each student when they begin the program and kind of ascertain at least a little bit about what their motivation is for entering the program and what their background is, both professional and personal.

> A lot of high schools here do what is called keyboarding or IS programs, where they're kind of introduced to desktop applications, like the (MS) Office programs. So what we really do is that we take that as the starting point. The students that come into my program generally don't come in without any background at all. So I'm taking what computer work they have already learned and we go from there [identifying]…standards of learning, plus [what they have learned] from high school.

Self-directed Learning. Respondents rated "self-directed learning" at the maximum, "5/Always", three out of four times. More importantly the ways that they worked to cultivate this characteristic were insightful. Some programs were entirely based on a self-paced format, used self-paced methods for some activities, and combined this approach with providing parameters and guidelines for the learners to be able to judge their own progress. While another program had the students provide a monthly-progress report of all of their work. One respondent also recognized that their work in developing critical thinking skills to solve problems was in fact cultivating self-directed learning. This area especially leads toward building patterns for lifelong learning. While they may not always be in formal classroom learning settings, adults are continually engaged in learning across the lifespan in both professional and personal arenas. Building strategies and a mindset about learning that incorporates self-directedness certainly lays the groundwork for lifelong learning perspectives and habits. The following quote from one interviewee illustrates self directed learning in the career and technical education context:

> [Ours is a] self-directed, self-paced program, so I don't have students in the same place at the same time. [For instance,] 5 in Photoshop, 2 in HTML, it depends on the student and how quickly they learn. They are required to keep a calendar that shows what they complete each day which they submit to me at the end of each month for a grade. That's like a time card for them; it helps them set a target date on that, helps them keep on track. [The] student sets the target date, based on my outline for them, a plan of study which shows them how many hours or weeks for each unit that they have to complete that.

Collaborative Learning. Most of the programs used "collaborative learning" in significant ways. One program however volunteered that they had plans to do more in this area. This fact primarily contributed to the large variance evident in the standard deviation of 1.00. In the following interview excerpt, one participant reveals how important collaborative learning is for her program's setting and plans to incorporate more it:

> That's something [collaborative groups] in which we could stand to do some improvement. And in fact, it's interesting- that's one of the things I have felt. Having individualized instruction, sometimes that makes group projects more difficult. They do already attend formalized, professional workshops in concepts like teamwork and resume writing...and communication workshops, but all students attend that. They attend in-house resume writing workshop and job interviewing workshops and also attend customer service workshops, which is also in-house from a variety of sources...This semester I am going to require every student to participate in a group project that's related to the learning that they are doing. So this is a pilot semester for that because I feel like that is something that has really been missing. So we do have that with a couple of the projects that we're running now, and by the end of the semester, every student will have had an opportunity to participate in a group project, and they will last anywhere from 4 weeks to 8 weeks depending on the project.

Team projects and small groups appeared in each program as techniques. However, one program articulated the strategy that they used to have learners constantly responsible to critique and assist each other; this practice was embedded within the concept parallel to field functions in the workplace. Additionally, one program had special workshops on communication and team building activities; again this formal approach simulates workplace experiences of human resources activities. Certainly, these programs had identified the need for collaborative experience and skills in the workplace and were incorporating them in the learning experiences. The following quotes clearly illustrate this connection:

> In the autobody program students are assigned to groups that they work in on a continual basis. This provides realistic experience of how they will work in their careers.

> Constant collaboration in the classroom, standing over another, critiquing their work, helping someone with something they've already learned, suggesting different, they work on a lot of different projects together.

> I have them set up in groups of 4 so that they can actually work as a team in certain situations we try to do building the network-they were assigned groups-that was a group project. They have to work in teams to figure it out. I'll give someone an example of a problem I worked on or someone else had and I say to the team, OK you need to figure this out. So they work in small groups or groups of 4 and occasionally with the class as a whole.

Climate. The practice of "building a climate of respect, encouragement, and/or support" was originally intended to capture the relationship among instructors and learners. Instead many of the respondents highlighted the cultivation of respect among the learners and upon further examination they had brought forth a valid point. Teachers and learners create the learning environment; therefore, the relationships, interactions, and communication among the learners can be very instrumental in setting the tone. Examples of working toward such a climate included conducting coursework in teams and small groups, having monthly presentations in which students could gain skill and confidence as the class supported their efforts, and celebrating the achievements of learners. The respondents revealed a real sense of individuals' needs in this area:

> I think that one [example of respect on support among] the students is when they present their monthly technology reports to each other, they don't really critique at the end of that; it's more about getting people to relax and so we all clap at the end of that. Regardless of how good or bad it was. They are encouraged to work with each other. So that if I'm not available, because I'm working with somebody else, they are encouraged to work with each other so that everybody kind of knows everybody, even on a personal level....When students pass their certifications; an important point nearing the completion, they are treated to lunch. We try to support and reward as well.

Learners in Planning. Regarding "involving learners in planning," the respondents indicated this had the lowest score (M = 4.25, SD = .50). While students participated in setting personal target dates and goals, it was not customary for them to directly contribute to the curriculum decisions. A striking exception to this observation is evident in one program in which the learners review objectives for the courses and make suggestions about content, activities, and assignments. The autonomy of the learners in this format really represented a different level of their involvement in and responsibility for their learning. It may be observed that such learner-centered planning is again providing a basis from which learners may easily develop lifelong learning skills. The two quotes provided here illustrate ways that programs are incorporating learner participation in planning:

> They went in there as a team and collaboratively [decided] what assignment could they be given this year. And what things did they want to know about that they think would help them. And they actually came up with homework assignments and I said don't be afraid that I am going to overload you; I would rather give you a relevant assignment than give you busy work. So they actually came up with suggestions about assignments and also kinds of companies that they would like to see speakers come from and things like that.

We provide for custom planning of their education. Their plan might be based on a learning disability or it could be on employer's goals for them. So although they are not involved in curricular planning, they are involved in instructional planning for themselves.

FINDINGS AND DISCUSSION—PROGRAM DOCUMENTS

The evaluation of the program description documents revealed similar rankings of the learning principles (see Table 7.3). "Learning for application" was certainly the predominate characteristic identified from the descriptions of the programs as 86.7% of the programs highlighted it. "Active learning" was also a prominent characteristic closely followed by "collaborative learning skills" and "self-directed learning." Many of these programs described careers and skills learners gain from the programs. In addition, they described how the learning proceeds. It is expected that these purposes may have brought some principles to light more frequently than others. However, it is noticeable that learners' planning and experience, where they would be more fundamentally involved in the direction of the on-going learning experience, were less often mentioned. It must also be remembered that these principles were identified in documents that publicly described the programs in contrast to the interviewer being able to query respondents regarding responses to specific inquiries. This difference certainly accounts for the wide difference in citation of items, however remarkably the ranking of them remained nearly constant. This fact likely speaks to the likelihood that these principles are indeed consistent within career and technical education as it is currently practiced.

Postsecondary and Secondary Comparison. Regarding the identification of adult learning principles postsecondary and adult programs aver-

TABLE 7.3 Frequency of Learning Principles Used Based on Documents

Learning principles	*N* yes	%
Learning for application	26	86.7
Involving learners in active learning	10	33.3
Cultivating collaborative skills	8	26.7
Cultivating self-directed learning	7	23.3
Building a climate of respect, encouragement, and/or support	4	13.3
Involving learners in planning	4	13.3
Building on learners' experience	3	10.0

Note: N = 30.

TABLE 7.4   Comparison of Frequency of Adult Learning Principles Comparing Programs

Learning principles	Adult and Postsecondary Programs (*N* = 10)		Secondary Programs (*N* = 20)	
	N yes	%	*N* yes	%
Learning for application	8	80	18	90
Involving learners in active learning	5	50	5	25
Cultivating collaborative skills	4	40	4	20
Involving learners in planning	3	30	1	5
Building a climate of respect, encouragement, and/or support	2	20	2	10
Building on learners' experience	2	20	1	5
Cultivating self-directed learning	1	10	6	30

Note: N = 30.

aged 2.50 indicators per program compared to secondary averaging 1.85. The distribution of the principles was also insightful as they followed nearly the same ranking order as the previous data (see Table 7.4).

Consistent with the evaluation across all programs, "learning for application" was the clear leader at 90% in secondary programs and 80% in adult programs. The next tier of responses included active learning, self-directed learning, and collaborative learning competing for second, third, and fourth rankings. Following fourth place, there was much variation. In the adult and postsecondary programs, "involving learners in planning" was 30% and "building a climate of respect" and "building on experience" were 20% with "self-directed learning" coming in last at 10%. In contrast, secondary programs rated "climate of respect" 10%, and both "involving learners in planning" and "building on learners' experience" 5%. Clearly the biggest variations were the much greater percentage of the principles being indicated in the adult and postsecondary programs and the higher ranking for "self-directed learning" in the secondary programs.

FINDINGS AND DISCUSSION—ADDITIONAL FINDINGS

Application to Secondary Students. In the interviews, the programs that merged both secondary and postsecondary learners in the same classroom explicitly demonstrated the viability of using adult learning principles with secondary students in this context. As documented in the following quote, those program representatives stated that the presence of the adults in the classroom raised the level of professionalism and seriousness about studies:

> It's [having adults and secondary together] an advantage instead of a disadvantage, and the reason why is because adults help to stabilize the classroom and my younger students are able to learn from them—I guess a lot of "adult" characteristics. And the adults pick up a lot of creativity from the high school students as well. They'll be working on a design that is specifically for a younger audience, and so they will go to the high school students and get tips on what is hip; [they get] input from them. It's impressive when you watch them interact. There's no division at all as far as adults and high school students are concerned. It is a learning experience for both. I always think adults come with a lot more baggage than high school students, but that's not always true, because of the harsh environments that the high school students are being raised in. They don't have family stability and this offers a stability that they can come to each day. I have real high attendance, very few problems with absences.

> I think in many situations there is a great advantage to having the high school and adult students mixed. We see that a lot. Most of our programs have high school students. High school students can learn a great deal from the adult students, in mentor-type relationships. Sometimes the high school students get on the adult students' nerves. They work well together; by and large it's beneficial to have a mixture.

The greater emphasis on learning for application, success in the workplace, and learner responsibility and involvement that we are accustomed to identifying with postsecondary career and technical education can be used with benefit among secondary learners. Rather than having a traditional teacher-centered learning environment throughout secondary studies, it may well benefit the learners by moving them towards perspectives and practices that will more closely resemble postsecondary career and technical education. Instead of a disjuncture as learners exit one system and enter the next, a more seamless transition could easily benefit learners immediately and in their future studies and work.

Softskills. It also became evident that these programs not only emphasized technical workplace skills, but also "soft skills," variously defined as workplace basic skills, employability skills, or generic skills, "the general skills that most workplaces require" (Brown, 2002) include communication skills, appropriate workplace behavior and dress, and project management, to name a few examples. Softskills are recognized as being instrumental in contributing to success in the workplace. These programs recognized this widely held perspective and incorporated them in many different ways- some programs did this more formally than others by having formal lessons and workshops on softskill topics. Other programs used relationships as a primary way of communicating softskill learning as instructors coached learners about etiquette, appropriateness, habits, protocol, and expectations through conversation, modeling, mentoring, and discussion. The learning principles that were recognized in this research also are consistent with softskills in that learning for application, collaborative learning, self-directed learning, and respect are all characteristics that do not just include technical knowledge. As the following quotes demonstrate, softskills were emphasized as a characteristic of these successful career and technical programs:

> Softskills are integral; our student organization-Skills USA [is conducted] every Wednesday-VICA-in my program and 20 percent of their grade is tied to their involvement in that. I require every one of my students to compete in a leadership contest and then those who qualify for the leadership contest (5) compete at the national level and it's considered a privilege. It's additional too. We placed in nationals last year—10 students to nationals who placed first at state, 1 placed 5, and others in the top 3. They work so closely in teams with that. [They] also work with developing resumes. Guest speakers come in and speak and talk to them about what it takes to be a good employee. I have a video library that I use and give them a sheet of paper when they go to watch it and they have to fill it in at the end on time management. Teamwork skills and "How to succeed in job interviews" complement that. [They also use the] Professional Development Plan-5 different books that help them assess career goals and help them reach those goals.

> One of the things we focus on is softskills and in computer networks that is customer service. So in order to know [technical skills] by the end of the two years and work with customers I expect them to treat each other in that manner. They are not allowed to cuss and they aren't allowed to put anyone down. We work on that very, very hard. They have dress up days; every Tuesday where they speak and they have to be not only respectful to the speaker, they have to turn off their monitors while the speaker is speaking. Also, if someone runs into trouble, they are expected to help bail each other out. We're not going to fail an individual; we are all going to fail. So we work on that a lot.

> You could go to a store or restaurant, and it's the same in business—if people don't understand you, can't read you work, or you don't treat them respectfully, you are not going to get or will have trouble keeping a job. You can be a great technician and super smart, but if you don't come to work on time, dressed appropriately [you will have problems]. I don't let tardies go, [these are] big etiquette issues.

STUDY LIMITATIONS

Case study limitations often include small sample sizes, potentially highly individualized settings, and the limited extent to which they may be generalized (Creswell, 1998; Yin, 2003). With this understanding, this study presents a basis to promote further discussion and research about how adult learning principles can be beneficially used in secondary and postsecondary career and technology education settings based on the success of theses programs. The concepts presented are an extended example of the use of adult learning principles within these specific contexts and settings and are not intended to be generalizable to all settings. These findings provide a basis for further consideration, discussion, and research.

IMPLICATIONS FOR A COMPULSORY VS. HIGHER EDUCATION (K–16) BRIDGE

What does this research show us about the composition and construction of a compulsory vs. higher education (K–16) bridge based on the strength of career and technical education? As we compare the adult education literature and the other findings of this study, what is the meaning for spanning the compulsory vs. higher education (K–16) gap? This research helps inform and delineate a framework for addressing these questions and relevant teaching and learning issues and trends.

Embedded in a grounded set of adult learning principles from the literature, this research study demonstrates several major implications that are connected: (a) principles of adult learning that can be contextually applied, (b) a vision of lifelong learning and ongoing professional development that can be cultivated earlier in learners' education, and (c) a focus on softskills in addition to technical or academic knowledge and skills.

Adult Learning. Regarding the adult learning principles, a clearly prominent emphasis is placed on application of learning and tandem simulation of the workplace that emerge as major themes over and again in the NC-CTE standards and programs. These data remind us that we need to point young or older adults toward how their learning fits into their needs and their world. Other programs can benefit by engaging their learners in active learning and simulations of and active participation in workplace projects and environments.

Vision. Closely ranked to these major points are the needs to build on learners' experience, cultivate self-directed learning, and learn collaborative skills. These strategies may be seen as laying groundwork for ongoing professional development and lifelong learning. As learners experience the freedom, ownership, and motivation of learning that meets their needs and includes autonomy and collaboration at various times, a wider spectrum of learning possibilities are experienced. The emphases and curriculum of these programs result in a vision or expectation of ongoing professional development, and more broadly, lifelong learning. Secondary education programs can benefit by introducing this perspective earlier to young adults so they begin to see the vast extension and application of learning into their futures. Revealing the relevance to and continuity of their current learning to their adult lives can likely have powerful possibilities for other secondary learners like it does for career and technical education learners.

Softskills. Finally, not just technical skill and knowledge were needed, but also "softskills" were emphasized in these programs. In an age of standards-based teaching and learning, we need to consider how we are accounting for valuable softskills in these standards and in our evaluation of learning. So often our secondary education becomes focused on achievement tests and college placement, but career and technical education provide us with some new considerations. How are we guiding learners in integrating their technical and content knowledge and skill with their perspective, attitudes, behavior, and work? Career and technical education programs provide a vivid lesson that softskills can be interwoven into the curriculum and extra-curricular activities alike. By bridging content knowledge with the learner's attitudes, behaviors, and other affective attributes, these programs and learners can experience many benefits including increased learner motivation, an elevated, "professional" classroom climate, increased transfer of learning, more successful work placement assignments, development of leadership and teamwork skills, and development of perspectives of a career rather than a more short-sighted "job."

RECOMMENDATIONS FOR BUILDING A STRONGER COMPULSORY VS. HIGHER EDUCATION (K–16) BRIDGE

As we consider the implications of this research, several recommendations emerge regarding how career and technical education can inform and strengthen a compulsory vs. higher education (K–16) bridge. Three areas of recommendation may be identified, those for educators, curriculum, and learners. These recommendations apply not only to secondary schools and educators, but also to career and technical programs. The professional development of educators is the cornerstone to success in this process. Through professional development we have the opportunity to introduce adult learning principles and strategies to a constituency who may not have been exposed before to them in terms of how they apply to their learners. Such professional development could take the form of not just lecture style presentations, but instead, interactive discussions, case studies, problem and project-based activities, reflective practice, and modeling the intersection of adult learning practices across the contexts of CTE (King, 2002, 2005; Lawler & King, 2000). Professional development can provide opportunities to discuss the meaning of lifelong learning and determine how to introduce it to their learners; likewise educators can consider and develop strategies for integrating softskills into their class experiences. By engaging educators in discussing these findings, they can work towards assessing and reflecting on what their classes and programs currently do and what else is possible. Critical to implementation is that the element that they make plans to operationalize what they have learned through these activities and determine needs to be done.

Regarding the curriculum, instructors and administrators can work towards not only learning about the principles and strategies, but also individually and collaboratively developing curriculum for their classes and across programs that reflect these findings. Even if an educational institution does not have a specialized career and technical program, their courses can be aimed to prepare students to become self-directed learners so that they can see application of their learning to contexts beyond the classroom. For instance, in our urban setting cultivating a vision of future "careers" for K–12 students is a critical shift from what they may have in their neighborhoods. Even without a CTE program, educators can integrate content into the traditional curriculum that discusses careers and activities that build skills that provide pre-career foundations for these students (King, 2007). Specifically, educators can determine the best ways to add or enhance the use of learning for application, active learning, collaborative learning, self-directed learning, building on learner experience, lifelong learning, and softskills in particular in their curriculum. They can explore new standards, new curricular materials, and new objectives and goals that might extend what they are already doing or bring them into new areas.

Finally educators can also look at what may be accomplished regarding the students' involvement. How can they be involved in the planning process? For instance how can they begin to experience taking some responsibility for the planning of their learning? Such a step would open wider the door to self-directed learning, learner responsibility, and perspectives of lifelong learning. Recommendations to accomplish this could be programmatic: student representatives on program advisory boards, extra-curricular: student participation and leadership in appropriate professional associations, or course specific: student participation in determining course goals, learning activities, and timetables. These are responsibilities that they will soon encounter as they cross the gap from secondary to postsecondary education and the workplace. The issue is how to best prepare them by building a bridge of learning experiences that reflects their need to shoulder these responsibilities successfully.

Each of these recommendations provides vibrant opportunities to reconsider "business as usual" and determine how secondary and postsecondary education might bridge the compulsory vs. higher education (K–16) gap. Examining secondary and postsecondary education from the perspective of career and technical education, through a lens of adult learning results in recommendations for educators, learners, and the curriculum. Educators today have the opportunity to refine or redefine their educational objectives based on these findings. Educational institutions hold the possibility of creating a compulsory vs. higher education (K–16) transition that is smoother so that learners' gains have the potential to be magnified and enduring. Beyond test scores and job placement, what are we doing to introduce learners to a culture of self-directed learning and a perspective of lifelong learning? This is a critical question that these recommendations can help us address.

FUTURE STUDY OF THE COMPULSORY EDUCATION VS. HIGHER EDUCATION (K–16) GAP

Many more questions for research emerge as we continue to consider how career and technical education can assist in bridging the compulsory vs. higher education (K–16) gap. Further research can focus on, how effectively do these principles and practices transition to the secondary context? How can these findings further inform practice in technical education, workplace learning, higher and further education? What adaptations work in different contextual and content areas? What additional benefits emerge as learners engage in taking increased responsibility for their learning? What impact does a perspective of lifelong learning and ongoing professional development have on learners immediately and as they progress in their work and learning through their adult years? What other challenges in secondary and postsecondary education might be addressed by bridging the compulsory vs. higher education (K–16) gap in these ways? And, as secondary education implements some of these changes, what complementary responses do we learn are needed in technical education, workplace learning, and postsecondary education? The desire is to continuously move ahead educational practice, theory, and research so that we can address the challenges facing our learners and our institutions. Addressing this gap through lessons learned from career and technical education does not provide final, definitive answers; instead it outlines a research-based framework for our efforts and reveals many more opportunities for us to explore.

REFERENCES

Bragg, D. D., & Reger, W. (2002). *New lessons about tech prep implementation*. St. Paul, MN: National Research Center for Career and Technical Education.

Brown, B. L. (1999). *Vocational certificates and college degrees, ERIC Digest No. 212.* Columbus, OH: ERIC Clearinghouse on Adult, Career, and Vocational Education. (ERIC Document Reproduction Service No. ED 434 248) Retrieved May 1, 2007, from http://eric.ed.gov/ERICDocs/data/ericdocs2/content_storage_01/0000000b/80/2a/2e/c3.pdf

Brown, B. L. (2002). *Generic skills in career and technical education; Myths and realities, No. 22.* Columbus, OH: ERIC Clearinghouse on Adult, Career, and Vocational Education. (ERIC Document Reproduction Service No. ED 472 363) Retrieved May 1, 2007, from http://eric.ed.gov/ERICDocs/data/ericdocs2/content_storage_01/0000000b/80/28/12/9c.pdf

Caffarella, R. S. (2002). *Planning programs for adult learners: A practical guide for educators, trainers, and staff developers* (2nd ed.). San Francisco: Jossey-Bass.

Castellano, M., Stringfield, S., & Stone, J. (2002). *Helping disadvantaged youths succeed in school.* St. Paul, MN: National Research Center for Career and Technical Education.

Cochran, J. (2007). Reactions to Western educational practice: adult education in Egypt. In K. P. King & V. C. X. Wang (Eds.), *Comparative adult education around the globe* (pp. 85–112). Hangzhou, China: Zhejiang University Press. (Worldwide distribution Transformation Education LLC www.transformationed.com)

Cooper, M., & Henschke, J. (2007). Expanding our thinking about Andragogy: Toward the international foundation for its research, theory and practice linkage in adult education and human resource development—A continuing research study. In K. P. King & V. C. X. Wang (Eds.), *Comparative adult education around the globe* (pp. 151–194). Hangzhou, China: Zhejiang University Press. (Worldwide distribution Transformation Education LLC, www.transformationed.com)

Creswell, J. (1998). *Qualitative inquiry and research design.* Thousand Oaks, CA: Sage.

Delci, M., & Stern, D. (1997). *Who participates in new vocational programs?* Berkeley, CA: National Center for Research in Vocational Education.

Imel, S. (1998). *Using adult learning principles in adult basic and literacy education.* Columbus, OH: ERIC Clearinghouse on Adult, Career, and Vocational Education. (ERIC Document Reproduction Service No. ED 425 336) Retrieved April 25, 2007, from http://eric.ed.gov/ERICDocs/data/ericdocs2/content_storage_01/0000000b/80/11/31/7d.pdf

Kerka, S. (2000). *Career and technical education: A new look.* Columbus, OH: National Dissemination Center for Career and Technical Education. (ERIC Document Reproduction Service No. ED 448319) Retrieved April 25, 2007, from http://eric.ed.gov/ERICDocs/data/ericdocs2/content_storage_01/0000000b/80/24/26/43.pdf

King, K. (2005). *Bringing transformative learning to life.* Malabar, FL: Krieger.

King, K. P. (2002). Testing the waters for distance education in adult education programs. *PAACE Journal of Lifelong Learning, 11,* 11–24.

King, K. P. (2007). Robotics—Prime opportunities for careers and student learning. In M. Gura & K. P. King (Eds.), *Classroom robotics: Case stories of 21st century instruction for millennial students* (pp. 133–144). Charlotte, NC: Information Age.

King, K. P., & Wright, L. (2007). New perspectives on gains in the ABE classroom: Transformational learning results Considered. In K. P. King & V. C. X. Wang

(Eds.), *Comparative adult education around the globe* (pp. 231–252). Hangzhou, China: Zhejiang University Press. (Worldwide distribution Transformation Education LLC, www.transformationed.com)

Lawler, P. A. (1991). *The keys of adult learning.* Philadelphia: Research for Better Schools.

Lawler, P. A., & King, K. P. (2000). *Planning for effective faculty development: Using adult learning strategies.* Malabar, FL: Krieger.

Levesque, K., Lauen, D., Teitelbaum, P., Alt, M., & Librera, S. (2000). *Vocational education in the United States: Toward the year 2000. Statistical Analysis Report.* Washington, D.C.: National Center for Education Statistics.

Merriam, S., & Caffarella, R. (1999). *Learning in adulthood,* (2nd ed.). San Francisco: Jossey-Bass.

National Centers for Career and Technical Education (NCCTE). (2002). *Exemplary programs: Outstanding practices.* Retrieved December 12, 2002, from http://www.nccte.org/programs/exemplary/Practices/definition.asp

National Centers for Career and Technical Education (NCCTE). (2003). *About: Vision.* Retrieved January 2, 2003, from http://www.nccte.org/about/aboutVision.asp

Scott, M., & Bernhardt, A. (1999). *Pathways to educational attainment and their effect on early career development.* Berkeley, CA: National Center for Research in Vocational Education.

Scribner, J. P., & Donaldson, J. G. (2001, Dec.). The dynamics of group learning in a cohort: From nonlearning to transformative learning. *Educational Administration Quarterly, 37*(5), 605–636.

United States Department of Labor. (2006). *Occupational outlook handbook 2006–2007.* Indianapolis, IN: Jist Works.

Vella, J. (2002). *Learning to listen, learning to teach.* San Francisco: Jossey-Bass.

Wonacott, M. E. (2002). *The impact of work-based learning on students.* Columbus, OH: ERIC Clearinghouse on Adult, Career, and Vocational Education. (ERIC Document Reproduction Service No. ED 472603) Retrieved April 25, 2007, from http://eric.ed.gov/ERICDocs/data/ericdocs2/content_storage_01/0000000b/80/2a/38/b0.pdf

Yin, R. K. (2003). *Case study research: Design and method* (3rd ed.). Thousand Oaks, CA: Sage.

CHAPTER 8

TRAINING IN CHINA

Victor C. X. Wang
California State University, Long Beach

This chapter reports the results of study designed to investigate the training preferences of Chinese trainers in light of the Western (i.e., United States) traditional trainer roles versus the performance consultant roles. Trainers from a Party school and two training colleges in Beijing, China, volunteered to respond to a survey comprised of thirteen statements about their training practices. Study results indicated that, while Chinese trainers agreed with Western trainers on the purpose of training, Chinese trainers clung to the role of traditional trainer instead of that of performance consultant as preferred by Western trainers. Study results also revealed the characteristic of training in China, a finding that was consistent with reports in the literature of training in China.

INTRODUCTION

Few things have more amazed Western scholars, than the fact that China's real GDP has grown 9.7% a year for the past two decades (Vachhani, 2005). As a direct result of this high-speed economic development, China has become the so-called "world factory" in the early 1990s. More and more mul-

Building Workforce Competencies in Career and Technical Education, pages 159–170
Copyright © 2009 by Information Age Publishing
All rights of reproduction in any form reserved.

tinational corporations have gained a foothold in China. Naturally, this has created a dire need for suppliers of training. Much of training has been conducted in China's Party schools and training colleges. What is clear to Western scholars is that China does produce what the rest of the world needs in terms of daily commodities. China is a labor-intensive market for profitable foreign businesses.

What puzzles Westerners is how training is conducted in China to promote desired changes in political ideology, socio-economic relations and human productive capabilities (Wang & Colletta, 1991). To Westerners, China is known as a strong ideological nation. First there was Confucius who emphasized moral cultivation and individual merit in training. Confucius' thinking has inspired generations of Chinese teachers and trainers. Then there were influential figures such as Marx, Lenin and Mao who inspired Chinese to engage in class struggle. Under the guise of "politics takes command," training was virtually next to non-existent in China during the Great Cultural Revolution, which lasted for ten years between 1966 and 1976. After China opened its door to the outside world in the early 1980's, there was much talk on training such as "system theory" and "decision making theory" in China. However, the reality in China has been that political aptitude and connections are still the all-important prerequisites to promotion and a degree in training is no shortcut.

Chinese cadres and workers are trained by Party schools and training colleges. Chinese trainers have been arguing over the importance of two controversial issues concerning training of their employees: moral cultivation or individual merit. Outside China, trainers are beginning to make a transition from traditional trainers to performance consultants. The traditional roles of trainers are somewhat outmoded as organizations improve their overall performance capacity to compete in a global economy.

Although the general mode of Chinese trainers may be imaginable to Western scholars, the question remains unexamined as to whether Chinese trainers still cling to their age-old mode of training, revolving around moral cultivation and individual merit. Western trainers have been advised to assume the roles of performance consultants to customize training to fit the organization and to align training to organizational goals. Has this form of training penetrated into Chinese training as a by-product of China's continuous use of foreign capital to develop its economy? Western scholars argue China must reform its training in order to keep up with the fast development of its economy. Without a sound form of training for its largest number of trainees in the world, China's form of training may be an impediment to learning.

In the context of increasing globalization, it seems appropriate to undertake a study of training in China, so China may effectively improve its human productive capabilities and Western trainers may customize training to fit the particular requirements of China's organizations. It is commonly argued that trainers' roles may either facilitate trainees' performance or inhibit it. While the goal of training in China is to train personnel for social-ist construction (Kaplan, Sobin, & Andors, 1979), the roles of the trainers are unclear to Western observers. Without a doubt, a study of the Chinese form of training may shed more light on the much- debated issues of tradi-tional trainer roles versus performance consultant roles. With this purpose in mind, the researcher formulated the following research questions: What are the training preferences of Chinese trainers in light of the Western training preferences relative to:

1. Learning needs versus performance needs;
2. Structured learning versus formation of performance models;
3. Measuring numbers of days and courses versus measuring perfor-mance;
4. Evaluating participant reaction and learning versus performance change and cost benefit;
5. Viewing training as a direct cost versus viewing training as an invest-ment?

In addition, the researcher was interested in the following question that is closely related to the research topic under study: What is the character-istic of training given China's special social setting with a background of semi-communism?

THEORY AND PRACTICE OF TRAINING IN NORTH AMERICA

Training in the United States was primarily influenced by three foreign training systems: the Russian system, the Sloyd system (Originated in Scan-dinavian countries), and the Arts and Crafts Movement (Originated in Eng-land) (Bott, Slapar, & Wang, 2003; Brehony, 1998; Grubb, 1998, Roberts, 1965; Roche, 1995). While the Russian training reaches large groups of trainees in the least possible time, the Sloyd training system encourages trainee self-direction and initiative, and the Arts and Crafts Movement em-phasizes the aesthetic and creative sides of work. Although these foreign influences are still felt to this day, training in the United States has gone in a different direction. First, the cost of training is high. According to Rob-inson and Robinson (1996), training in North America has become a $50 billion enterprise. If the cost of having employees attend training off the job is added into the equation, the total expenditure in formal training and development of employees may exceed well over $300 billion. Second, one in eight Americans receives training every year. The American Society for Training and Development (ASTD) specifies different training categories for American workers:

1. Executive & Supervisory;
2. Customer Service;
3. New Technology;
4. Basic Skills. (Wang, 2003, p. 32)

As its overall purpose, training in North America must help organization improve its overall performance capacity so it can compete in a global economy (Gilley, 1998, p. 111). Caffarella (2002, p. 11) divides the purpose of training into three kinds of change: individual change related to acquisition of new knowledge, building of skills, and examination of personal values and beliefs; organizational change resulting in new or revised policies, procedures, and ways of working; and community and societal change that allows for differing segments of society.

Based on the purpose of training, trainers in North America have traditionally focused on identifying and addressing *learning* needs of employees. Training programs have produced *structured learning* experiences such as self-paced packages, and computer-based programs. Training has been viewed as *an end*; if trainees have learned; then, the desired output from the traditional trainer role have been achieved. Measures concentrate on *number* of participant days, instructor days, and courses. The implication is "more is better." Training evaluations have focused on participant *reaction* and *learning*. Trainers have only identified the training needs of employees. Trainers have viewed training as a *cost* and training programs have been viewed as having a *limited, acknowledged* linkage to business goals.

As competition has become one of its survival skills for organizations in this global economy, organizational decision makers are demanding that trainers produce results that improve organizational effectiveness (Gilley, 1998). Trainers no longer assume the role of just being trainers. To bring about organizational change, trainers in North America are required to assume a new role of becoming performance consultants. The traditional role of trainers is still useful. However, the new role of becoming performance consultants requires more. Trainers in North America need to make the transition from trainers to performance consultants. In contrast to its traditional trainer role, performance consultants identify and address *performance* needs of people. Performance consultants provide services that result in changing or improving performance. Training programs should include formation of performance models and guidance in addressing work environment obstacles. Training is viewed as a *means* to an end. Employees learn to transfer what they learn to their jobs. Consultants learn to establish and maintain partnerships with managers and others in the organization. Measures focus on performance of people in the organization. The results and non-training actions are measured for *performance change and cost benefit.* Assessments focus on determining performance gaps and the reasons for these gaps. The work environment is required to support required performance. Training is seen as producing measurable results. Training programs and services have a *high* linkage to the organization's goal.

To make a successful transition from trainers to performance consultants, training leaders advocate that trainers in North America must learn to do the following:

- Develop thorough knowledge of organizations.
- Foster critical consulting skills.
- Learn a cross-cultural perspective of training.
- Adopt and adapt the responsibilities and roles of performance consultants.
- Apply the consulting skills.

HISTORY AND PRACTICE OF TRAINING IN CHINA

Although the Chinese pioneered the system of education and training for public service as early as the 10th century AD (Paltiel, 1992), this entire tradition disappeared by the 1960s as a result of the Great Cultural Revolution launched by Mao as a result of power struggle. Since then, the Chinese authorities have had tremendous difficulties in establishing even the minimal standards of training for public officials. Starting in the early 1980's, the educated elite of China began to re-establish the same intimacy with prestige and power that training had in traditional times. However, training in China has been revolving around two priorities: professionalism and moral competence as advanced by Confucius. Although Confucius suggested selecting members of the ruling class on the basis of individual merit, Chinese officials nowadays have tended to favor moral cultivation in training. Traditionally, Mao rejected formal training as the basis of his new hierarchy, but insisted on individual cultivation of moral worth as a means of inculcating revolutionary solidarity in a collective setting. The task of training Chinese cadres rested with the trainers in Moscow. The Soviets, interested in indoctrinating Chinese youth with revolutionary spirit in China, tapped the hunger for training among Chinese youth by establishing training colleges for Chinese on Soviet territory. Later, a Marxist-Leninist Training Academy was established on Chinese territory. These training academies were later known as "May Seventh Cadre Schools." Training in these schools took the form of reading a Party document or texts of Marx, Engels, Lenin and Mao.

After the reading, the trainees were sent down to gain practical experience in lower-level line positions. Mao's trainers argued that Western training focused on narrow utilitarianism. Instead, Mao made "redness", i.e., political motivation, a priority in recruiting and promoting cadres.

After the hiatus of the Cultural Revolution, the industrialized West became the model for Chinese reformers. Priority was given to induce older, less-educated cadres from the Party's guerrilla days to retire and yield their place to younger, better-trained personnel. The purpose of training has begun to attach importance to educational background and academic record as well as to experience and achievements in work. All Party schools and training colleges must revise their teaching plans and shoulder the regular training of cadres for socialist modernizations. In addition to systematic training in Marxist theory, trainees should receive training in economics, management, law, and scientific leadership methods. Professional training should constitute 70% of the curriculum in these Party and training schools.

Although Chinese training programs have been expanded, all the long and short-term training courses are prescribed by the Ministry of Education. The trainers, normally teachers from universities with no real world experience, are expected to teach experienced employees. Textbooks and training programs conveniently repeat abstract generalizations and manipulate buzzwords like "system theory" and "decision making theory." Although trainers and trainees in China argue that training is a matter of technical competence rather than political commitment to the Party and the people, political aptitude and connections are still the all-important prerequisites to promotion and a degree in training is no shortcut. Numerous Chinese graduates of MBA programs at the institutions of American higher learning have difficulty finding appropriate positions in China. Some have taken the jobs of teaching English as a foreign language for Chinese universities.

As far as expenditure is concerned, Chinese trainers view training as a direct cost. Virtually no employers are willing to offer high costs to train their employees. As more and more foreign enterprises and joint ventures have gained a foothold in China, terms such as performance consultants are used more and more frequently to refer to HRD professionals. However, the question remains unanswered as to whether training in China is comparable to the traditional focus or the current focus of training in North America (i.e., the United States).

METHODOLOGY

The site of this study was comprised of a small Party school (enrollment 900) and two training colleges in Beijing, China, with a population of well over 10 million. Since the Chinese communists came to power in 1949, these Party schools and training colleges throughout China have shouldered the responsibilities of training China's cadres and workers. Trainers in these schools are tenured teachers or teachers from other universities. They have been using training methods prescribed by either the Ministry of Education or other higher authorities. To make their training popular, these trainers like to use Western terms such as "system theory" and "decision-making theory."

During June 2005, 49 participants (100%) were contacted and volunteered to return questionnaires. Thirty were male trainers and 19 were female trainers. Of these trainers, 95% were between the ages of 45 and 65.

Data were collected by means of a questionnaire containing 13 items. The instrument was developed using the well-accepted traditional trainer roles versus the performance consultant roles by Robinson and Robinson (1996) in an easily understood format with a 1–7 Likert continuous scale: (1) strongly disagree and (7) strongly agree. All information used in this analysis was derived from the questionnaire data. This questionnaire had been developed by the researcher and tested at one institution of higher learning in the United States before its use in Beijing, China. It was proved to be content-valid. The reliability of the questionnaires was alpha .92, N of cases = 49, N of items = 13.

Data collected in this study were analyzed using SPSS (12.0 for Windows) software. High mean scores on statements 1, 2, 3, 4, and 5 represent support for the traditional trainer role. High mean scores on statements 6, 7, 8, 9, and 10 indicate support for the performance consultant role. For statements 11–13, high mean scores reflect support for the traditional Chinese mode of training. Low mean scores show support for a different mode of training.

FINDINGS

In Table 8.1, statements 1, 2, 3, 4, and 5 dealt with the traditional trainer role specified by Robinson and Robinson (1996). In Table 8.2, statements 6, 7, 8, 9, and 10 represented the performance consultant role based on Robinson and Robinson (1996). In Table 8.3, statements 11, 12, and 13 reflected the characteristic of Chinese training. The standard deviation scores for these trainers are also provided in the tables.

Table 8.1 indicates that Chinese trainers had high scores on all five statements that make up the traditional trainer role. Their scores in statements 3 and 5 were even higher. These results suggest that Chinese trainers favored the traditional trainer role over the performance consultant role. Neither their training nor their training evaluations focused on performance. They

viewed training as a direct cost. They did not view training as an investment. They believed that the linkage between training and business goals
was limited.

TABLE 8.1   Mean Responses: Traditional Trainer Role

Statements	M	SD
1. Trainers should identify and address learning needs of trainees.	4.31	1.69
2. Trainers should produce structured learning experiences such as training programs, self-paced packages, and computer-based training programs.	4.73	1.18
3. Trainers should measure number of participant days, instructor days, and courses.	5.11	1.38
4. Training evaluations should be completed for participant reaction and learning.	4.25	1.34
5. Training reflects a direct cost. Therefore, training programs and services have a limited linkage to business goals.	5.21	1.47

Note: $n = 49$; $N = 49$

TABLE 8.2   Mean Responses: Performance Consultant Role

Statements	M	SD
6. Trainers should identify and address performance needs of trainees.	3.31	1.29
7. Trainers should formulate performance models for trainees.	3.73	0.28
8. Trainers should measure performance of Trainees.	3.41	0.18
9. Training evaluations should be completed for performance change and cost benefit.	3.05	1.34
10. Training reflects an investment. Therefore, training programs and services have a high linkage to business goals.	2.01	0.47

Note: $n = 49$; $N = 49$

TABLE 8.3   Mean Responses: Characteristics of Chinese Training

Statements	M	SD
11. The Ministry of Education should prescribe training courses.	4.11	1.35
12. Moral cultivation and connections are important prerequisites to promotion in China.	5.73	1.36
13. The purpose of training is to improve one's record and achievements in work.	5.11	1.38

Note: $n = 49$; $N = 49$

Table 8.2 describes the trainers' responses for the performance consultant role. It illustrates that Chinese trainers had low scores on all five statements that make up the performance consultant role. These results suggest that Chinese trainers did not assume the performance consultant role. Their training or training evaluations focused on the traditional trainer role. They viewed training as a direct cost. They did not view training as an investment. They did not believe that the linkage between training and business goals was high. These results verified the results from Table 8.1.

Table 8.3 contains the trainers' responses for their mode of training in China. The table shows that Chinese trainers had high scores on all three statements that make up the characteristic of training in China. These results indicate that Chinese trainers believed that moral cultivation and connections were prerequisites to promotion in China, although they agreed with Western trainers on the purpose of training. These results also show that training in China was top-down.

DISCUSSION

The purpose of this study was to determine Chinese trainers' training preferences in light of the Western traditional trainer roles versus the performance consultant roles. An additional purpose of the study was to determine the characteristic of training in China. The findings showed that trainers in China surveyed supported the traditional trainer role. In other words, Chinese trainers identified and addressed learning needs of trainers and produced structured learning experiences such as training programs, self-paced packages, and computer-based training programs. They measured number of participant days, instructor days, and courses and their evaluations were completed for participant reaction and learning. Above all, Chinese trainers viewed training as a direct cost. They did not see a high linkage between training and business goals. The findings also indicated that these Chinese trainers viewed moral cultivation and connections as important prerequisites to promotion, although they did believe that the purpose of training was to improve human capabilities. These Chinese trainers relied on the Ministry of Education to prescribe training courses to them in China.

These findings confirmed Wang and Bott's 2004 research concerning Confucian Heritage Cultures. According to Wang and Bott (2004), Chinese trainers or educators prefer a liberal philosophy in training. Wang's (2005) research on teaching philosophies of Chinese vocational education instructors further confirmed the liberal philosophy in training. Trainers are regarded by their trainees as an unchallengeable authority. Trainers focus on structured learning experiences in which they serve as directors or coaches, whereas trainees assume the submissive roles of simply following their trainers. Chinese trainers provide less hands-on experience because they view training as a direct cost. The fact is if these Chinese trainers have to follow directives from the Ministry of Education, it is really hard for them to make the transition from the traditional roles of trainers to the current Western roles of performance consultants because their roles have been predetermined by higher authorities. Numerous studies have suggested that compliance with authority is highly valued in the Chinese culture (Pratt, 1988, 1993).

What is wrong with the traditional roles of trainers is that structured learning does not offer trainees freedom to transfer what they learn to their jobs. Both trainers and trainees need to be aware that performance is needed to achieve business goals. To have such desired performance outcomes, trainees need to be given the Western trainee-centered learning approach in which trainees become responsible for their own learning. Naturally, trainees are in a position to transfer what they learn to their jobs. This is not to say that trainees under the traditional mode of training cannot perform their jobs. Rather, the current Western roles of performance consultants may lead to maximized performance needed by businesses. For example, performance consultants measure the contribution to improving the performance of people in the organization. They measure performance change and cost benefit. Above all, they identify performance gaps. All of these roles point in one direction—performance of the trainees. To remain competitive in this globalization, human productive capabilities are equally as important as political ideology and socio-economic relations.

The United States of America cannot remain the only superpower in the world without its highly trained scientists, engineers in Silicon Valley and its well-trained career and technical workers elsewhere in the country. In training, U.S. trainers have adopted and adapted a series of foreign training methods (Wang & Redhead, 2004). It seems for now that the performance consultant role has become more pronounced in the Western hemisphere because Western trainers believe that success in the training world is determined by job performance (Rossi, 2005). The traditional trainer role seems to have become outmoded in the new context of globalization. That Chinese trainers view training as a direct cost is shorted sighted in light of the Western performance consultant role. Although China's economic development is impressive, China cannot remain competitive unless its trainers believe that completed work has a high linkage to the organization's goal. To put this in more concrete terms, China needs to make training a multi-billion dollar enterprise just like its American counterpart. And the Western role of performance consultants cannot be neglected in the context of globalization. In the years that follow, the relation between performance professionals and consultants will increase in importance in the training world (Suleiman, 2004).

IMPLICATIONS

This study was designed to determine the training preferences of Chinese trainers in light of the Western training preferences of being performance consultants in the new context of globalization. The Western preferred training methods have evolved from foreign training methods such as the Russian, the Sloyd and the Arts and Crafts Movement (Bott, Slapar, & Wang, 2003). Over the years, American trainers have adopted and adapted a series of foreign training methods to help organizations improve their overall performance capacity, so its organizations can compete in a global economy.

However, this beautifully, well-reasoned performance consultant role meets with resistance from an authoritarian culture. For Western suppliers of training to be successful in China, particular attention must be given to local social contexts. Most importantly, social norms and type of government predetermine whether Chinese trainers need to cling to the traditional role of training or the Western performance consultant role. Since training in China is seen as training from above, for Western trainers to be successful in China, it is best to convince Chinese higher authorities of the effective performance consultant role before they try to persuade Chinese trainers to buy into their training mode.

This chapter supports a fresh look at the traditional trainer roles versus the performance consultant roles through the lens of Chinese trainers. The study implies that social norms, the type of government in which training takes place, cannot be ignored. An ideological country like China with approximately 1.3 billion people needs to realize that training to improve human productive capabilities is just as important as political ideology and socio-economic relations. Training should be viewed as a means to an end. It is the performance of trainees that needs to be evaluated. Performance is needed to achieve business goals. Further research is necessary, especially in the area of why Chinese trainers prefer the traditional trainer role to the performance consultant role. In-depth observations and interviews may facilitate such an undertaking in the future.

REFERENCES

Brehony, K. J. (1998). 'Even far distant Japan is showing an interest': The English Froebel Movement's turn to Sloyd. *History of Education 27*, 279. Retrieved May 21, 2005, from EBSCOHost Academic Search Elite database.

Bott, P. A., Slapar, F. M., & Wang, V. (2003). *History and philosophy of career and technical education*. Boston: Pearson.

Caffarella, R. S. (2002). *Planning programs for adult learners* (2nd ed.). San Francisco: Jossey-Bass.

Gilley, J. W. (1998). *Improving HRD practice*. Malabar, FL: Krieger.

Grubb, W. N. (1998). *Preparing for the information-based workplace: Pedagogical issues and institutional linkages*. Retrieved May 22, 2005, from http://mitsloanMIT. edu/iwer/papers.html

Kaplan, F. M. , Sobin, J. M. , & Andors, S. (1979). *Encyclopedia of China today*. New York: Harper & Row.

Paltiel, J. (1992). Educating the modernizers: management training in China. In R. Hayhoe (Ed.), *Education and modernization: The Chinese experience* (pp. 337–357). New York: Pergamon Press.

Pratt, D. D. (1988). "Andragogy as a relational construct." *Adult Education Quarterly, 38*, 160–181.

Pratt, D. D. (1993). *"Andragogy after twenty-five years."* New Directions for Adult and Continuing Education, No. 57. San Francisco: Jossey-Bass.

Roberts, R. W. (1965). *Vocational and practical arts education: History, development, and principles* (2nd ed.). New York: Harper & Row.

Robinson, D. G., & Robinson, J. C. (1996). *Performance consulting moving beyond training*. San Francisco: Berrett-Koehler.

Roche, J. F. (1995). The culture of pre-modernism: Whitman, Morris, and the American Arts and Crafts Movement. *ATQ, 9*(2), 1–12. Retrieved May 20, 2005, from EBSCOHost Academic Search Elite database.

Rossi, J. (2005). Putting performance into practice. *Training & Development, 59*(5), 18.

Suleiman, A. (2004). Consultants: the trainer's friend. *Training & Development, 58*(11), 4.

Vachhani, A. (2005). India and China—A game of one-upmanship. Retrieved May 1, 2005, from http://www.blonnet.com/2005/04/04/stories/2005040400090800.htm

Wang, J. L., & Colletta, N. (1991). Chinese education problems, policies, and prospects. In I. Epstein (Ed.), *Chinese education problems, policies, and prospects* (pp. 145–162). New York: Garland.

Wang, V. (2003). *Principles of adult education*. Boston, MA: Pearson.

Wang, V. (2005). Teaching philosophies of Chinese vocational education instructors. *International Journal of Vocational Education and Training, 13*(1), 7–21.

Wang, V., & Bott, P. A. (2004). Modes of teaching of Chinese adult educators. *Perspectives: The New York Journal of Adult Learning, 2*(2), 32–51.

Wang, V., & Redhead, C. K. (2004). Comparing the Russian, the Sloyd, and the Arts and Crafts movement training systems. *International Journal of Vocational Education and Training, 12*(1), 42–58.

CHAPTER 9

TEACHING PHILOSOPHIES OF CHINESE CAREER AND TECHNICAL INSTRUCTORS AND U.S. CAREER AND TECHNICAL INSTRUCTORS

Victor C. X. Wang
California State University, Long Beach

This chapter compares the teaching philosophies of vocational education instructors teaching in Chinese vocational agricultural universities and American land-grant universities. A researcher-made survey instrument called the Philosophies of Vocational Education Scale (PVES) was employed to measure which of six philosophical approaches drove the teaching of these instructors in a given situation. Data were collected from 64 (74%) of 87 randomly polled instructors at the Chinese vocational agricultural universities and 64 (74%) of 87 randomly polled instructors at the American land-grant universities to determine and compare their teaching preferences. The results of the study showed while the two groups of instructors

Building Workforce Competencies in Career and Technical Education, pages 171–190
Copyright © 2009 by Information Age Publishing
171

were from different social settings, both groups were liberal, progressive, behaviorist and somewhat humanistic and radical but not analytic in their philosophy of instruction (the difference between the means of Chinese CTE instructors and U.S. CTE instructors was not statistically significant: $p > 0.05$).

INTRODUCTION

It is well known to educators in the field of career and technical education that manual training was first introduced in the United States in 1876 by the Russian educator Victor Della Vos, who was the director of the Moscow Imperial Technical School (Bott, Slapar, & Wang, 2003, p. 36; Roberts, 1965). Not only did Della Vos bring the method of manual training to the United States, but also he brought with it the notion of competency-based education (also known as performance-based education in the field of career and technical education). "Competency-based" education (CBE) has been synonymous with American Vocational Education since its early inception in 1876. The Russian version of CBE places great emphasis on the skills aspect of work, and it has been the basis of many curricula, including the "Modules of Employable Skills" developed by the International Labor Office, the Developing a Curriculum (DACUM) process initiated in Canada and the *serie metodica ocupacionis*, or shopwork methodological series, developed in Brazil and disseminated throughout South America (Wang & Redhead, 2004, p. 50).

Numerous U.S. secondary schools have integrated competency-based curricula in vocational education since the 1960s, as have schools in Australia and Great Britain (Grubb, 1998). The behaviorist philosophy has been playing a major role in making educators adopt CBE in the Western Hemisphere and the chief proponent of this philosophy was Skinner who advocated his behavior theory (1968). Not surprisingly, behaviorism has become American and mirrors the turn-of-the 20th century notion that all people could achieve great accomplishments given the opportunity (stimulus), individual initiative (response), and fair treatment (rewards) (Knowles, Holton, & Swanson, 1998, 2005). Because CBE programs specify in behavioral terms the goals and objectives to be met, the learning experiences to be engaged in and the method of evaluation used to demonstrate achievement of the predetermined goals, CBE has been popular with American vocational education instructors (Elias & Merriam, 1995, 2005).

China began to adjust its economic and educational policies in the early 1980s in order to catch up with the developed countries in the world. Thus, vocational education has assumed the objective of providing the people of China with the skills required for rapid economic development. As Chen

(1981) put it, the overriding aim of vocational education in the post-Mao era is to serve the needs of the modernization program (p. 153). Towards this end, China began training hundreds of thousands of skilled workers. At the same time, vocational education was expected to develop an array of technical fields specially tailored to national development goals. According to Ministry of Education in China, China will invest 14 billion Yuan (1.75 billion U.S. dollars) during the 11th five-year-plan period (2006–2010) to develop technical and skills training for young workers (Xinhua, 2006).

In spite of the popularity of vocational education in China, however, the philosophies adopted by Chinese vocational education instructors, especially with regard to the six prevalent Western (U.S.) philosophies, have remained unexamined. Of particular interest is the question of whether vocational education in China is delivered using primarily liberal methods, given China's Confucian heritage. In the Confucian tradition, educators prefer didactic teaching and rote learning to critical thinking and are regarded by their students as an unchallengeable authority; Confucian educators rely on lecture and externally established examinations (Wang & Bott, 2004, p. 47). Another compelling reason to examine whether Chinese career and technical instructors have adopted the six Western philosophies is that outsiders are well aware: besides, Confucianism, *Marxism, Maoism and Leninism* had influenced Chinese teaching philosophies in general. Although China began to send hundreds of scholars and students to industrialized nations to study Western advanced science and technology and advanced notions of education in the early 1980s, the number of returning scholars and students has been very low. Those who have returned to work for China may not be in leadership positions. Therefore, to determine the teaching philosophies of Chinese career and technical instructors in light of those of U.S. career and technical instructors will assist career and technical educators in adopting and adapting appropriate teaching philosophies in the field of career and technical education according to their respective social settings. As globalization brings different cultures together, it is really hard to tell which philosophies are Western and which are Chinese. In spite of cultural integration, one's teaching philosophies should be clear and sound. Otherwise, instructional outcomes cannot be resulted from meaningful philosophies.

To address these questions, this chapter was designed to investigate the philosophical preferences of Chinese vocational educators and compare their preferences to those of U.S. vocational educators. Specifically, the purpose of this chapter was to carry out a comparison of teaching philosophies of Chinese vocational education instructors with those of U.S. vocational education instructors, particularly in light of Western behaviorism characterized by competency-based education or performance-based education. To determine the generally accepted philosophy of Chinese vocational education instructors, the following research question was formulated: What is the philosophy of Chinese vocational education instructors relative to *liberal* vocational education, *progressive* vocational education, *behaviorist* vocational education, *humanistic* vocational education, *radical* vocational education and *analytic* vocational education as practiced by Western vocational education instructors, particularly at land-grant universities?

PHILOSOPHIES OF VOCATIONAL EDUCATION IN THE UNITED STATES

According to Elias and Merriam (1995, 2005), philosophy inspires one's activities and gives direction to practice. They further pointed out that the power of philosophy lies in its ability to enable individuals to better understand and appreciate the activities of everyday life. On this basis, it can be argued that the philosophy adopted by vocational education instructors can be expected to lead to specific instructional outcomes. Elias and Merriam (1995, 2005) described how instructors' philosophies influence their modes of instruction as follows:

- Liberal vocational education has its emphasis upon liberal learning, organized knowledge, and the development of the intellectual powers of the mind. Therefore, instructors recognize the lecture method as an efficient instructional strategy.
- Progressive vocational education emphasizes such concepts as the relationship between education and society, experience-centered education and democratic education. Instructors with this philosophy may organize, stimulate, instigate, and evaluate the highly complex process of education.
- Behaviorist vocational education emphasizes control, behavioral modification, learning through reinforcement, and management by objectives.
- Humanistic vocational education emphasizes freedom and autonomy, trust, active cooperation and participation, and self-directed learning. Instructors with a preference for this philosophical approach may implement group dynamics, group relations training, group process, sensitivity workshops, encounter groups, and self-directed learning.
- Radical vocational education emphasizes an awareness of social action. Instructors with philosophical orientation may implement libertarian, dialogic, and problem-posing education.
- Analytic philosophy of vocational education focuses on clarifying concepts, arguments, and policy statements used in vocational edu-

cation. Instructors with this philosophical orientation may attempt to eliminate language confusions.

American vocational instructors' preference for the behaviorist philosophy can be traced to industrial revolution. The Russian training method and the Sloyd system (which originated in the Scandinavian countries and was brought to the U.S. by Lars Erickson and Gustaf Larsson, both of Sweden in the 1880s) both emphasize the skills aspect of work. These two approaches were adopted primarily in response to the sharply increased demand for skilled workers during the period of the industrial revolution (Wang & Redhead, 2004, p. 42). Roberts (1965) and Grubb (1998) argued that both the Russian system and the Sloyd system contributed to the remodeling of the U.S. vocational educational system and that the influence of these two approaches can still be felt to this day.

Competency-based education in vocational education is associated with behaviorist philosophy because instructors who prefer behaviorist philosophy to other philosophies design and implement programmed learning and behavioral learning objectives. Although CBE remains a buzzword in American vocational education, other philosophies successfully co-exist in American vocational education. For example, John Dewey (1961) popularized the progressive philosophy that occupations should be used as vehicles of instruction in vocational education (Bott et al., 2003; Roberts, 1965). Progressive education's emphasis upon vocational and utilitarian training, learning by experience, scientific inquiry, community involvement and responsiveness to social problems may account for the hands-on nature of vocational education.

Although vocational education literature suggests the dominance of the behaviorist philosophy in vocational education in the United States, other philosophies clearly play a role in American vocational education. These other philosophies often supplement and enhance the CBE approach preferred by American vocational education instructors. The present chapter was intended to investigate whether a similar dynamic operates in the context of a Confucian tradition such as China's and if Chinese vocational education has been shaped by the same Russian and Sloyd systems. It must be pointed out that the Russian and Sloyd systems never reached China because when the two systems were adopted in North America, China remained an agricultural country. On the other hand, Dewey lectured in China between 1919 and 1921 (Kaplan, Sobin, & Andors, 1979) and he produced numerous articles, addressing education in China. Although an outspoken proponent of progressive philosophy, it is questionable how much influence Dewey may have exerted on career and technical education in China (Wang, 2007a).

THEORY AND PRACTICE OF VOCATIONAL EDUCATION
IN CHINA

Chinese education has been profoundly influenced by the ideas of Confucius, Mao and Marx, so dialectical materialism is the preferred process for identifying the objective facts of any situation. Thus, both the methodology and subject matter of China's schools are expected to rely on a "scientific" (i.e., dialectical) approach. This mode of education is grounded on the value of seeking truth from facts, objective truth and the unity of theory and practice (Kaplan, Sobin, & Andors, 1979, p. 218).

A significant application of these values for vocational education, however, was an approach enunciated by Mao in Chapter Four in *Selected Works of Mao Tse-tung* (1957), "On the Correct Handling of Contradictions Among the People." According to Mao, formal education was to be combined with vocational education in order to produce a cultured, Socialist-minded worker (Cheng & Manning, 2003). It was Mao's intent that China's educational system would be open to the masses.

In December 1949, Liu Shih, head of the Supervision Department of the Ministry of Education, stated that the country's new educational system "will guarantee that all working people and their children will have the opportunity to enjoy educational facilities, thus enabling the country to cultivate more effectively every type of constructive talent from among the people" (Kaplan et al., 1979, p. 218). With regard to vocational education, the school system took special care to enroll children of worker-peasant backgrounds, as well as to provide a wide range of spare-time programs and short-course primary and middle schools for adults (Wang & Colletta, 1991). Because of this favorable educational policy initiated since the founding of China, vocational education developed rapidly. During the years when politics took precedence over education, vocational education suffered from decreased enrollments. Since China began to implement economic and educational reforms in the early 1980s, there has been growing demand for trained personnel with applicable skills in the Chinese society (Yang, 2005).

While vocational training was initially given priority over the education of children, a broad network of schools was eventually established at all levels. The system was characterized by a high degree of administrative decentralization and local flexibility. In rural areas, vocational education was introduced with the full cooperation of local residents and structured so as to meet their needs and schedules (Kaplan et al., 1979). Most schools undertook as minimum goals a standard of functional literacy, basic arithmetic skills and practical instruction in skills applicable to the local economy.

In the area of vocational curriculum, the Ministry of Education issued lists of authorized primary and secondary texts; guidelines were issued that cautioned against narrow-minded utilitarianism or empiricism that refuses theoretical learning (Kaplan et al., 1979). As Yu and Xu (1988) put it, the development of curriculum and specialties is closely related to the development of economy, science and technology in the larger context (p. 13). All courses of study and training methods were to reflect these central directives and were, furthermore, to be submitted for approval by the ministry.

Although there are some differences between Western vocational education and Chinese vocational education, the Chinese "double-track" system is not unfamiliar to Western vocational education instructors. In this system, "little treasure pagoda" schools are maintained as full-time, state-aided institutions preparing students for advanced studies and, ultimately, professional careers. The remainder of the system focuses on training industrial and agricultural workers.

Although multiple philosophical traditions, including Confucianism, Marxism and Maoism have influenced education in China, Chinese vocational education does not appear to reflect a dominant philosophy. No empirical study has been conducted to determine what philosophy drives the teaching activities implemented by Chinese vocational education instructors. China has been doing business with USA since the early 1980s. Has the notion of competency-based education been brought to China as a result of China's open door policy? Has American behaviorism influenced vocational education in China like Confucianism, Marxism and Maoism? If so, to what extent have Chinese vocational education instructors adopted and adapted American performance-based education? A comparison of teaching philosophies between Chinese vocational education instructors and American vocational education instructors will definitely shed some light on the above questions.

METHODOLOGY

Design

The study used a quantitative survey design. A researcher-designed questionnaire was administered to a sample of vocational education instructors teaching at institutions of higher education in China and the U.S. The survey instrument was designed to elicit the instructors' preferences for teaching methods or modes of instruction that are consistently associated with six clearly defined philosophical orientations. Thus, instructors' scores could be interpreted as reflecting the instructors' philosophical preferences.

Sample

A survey of 64 vocational education instructors at five vocational agricultural universities representing the northeast, the northwest, the south-east, the southwest and the central regions of China was conducted. These vocational agricultural universities enroll thousands of students per year, and their instructors shoulder a heavy load of teaching responsibilities. These vocational education instructors are bona fide vocational education instructors, fulfilling the goal of educating and training industrial and agricultural workers for China's rapid economic development. The vocational education instructors teaching in these vocational agricultural universities range in age from 29 to 65. They are full time faculty at these institutions of higher learning but are also employed at other universities as part time faculty. Most of these instructors choose to work part-time at other universities to supplement the low pay they receive from their home institutions.

The same survey was administered to 64 vocational education instructors at five land grant universities representing the South and Midwest of the United States of America. These land grant universities all have departments of vocational education where such vocational education leaders as Roberts (1971) and Miller (1985) worked to shape the teaching philosophies of vocational education instructors in the West. For example, Roberts developed and classified teaching philosophies into organization, administration, and instruction (Bott et al., 2003; Roberts, 1965); Miller grouped the philosophies of vocational education into people, programs, and processes as a matter of convenience (Bott et al., 2003; Roberts, 1965). While the terms of these taxonomies differed, they are all closely related to the six prevalent Western philosophical perspectives: *liberal, progressive, behaviorist, humanistic, radical* and *analytical.* The influence of these two leaders is still felt today, and their philosophies of vocational education are still taught in the approximately 100 universities of vocational education in the United States.

Instrumentation

The researcher designed a survey instrument called the Philosophies of Vocational Education Scale (PVES) to determine what type of philosophy drove the teaching of these instructors in a given situation. The survey instrument design was based on Elias and Merriam's (1995, 2005) description of what instructors may do if they possess one of six philosophical orientations: *liberal, progressive, behaviorist, humanistic, radical* and *analytic.* The overall PVES score was comprised of six subscales measuring the six factors that reflect the above-mentioned philosophies in vocational education.

The survey utilized a Likert scale from five to zero with five being the highest (support for the philosophy implied in the factor name) and zero the lowest (support for a different philosophy). For this study, survey responses were used to identify the general philosophy of vocational education instructors in order to develop the base of data. The vocational instructors' mean scores on each of the six PVES factors were calculated using the Statistical Package for Social Sciences (SPSS-16.0 for Windows). The mean score of 2.5 represented the midpoint between 0 and 5.

High mean scores for factors represent support for the philosophy implied in the factor name. Low mean scores indicate support for a different philosophy. If a mean score nears the mean score (2.5), it may indicate support for the philosophy implied in the factor name; it may also indicate support for a different philosophy.

The researcher clearly defined the six factors in the PVES instrument as follows:

In Factor One, liberal vocational education is indicated by 2 positive items in the instrument. Those who support a liberal vocational education use lecture method as an efficient instructional strategy and develop students' intellect through reading, reflection, and production.

Factor Two is concerned with progressive vocational education. This factor is comprised of 4 positive items. Instructors who scored high in this factor organize, stimulate, instigate and evaluate the highly complex process of education. They provide the setting that is conducive to learning. While being a helper, guide, encourager, consultant and resource person, they also become a learner in the learning process.

Factor Three relates to behavioral vocational education and consists of 2 positive items. Instructors who supported this factor design an environment that elicits desired behavior for meeting educational goals and extinguishes behavior that is not desirable. These instructors are contingency managers, environmental controllers or behavioral engineers who plan in detail the conditions necessary to bring about desired behavior.

Factor Four is made up of 4 positive items and 1 negative item. Instructors who score high on this factor prefer a humanistic approach to vocational education. Humanistic instructors implement group dynamics, group relations training, group process, sensitivity workshops, encounter groups, and self-directed learning.

Factor Five is concerned with radical vocational education and contains 3 positive items and 1 negative item. Instructors who support this philosophy offer problem-posing education to students.

Factor Six includes 1 negative item and 1 positive item. Instructors who score high on this factor seek to eliminate confusion with language and do not construct explanations about reality.

A total of ten vocational education instructors in the department of vocational education in a land grant university in the Midwest of USA and in a vocational agricultural university in northeast China, who were not included in the sample, completed the PVES in a pilot study to validate the instrument. Data gathered from the validation study were not included in the study but were used to determine whether revisions to the instrument were needed. The validation study was also used to test to clarity and comprehensibility of the questionnaire items. Validation study results indicated revisions to the instrument were not needed since the vocational education instructors in the validation study understood clearly the questions in the survey instrument. In sum, the questions used could be considered content valid. The alpha reliability coefficient for the instrument was 0.92.

The quantitative survey instrument for this study was emailed as an attached electronic file to vocational education instructors at participating universities of vocational education in China and in the United States.

Data Analysis

Data collected in this chapter were analyzed using SPSS (16.0 for Windows) software. Since the survey instrument called PVES (Philosophies of Vocational Education Scale) contains both positive items and negative items, different values were assigned to these items. For positive items, the following values were assigned: "Always" equals five, "almost always" equals four, "often" equals three, "seldom" equals two, "almost never" equals one and "never" equals zero. For negative items, the following values are assigned. "Always" equals zero, "almost always" equals one, "often" equals two, "seldom" equals three, "almost never" equals four and "never" equals five. Omitted items are assigned a neutral value of 2.5.

Analysis was conducted for each factor specified in the research question. For descriptive statistics, mean scores and standard deviations were reported for the vocational educators' responses. To provide a better picture of the population surveyed, the overall scale mean scores and standard deviations were also calculated. The findings were entered into tables and figures, and a narrative was developed to report the findings.

FINDINGS

This chapter was designed to identify the teaching philosophies identified in this studied as preferred by Chinese vocational education instructors in terms of six dominant philosophical systems: liberal, progressive, behaviorist, humanistic, radical and analytical. Using a Likert-type scale instrument, respondents were asked to indicate their preference for teaching methods or modes that consistently reflect the six specified philosophical orientations to education. Sixty-four Chinese vocational education instructors answered survey questions, using the researcher' survey instrument called PVES. Another sixty-four American vocational education instructors answered the same survey questions.

The tables presented below summarize the survey results. The mean scores for these vocational educational instructors on each of the six factors are presented in separate tables. Each of the six factors contains several items that make up the instructor's general philosophy. The standard deviation scores for these vocational education instructors are also provided in the tables.

Table 9.1 summarizes the vocational education instructors' responses for Factor One. Table 9.1 indicates that vocational education instructors had high scores in the two variables that make up Factor One. The results suggest that both Chinese and American vocational education instructors favored liberal philosophy in their teaching. They tended to use the lecture method as an efficient instructional strategy and supported the notion of developing students' intellect through reading, reflection, and production. Table 9.2 summarizes the vocational education instructors' responses for Factor Two.

TABLE 9.1   Mean Responses: 64 Vocational Education Instructors from China and the United States

	China		United States	
Factor One: Liberal Philosophy	M	SD	M	SD
1. I use the lecture method as an efficient instructional strategy.	3.73	0.50	3.00	1.41
19. I develop students' intellect through reading, reflection, and production.	3.68	0.89	4.00	1.00

Note: n = 64; N = 87

TABLE 9.2   Mean Responses: 64 Vocational Education Instructors from China and the United States

	China		United States	
Factor Two: Progressive Philosophy	M	SD	M	SD
3. I organize, stimulate, instigate, and evaluate the highly complex process of education.	3.64	0.82	3.65	1.18
6. I am a helper, guide, encourager, consultant, and resource instead of a transmitter, disciplinarian, judge and authority.	4.02	0.62	4.22	1.18
7. I provide the setting that is conducive to learning.	3.89	0.77	4.30	1.08
8. I become a learner in the learning process.	3.85	0.82	4.30	1.08

Note: n = 64; N = 87

Table 9.2 shows that both Chinese and American vocational education instructors had high scores on the four variables that comprise Factor Two. These results indicate that these vocational education instructors applied progressive philosophy in their teaching. First, they provided a learning setting in which they became a co-learner, a helper, guide, encourager, consultant and resource person. They also organized, stimulated, instigated, and evaluated the highly complex process of education.

Table 9.3 summarizes the vocational education instructors' responses for Factor Three. Table 9.3 indicates that both Chinese and American vocational education instructors had high scores on the two variables in Factor Three, Behavioral Philosophy. The results show that vocational education instructors designed an environment that elicited desired behavior toward meeting educational goals and to extinguish behavior that was not desirable. They were contingency managers, environmental controllers or behavior engineers who planned in detail the conditions necessary to bring about desired behavior. These results indicate that Chinese vocational education instructors favored behavioral philosophy in their teaching.

Table 9.4 summarizes the vocational education instructors' responses for Factor Four. Thus, Table 9.4 indicates that both Chinese and American vocational education instructors had high scores in four of the five variables that make up Factor Four. These results suggest that these vocational education instructors basically favored humanistic philosophy in their teaching except that they provided information to their students, which is something humanistic instructors do not do. The results show that these vocational education instructors were facilitators, helpers, and partners in the learning process; they created the conditions within which learning could take place; they trusted students to assume responsibilities for their learning and

TABLE 9.3   Mean Responses: 64 Vocational Education Instructors from China and the United States

	China		United States	
Factor Three: Behavioral Philosophy	M	SD	M	SD
4. I design an environment that elicits desired behavior toward meeting educational goals and to extinguish behavior that is not desirable.	3.91	0.68	3.89	1.13
5. I am a contingency manager, an environmental controller, or behavioral engineer who plans in detail the conditions necessary to bring about desired behavior.	3.75	0.69	2.97	1.24

Note: n = 64; N = 87

TABLE 9.4   Mean Responses: 64 Vocational Education Instructors from China and the United States

Factor Four: Humanistic Philosophy	China		United States	
	M	**SD**	**M**	**SD**
11. I trust students to assume responsibility for their learning.	3.74	0.70	3.97	1.07
12. I respect and utilize the experiences and potentialities of students.	3.64	0.96	4.46	0.77
13. I provide information to my students.	1.19	0.97	0.49	0.77
14. I am a facilitator, helper, and partner in the learning process.	3.88	0.94	4.49	0.69
15. I create the conditions within which learning can take place.	3.88	0.96	4.30	0.91

Note: n = 64; *N* = 87

TABLE 9.5   Mean Responses: 64 Vocational Education Instructors from China and the United States

Factor Five: Radical Philosophy	China		United States	
	M	**SD**	**M**	**SD**
9. I offer a libertarian, dialogic, and problem-posing education.	3.87	0.58	3.27	1.07
10. I emphasize the importance of dialogue and equality between teacher and learners.	4.02	0.92	4.08	0.95
16. I am open to clarifications and modifications.	3.67	1.06	4.65	0.63
17. I determine the themes that serve to organize the content of the dialogues.	1.46	0.89	1.35	0.79

Note: n = 64; *N* = 87

respected and utilized the experiences and potentialities of students. Humanists do not provide information to students. However, these vocational education instructors provided information to their students.

Table 9.5 summarizes the vocational education instructors' responses for Factor Five. It demonstrates that both Chinese and American vocational education instructors had high scores in three of the four variables that comprise Factor Five. These results indicate that vocational education instructors generally applied radical philosophy in their teaching except that they determined the themes that served to organize the content of the dialogues, which is something radical instructors do not do.

Table 9.6 summarizes the vocational education instructors' responses for Factor Six. Table 9.6 indicates that both Chinese and American vocational education instructors did not favor analytic philosophy in their teaching. Although they eliminated language confusions, they constructed explanations about reality, which is not a practice of analytic instructors.

Table 9.7 summarizes the vocational education instructors' responses for Overall Scale Means and Standard Deviations on the Six Factors. Further examination of Table 9.7 demonstrates that both Chinese and American vocational education instructors had high scores on Factor One, Factor Two and Factor Three. This result suggests that Chinese and American vocational education instructors were liberal, progressive and behavioral in their instruction. They had relatively high scores on Factor Four and Factor Five. Although these vocational education instructors had relatively high scores in Factor Four and Factor Five, the low score one item from each of these two factors indicated that they were not humanistic or radical in their teaching. Their score on Factor Six was low, indicating that these vocational education instructors were not analytic in their instruction.

TABLE 9.6   Mean Responses: 64 Vocational Education Instructors from China and the United States

	China		United States	
Factor Six: Analytic Philosophy	M	SD	M	SD
2. I eliminate language confusions.	3.91	0.77	3.95	1.37
18. I construct explanations about reality	1.57	0.87	1.54	1.37

Note: n = 64; N = 87

TABLE 9.7   64 Vocational Education Instructors from China and the United States

	China		United States		Difference	
Factors	M	SD	M	SD	M	SD
1. Liberal Philosophy	3.71	0.70	3.50	1.21	0.21	−0.51
2. Progressive Philosophy	3.85	0.76	4.12	1.13	−0.27	−0.37
3. Behavioral Philosophy	3.83	0.69	3.43	1.19	0.40	−0.50
4. Humanistic Philosophy	3.27	0.91	3.54	0.84	−0.27	0.07
5. Radical Philosophy	3.26	0.86	3.34	0.86	−0.08	0.00
6. Analytic Philosophy	2.74	0.82	2.75	1.23	−0.01	−0.41

Note: n = 64; N = 87

DISCUSSION

The purpose of this chapter was to identify the general philosophies (i.e., *liberal, progressive, behavioral, humanistic, radical or analytic*) practiced by Chinese vocational education instructors in light of the predominant "competency-based" education (behavioral philosophy) in American vocational education. The findings indicated that there were no significant differences in the teaching philosophies between Chinese vocational education instructors and American vocational education instructors ($p > 0.05$).

The study's findings showed that the Chinese vocational education instructors surveyed supported *liberal, progressive* and *behavioral* philosophies in their teaching. These were the same teaching philosophies preferred by American vocational education instructors. They used the lecture method as an efficient instructional strategy and supported the notion of developing students' intellect through reading, reflection, and production. They provided an environment in which they were co-learners, helpers, guides, encouragers, consultants and resource persons. They organized, stimulated, instigated and evaluated the highly complex process of education. They designed a learning setting that elicited desired behavior toward meeting educational goals and to extinguish behavior that was not desirable.

The probability (0.10) associated with the test statistics ($t = -0.01$) is greater than alpha (0.05), there was no difference between teaching philosophies of Chinese CTE instructors and U.S. CTE instructors. The findings also indicated that both Chinese and American vocational education instructors were *humanistic* and *radical* in their instructions in that they trusted students to assume responsibilities for their learning and respected and utilized the experiences and potentialities of students. They offered a problem-posing education and they were open to clarifications and modi-

TABLE 9.8 Independent Samples *t*-Tests for the 64 Vocational Education Instructors in China and the United States

Factor	*t*-Value	*p*-Value
1. Liberal Philosophy	0.41	0.72
2. Progressive Philosophy	−1.52	0.18
3. Behavioral Philosophy	0.86	0.48
4. Humanistic Philosophy	−0.30	0.77
5. Radical Philosophy	−0.09	0.93
6. Analytic Philosophy	−0.003	0.10
Independent Samples *t*-test for all factors	−0.01	0.10

fications. The findings demonstrated that they were not *analytic* in their teaching (China: M = 3.91, M = 1.57; USA: M = 3.95, M = 1.54). Although these vocational education instructors were basically *humanistic* and *radical*, there were situations in which they were not *humanistic* and *radical*.

It is not out of the ordinary to Western scholars that Chinese vocational education instructors apply liberal philosophy in their teaching because this finding corroborated Wang and Bott's 2004 research concerning the modes of teaching of Chinese educators. Wang and Bott (2004) found that Chinese educators in general have been clinging to a liberal philosophy in education that views instructors as having absolute authority over learners. Wang and Bott's 2004 research further indicated that Chinese vocational education instructors supported a teacher-centered mode of teaching, viewed lecturing as a superior method and considered themselves as providers of knowledge rather than facilitators.

The current study also confirmed the Chinese educational belief that there is always a truth proposition (knowledge) or an accepted theory that can be disseminated through the agency of the teacher (as cited in Wang, 2007, p. 114). This very belief is manifested in the liberal philosophy in education. Other scholars such as Paine (1992) explain that Chinese teaching philosophies are designed to help students master teaching materials, apply these teaching materials, and help the student master the basic function of each instructional segment (p. 189). To achieve this instructional goal in vocational education, memorization is viewed as an optimal method in teaching and learning in general.

Based on the literature review of Chinese vocational education, it appears that Mao and Marx's teachings have become the central directives in Chinese vocational education in that theories and practice must be united. Chinese vocational education instructors are opposed to the Western "narrow-minded utilitarianism or empiricism that refuses theoretical learning." This is probably why Westerners often see Chinese educators expound in minute detail on textbook materials in their classes to enhance theoretical learning. Chinese cooperative arrangements are not unfamiliar to Western vocational education instructors. The fact that Chinese vocational education instructors are progressive suggests that they value interaction between learners and the environment and that they value the function of helpers more than that of disciplinarians.

Although "competency-based" education (CBE) is typical American vocational education (behavioral philosophy), this mode of education is not unfamiliar to Chinese vocational education instructors. For example, since China opened its door to the outside world in the early 1980s, vocational education has had the concrete task of providing the people with the skills required for rapid economic development. Short training courses have been offered toward this end, and courses typically contain specific learning objectives. And it is natural that Chinese vocational education instructors use programmed instruction to achieve their teaching goals. Although Mao and Marx shaped Chinese education in general, China has a history of seeking Western influence in education. In 1922, Chinese education showed a marked shift from Japanese to U.S. influences (Kaplan et al., 1979, p. 219). John Dewey, the most prominent U.S. educator of the time, spent 26 months lecturing in China between 1919 and 1921. Dewey's progressive philosophy and Western behavioral philosophy may have spread throughout China as a result of his influence.

The fact that Chinese vocational education instructors are humanistic in their teaching should also not surprise Western scholars in vocational education because it was Confucius who advanced humanism first in China twenty-five centuries ago (Wang & King, 2007, p. 256). The writings of Confucius reveal abundant examples of humanism, and even Western scholars such as Rogers (1969) and Knowles (1975) were heavily influenced by Confucian teachings. Humanists maintain that humans have unlimited potential for learning and that they are capable of self-direction in learning.

The confirmation of Chinese vocational education instructors' radical philosophy in teaching is somewhat surprising given Chinese educators' reputation for preferring spoon-feeding methods to problem-posing education (Wang, 2007b). Chinese educators are known for promoting rote learning instead of critical thinking in their teaching. However, since China opened its door to the outside world in the early 1980s, the Western democratic approach to teaching (e.g., dialogue, and discussion) has been experimented with and implemented on a trial basis.

Analytic instructors are not expected to construct explanations about reality. That Chinese vocational education instructors like constructing explanations about reality may reflect their preference for liberal philosophy over an analytical approach to education. Instructors with this liberal philosophy view themselves as unchallengeable authorities. Naturally, authorities should provide answers to "all" questions and problems, without any limitations whatsoever.

IMPLICATIONS

This chapter was designed to identify the general philosophies (i.e., *liberal, progressive, behavioral, humanistic, radical or analytic*) practiced by Chinese vocational education instructors in comparison to the predominant "competency-based" education (behavioral philosophy) in American vocational education. Western scholars may have preconceived notions about the kinds of philosophies Chinese vocational education instructors may hold. However, the reality is that Chinese vocational education instructors have also adopted the Western "competency-based" education to effectively cultivate every type of constructive talent among the Chinese people. The lesson drawn from this study is that teaching philosophies preferred by Western educators are also applicable to Chinese educators regardless of the differences in social environments. Confucianism, like the teachings of Socrates and Plato, has influenced educators globally for generations. If one's teaching philosophy seeks only to promote "competency-based" education, learning objectives are unlimited. The fact that Chinese vocational education instructors are liberal, not analytic in their approach represents a perfect example of how educational objectives can shape teaching philosophies.

For example, in the area of vocational curriculum, the Ministry of Education issues lists of authorized primary and secondary texts. This policy leaves no room for Chinese vocational education instructors to pursue an analytic approach. Rather, they must conform to the liberal philosophy in teaching. At the same time, to restrict teaching philosophies to a particular social environment is becoming impractical, especially when the world is becoming a global village where teaching must foster "competency-based education." To label teaching philosophies as Western or Chinese is extremely problematic, especially when Western educators and Chinese educators borrow effective teaching philosophies from one another via educational ambassadors such as John Dewey and most current ones. Finally, to say which of the philosophies leads to better learning is probably impossible since each of us who teaches engages in not only a time-honored process but one that is quite unique to the immediate situation in which we are actually teaching (Jarvis, 2002, p. 29). No single philosophy of vocational education should dominate the field (Wang, 2007b, p. 149). The best way of making one's philosophy work for the best teaching/learning results is to adopt and adapt a philosophy according to one's specific teaching/learning situation that may involve a plethora of other factors such as learner needs, learner styles, learner experience and learner motivation.

The present chapter supports a fresh look at the prevalent philosophies through the lens of the Chinese and American vocational education instructors. The study implies that specific educational goals and objectives may shape educators' philosophy of teaching. Most importantly, the chapter has provided insight into vocational education and training, particularly as globalization brings different cultures together to learn from each other. It is the researcher's intent that by examining the acts of others we improve our own practice in teaching. Further research is needed, especially in the form of qualitative investigation, to understand the influences and motivations that lead Chinese and American vocational education instructors to hold certain philosophies in teaching.

REFERENCES

Bott, P. A., Slapar, F. M., & Wang, V. (2003). *History and philosophy of career and technical education.* Boston: Pearson.

Chen, T. H. (1981). *Chinese education since 1949: Academic and revolutionary models.* New York: Pergamon Press.

Cheng, Y., & Manning, P. (2003). Revolution in education: China and Cuba in global context, 1957–76. *Journal of World History, 14*(3), 359–391.

Dewey, J. (1961). *Democracy and education.* New York: Macmillan.

Elias, J. L., & Merriam, S. B. (1995). *Philosophical foundations of adult education.* Malabar, FL: Krieger.

Elias, J. L., & Merriam, S. B. (2005). *Philosophical foundations of adult education* (3rd ed.). Malabar, FL: Krieger.

Grubb, W. N. (1998, December). *Preparing for the information-based workplace: Pedagogical issues and institutional linkages.* Paper prepared for "Learning Now: An International Symposium on Skill for the Information Economy", Chapel Hill, NC, Dec. 13–15, 1999; and for "Labor Organizations and Labor Market Institutions in the New Economy: Lessons from Silicon Valley", San Jose, Jan. 29–30, 1999. Retrieved May 23, 2007, from http://mitsloan.mit.edu/iwer/pdf/tfgrubb.pdf

Jarvis, P. (2002). Teaching styles and teaching methods. In P. Jarvis (Ed.), *The theory & practice of teaching* (pp. 22–30). London: Kogan Page.

Kaplan, F. M., Sobin, J. M., & Andors, S. (1979). *Encyclopedia of China today.* New York: Harper & Row.

Knowles, M. S. (1975). *Self-directed learning.* New York: Association Press.

Knowles, M. S., Holton, E., & Swanson, A. (1998). *The adult learner.* Houston, TX: Gulf.

Knowles, M. S., Holton, E., & Swanson, A. (2005). *The adult learner* (6th ed.). Boston, MA: Elsevier Butterworth Heinemann.

Mao, T. T. (1957). *Selected works of Mao Tse-tung: On the correct handling of contradictions among the people.* Retrieved February 24, 2005, from http://www.marxists.org/reference/archive/mao/selected-works/volume-5/mswv5_58.htm

Miller, M. D. (1985). *Principles and philosophy for vocational education.* Columbus, OH: Ohio State University.

Paine, L. (1992). Teaching and modernization in contemporary China. In R. Hayhoe (Ed.), *Education and modernization: The Chinese experience* (pp. 183–209). New York: Pergamon Press.

Roberts, R. W. (1965). *Vocational and practical arts education: History, development, and principles* (2nd ed). New York: Harper & Row.

Roberts, R. W. (1971). *Vocational and practical arts education: History, development, and principles* (3rd ed.). New York: Harper & Row.

Rogers, C. R. (1969). *Freedom to learn.* Columbus, OH: Merrill.

Skinner, B. F. (1968). *The technology of teaching.* New York: Appleton-Century-Crofts.

Wang, J. L., & Colletta, N. (1991). Chinese education problems, policies, and prospects. In I. Epstein (Ed.), *Chinese education problems, policies, and prospects* (pp. 145–162). New York: Garland.

Wang, V. C. X. (2007a). Chinese knowledge transmitters or western learning facilitators adult teaching methods compared. In K. P. King, & V. C. X. Wang (Eds.), *Comparative adult education around the globe* (pp. 113–137). Hangzhou, China: Zhejiang University Press.

Wang, V. C. X. (2007b). How contextually adapted philosophies and the situational roles of adult educators affect learners' transformation and emancipation. In K. P. King, & V. C. X. Wang (Eds.), *Comparative adult education around the globe* (pp. 139–150). Hangzhou, China: Zhejiang University Press.

Wang, V. C. X., & Bott, P. A. (2004). Modes of teaching of Chinese adult educators. *Perspectives: The New York Journal of Adult Learning, 2*(2), 32–51.

Wang, V. C. X., & King, K. P. (2007). Confucius and Mezirow—Understanding Mezirow's theory of reflectivity from Confucian perspectives: A model and perspective. In K. P. King, & V. C. X. Wang (Eds.), *Comparative adult education around the globe* (pp. 253–275). Hangzhou, China: Zhejiang University Press.

Wang, V. C. X., & Redhead, C. K. (2004). Comparing the Russian, the Sloyd, and the arts and crafts movement training systems. *International Journal of Vocational Education and Training, 12*(1), 42–58.

Xinhua. (2006). *China to invest 14 billion Yuan to develop technical training.* Retrieved January 9, 2007, from http://www.zju.edu.cn/english/news/2006/news061115.htm

Yang, D. P. (2005). China's education in 2003: From growth to reform (J. Eagleton, Trans). *Chinese Education and Society, 38*(4), 11–45. (Original work published in 2003)

Yu, B., & Xu, H. Y. (1988). *Adult higher education: A case study on the workers' college in the People's Republic of China.* UNESCO: International Institute for Educational Planning.

CHAPTER 10

FOUNDATIONS OF E-LEARNING IN CAREER AND TECHNICAL EDUCATION

Using the Medium to Meet Learners' Needs

Kathleen P. King
Fordham University

INTRODUCTION

Distance learning has a history that spans hundreds of years, far predating technology-assisted efforts. Indeed, many nations and cultures delivered critical educational information by foot with human messengers and couriers (e.g., Greece, Africa). By the mid 1800s, mail correspondence courses for formal educational efforts were appearing, and by the 1940s, not only was mail correspondence used for many efforts, but learning via radio was widely utilized for educational purposes, primarily informally by educational and religious groups across Asia and Africa. Since the 1960s, television has been used extensively for formal and informal learning as well (Moore

Building Workforce Competencies in Career and Technical Education, pages 191–211
Copyright © 2009 by Information Age Publishing
191

& Kearsley, 1996). With this extensive foundation of efforts in bridging the expanses of distance for the purposes of education, it is surprising that it has taken 40 years for e-learning to mature significantly for formal educational efforts (King & Griggs, 2006).

Traditional educational organizations are not swift to adopt change: traditions run deep in academia, therefore the adoption of videoconference, teleconferencing, and then e-learning from the 1970s through the 2000s was not widely embraced in the United States until 2005. A significant marker in this timeline is 2008/2009 when the US Department of Education (USDOE) made financial aid available to postsecondary students enrolled in online courses (Woods, 2001).

Within the larger context of distance learning, the history of e-learning provides a backdrop for our discussion of e-learning in career and technical education (CTE). Educational institutions and teachers have vibrant opportunities to use e-learning to model *technology in action* for exploring and supporting career development, cultivating learning communities, learning cutting-edge applications, developing connections to experts in the field, and facilitating ongoing communities of experts. Career and technical education has much to gain from e-learning; therefore, we find some of the most advanced demonstrations of technology in instructional applications emerge from CTE even today.

This chapter provides a thorough discussion of e-learning in CTE. Drawing on the literature and using examples, the chapter describes CTE and e-learning specific benefits, evolution of use, current and creative learning practices, recommendations and strategies for teaching and learning and emerging trends and future. The chapter is meant to develop a vision of e-learning for CTE, grounded in the accomplishments of the past, and fueled by the possibilities of creating learning communities and experiences beyond the boundaries of time and space.

THE HISTORICAL BACK STORY

While the need for technology specialists ("techies") or complex, pricey solutions like proprietary video conference hookups dominated the early years of distance learning and e-learning adoption, e-learning is much more accessible today. Part of this transition started with the distribution of the *personal computer (PC)* in the late 1980s. There were three other major contributors to this phenomenon documented over the last 30 years. First was the open source standardization of *HTML* for the World Wide Web in 1990. Second, the continuing rollout of *broadband Internet* access at affordable prices across the world fueled adoption. The third major influence is *social adoption.* This momentous transition happened circa 2005 as Web use for personal, everyday, workplace, and educational use became not only ubiquitously available, but expected and utilized. Critical barriers of computing capability, affordability, and scalability were broken down.

Indeed, the phenomena of 2005 were a confluence of several factors of which e-learning and education need to take notice: availability, affordability and usability created a synergy. The availability and affordability of hardware (powerful enough to conduct interesting and compelling activities), the availability of abundant information, news, social media, business, finance, and entertainment to drive non technophiles over the hurdle of learning (e.g., think of Google.com, Amazon.com, e-Trade.com (stocks), and University of Phoenix). The abundance of user-friendly recreational and social media resources broke down the barriers of usability and affordability (many free). These were dynamic and user-driven platforms and activities, drawing mass numbers and the purchasing power of Digital Natives (Prensky , 2001) to them in the millions (think YouTube, Facebook.com, MySpace.com, World of Warcraft, Second Life, and iTunes). From cell phones to iPods, low-cost laptops to iPhones, mini-laptops to large screen HDTVs, the focus of the technology, business, commerce, and service industries was the race to develop user-friendly applications. These highly desired gadgets were less expensive, easy to learn, and enhanced with any online connection.

In 2009, computer users' every day concerns changed from, "Where can I find Internet access?" to "Which access should I use?" as we have a plethora of connectivity devices and options for platforms. We are constantly connected via cell phone, MP3 player, car satellite, and laptop. We no longer solely consume the masses of information flooding our inboxes, but now *create* content and electronically launch it across the globe.

In the midst of this social revolution has been the challenge for traditional education to find its place. Thankfully, innovative pioneers have gone before us: they were thrashing through the tangles of wires as we waited for the Wireless Age; breaking through the mainframes, as we were dreaming of the handheld computer; and coping with modems until broadband reached us all. We can build on the shoulders of these giants to advance CTE even further over the next few decades. CTE can use these new levels of technology advancement to reach beyond geographical barriers, scaffold resources, and evolve new models of teaching e-learning. The medium *is* the message—CTE can be the life and blood of e-learning.

Early distance learning classes had many problems, as costs were voluminous, connections failed frequently, and poor coordination between sites made traditional classroom management look like child's play. In addition, we had educators and administrators who could not envision a new form of teaching. They were intent on forcing the familiar paradigm into the new. In the case of online courses, the result was yellowed lectures notes typed up and posted on a webpage being called a course—no instructor interaction, alternate media, activities, nor dialogue.

In 2009 and beyond, we seem light-years further ahead as we engage in dialogue-based, problem-based learning affording dynamic virtual classroom experiences. Consider harnessing Second Life and iTunes for CTE, using the roller coasters in a virtual world to teach Physics, or conducting medical lab tests and surgeries in a virtual laboratory. We do not need to imagine the future is here. Incorporating such vibrant interactive activities into the convenience and power of well-designed e-learning is opening the opportunities of CTE wider every moment.

CURRENT AND CREATIVE PRACTICE

Our discussion of the current uses and creative practices of e-learning today includes not only the teacher's perspectives, but also a fuller picture of the learning community. It is because of the needs of students that the e-learning experience has become so vitally possible. If they did not see a need, and if they did not see value, they would not be enrolling for e-learning classes. In addition, in order to provide the credits and degrees our students need, and the support so essential for academic and online success, institutional perspectives and needs must be met.

Student Perspectives

Considering e-learning from the student perspective provides a multitude of benefits, yet some realistic hesitations. Along with a firsthand student perspective, the first portion of the section provides a brief overview of benefits. The final portion will discuss three primary hesitations, which arise as students consider e-learning.

Consider the following reflection about e-learning written by a teacher who enrolled in her second online graduate class responding to the question, "What are the student benefits of distance learning?"

> The benefits to distance learning are endless. As a learner, it gives you the flexibility to manage your time and to balance your life both personally and professionally. For example, without distance education I would never have been able to pursue a Masters Degree with a full time job that requires 50% travel and still be able to spend quality time with my husband, family, and friends.
>
> In addition, working online gives the participant access to an overabundance of resources. Everything is literally at your fingertips!

Perhaps one of the greatest benefits to online learning is that it knows no geographical boundaries and so classmates can work together collaboratively even though they may live in a different state or country!

Working online is also a tremendous cost savings to the student. There is no fee for room and board, and with the rising cost of gas, it's great not to have to fill up before "heading to class."

Do you have anxiety about social situations? Online learning puts participants at ease, allowing them to contribute to discussions and make friends with their classmates in a non-threatening environment.

Students with learning disabilities can work at their own pace. This is extremely helpful, for example if you have a student with word retrieval problems. In a classroom setting, [that] student... may have difficulty responding immediately to a question posed by the instructor and consequently get dinged on their final grade for not participating enough. Posting the questions in a discussion board levels the playing field and gives everyone an equal opportunity to participate. (Brianna)

This concise response effectively captures most of the critical elements of distance learning for which students are hungering in the 21st century. They are searching for convenience and flexibility, both in high school and post-secondary education as many concurrently work or have family demands. She also refers to the abundance of resources readily available to support learning in the same way our students work and engage in entertainment. Additionally, the opportunity to benefit from global collaboration in her studies is a dimension she enjoys while also saving money on transportation, room and board. Finally, as a teacher in training, she realizes the benefits to students with needs, which may be different from her own. The online learning environment offers the capability to adjust one's work pace, find a save environment for dialogue, and as she says, "Level the playing field" for those hesitant to speak up in class. I can add that to this teacher's perspective as I have seen online dialogue encourage students to participate in class (King, 2001; 2008). Empowerment through collaboration virtual or not is a welcome outcome for such students.

CTE students stand to gain even more as they have access to specialized courses, which may not be available in their area, such as experts, resources, high-end simulations, and global experiences. The potential science and technology classes have to reach beyond laboratories has been demonstrated by participation in classroom video field trips to observe robotic assisted surgery (Tood & Himburg, 2007), to web-based simulations of pig dissections, and student internships in real-life civil engineering projects (International Education and Resource Network, 2008).

On the other hand, the same student, "Brianna," who shared the benefits of distance learning, articulates significant difference she has seen compared to traditional classrooms:

> It's important to note that while there are many benefits to online learning, it's not for everyone. Students who are the most successful with this learning environment are "...self-motivated, have clear goals, have set aside appropriate time, and are Web-savvy..." (Distance Education Clearinghouse "Overview and FAQs"). The disadvantage to online learning is that since you don't have a set time for class, work might get pushed aside with all of the other commitments begging for your time...especially when your boss is breathing down your neck! You must be disciplined enough to make yourself work when there is no teacher standing directly over your shoulder, and you must be able to dedicate the time necessary to visit Blackboard (for example) regularly and be a steady contributor to the class. ("Brianna")

In this quote, she vividly describes the need for students to be self-disciplined. She identifies the fact that students cannot "coast" through class, bearing little accountability. Instead integrated in the e-learning experience is the need to cultivate those valuable softskills, recognized in CTE programs and demanded in the workplace as well: timeliness, meeting deadlines, setting goals, time management, collaboration skills, interpersonal relationships, and coping with competing demands (Bancino & Zevalkink, 2007; Boutelle, 2007). Learners who develop self-directed skills greatly increase their career chances in the competitive global market of the 21st century (ASTD Public Policy Council, 2006).

Finally consider the hesitations. Among these are the desires of students for face to face interaction with teacher and classmates: this is a real need and innate to some certain personality types and learning styles. However, in my experience, once students engage in interactive learning communities, they realize how much more they get to know their colleagues than in a race in and out of class format. While everyone is pressed for time, all the time, when students engage in discussion boards, there is unlimited time for reflecting, gathering their thoughts, posing their response, and responding to others. Simple analysis of most online classes demonstrates that when teachers empower students with strategies and assignments, which encourage online dialogue, they participate much more than ever would be possible in an on-campus class. Frequently a single discussion question/posting in online classes of 15 students, yields 30–90 learner responses. Therefore, one finds students, once encouraged to participate online, learn that it is a very different experience than they expected. It turns out that an unknown or preconceived expectation is what they often oppose.

Another obstacle is accessibility, which institutions can address. In fact, most programs do not require students to have very new or expensive computers. This barrier is additionally diminishing with the falling price of computer hardware. The bigger issue is broadband access, which becomes a critical issue for many rural people and those with less socioeconomic means. Institutions may help students budget for this expense by incorporating the cost of broadband access, as customary e-learning student cost on the school website, just like books.

Finally, students may feel inadequately prepared or skilled to use e-learning technologies. In the case of CTE programs, this should not be an enduring obstacle as the "Medium *is* the message." By engaging in online programs and courses, students address the outcomes and competencies influenced in their course of study. A hallmark of CTE programs is that they prepare students to enter today's workforce immediately. For the last 15 years, we have seen a rapid integration of technology in the workforce, and yet education has lagged far behind. CTE e-learning provides situated learning experiences for students to use technology while earning their credits, concurrently better preparing for the 21st century workplace (The Partnership for 21st Century Skills, 2004; ASTD Public Policy Council, 2006; Lave & Wenger, 1991).

Institutional Perspectives

Regarding the current and creative practice for e-learning in CTE, educational institutions have many sectors to consider and juggle in order to be successful. However, the sections above demonstrate that there are great student needs for this educational delivery system, and that we stand to gain much from higher education's prior experience with distance learning.

Additional trends among these patterns and possibilities are most telling. In 2007–2008, it became clear that two-year colleges were leading the innovative efforts of distance learning (Allen & Seaman, 2008). In fact, one article reported results conducted by the American Association of Community Colleges demonstrates that 64% of all the colleges offered online courses (Jashik, 2008). What does this mean for CTE? It is significant because two-year colleges have been primary providers of CTE programs. This institutional trend reveals an infrastructure and readiness on the postsecondary level which has been sorely needed in the past. More specifically, this pattern was perceived as far back as 2003 when Johnson Benson, Duncan, Shinkareva, Taylor, and Treat published that according to a national survey, 76.3% of community colleges offered CTE courses and programs through some type of distance learning.

Indeed, several states in the United States have taken on the task of developing CTE e-learning initiatives in order to meet the many needs of their students. Kentucky's Area Technology Centers (ATC's) system is one example, which has been successful and is developing its Virtual Area Technology Center (VATC). This example is of prime importance because the institution of the state educational department, CTE department, and the schools agree to provide two forms of instruction (local and remote), both of which are focused on enhancing student learning (Stone, 2007).

When organizations recognize student learning is fundamental, they embrace the power of e-learning to meet the need. In the case of the ATCS and VATC, the programs either supplement support of the traditional classroom, or serve remote students. Both are classic uses of distance learning in K–12 settings. These programs understand the power of multiplying their efforts through e-learning, broadening their course offerings, and resources, while also serving a larger constituency (Wonacott, 2001). Traditional strategies of weighing costs vs. benefits reveal that this approach makes sense while accomplishing the greater scalability.

Having a broad based program with low cost technologies and ease of use are all winning practices for scalable e-learning. Scaling a program means that offering what is in one location or place with little difficulty in other locations.

Several state colleges have also launched programs to offer CTE programs via distance learning, including a significant sample of Jefferson State Community College (Birmingham, AL), St. Petersburg College (St. Petersburg, FL), and County College of Morris (Randolph, NJ) (Benson, Johnson, Taylor, Treat, Shinkareva, & Duncan, 2004). This group of community college programs is important because they were the subject of a study conducted by Benson et al. published in 2004 demonstrating that CTE programs could effectively use e-learning to prepare students in both content and skills central to CTE fields.

Up until this point, the literature repeatedly raised the issue of skills attainment (Johnson, et al., 2003; Zirkle, 2004). Therefore, this study is a significant turning point. In this matched mixed-method research study, the same curriculum and teacher were used with different students at a distance and face-to-face. The results among a total of 193 participants across these three CTE college courses, revealed e-learning students and traditional classroom students performed equally well and appeared to be as equally motivated and satisfied (Brown et al., 2003).

Institutions delivering CTE programs know that student needs, student skills, and student achievement can be met reliably with appropriately designed e-learning by building upon a solid history of distance learning, continuing to incorporate better teaching and learning strategies through new technologies.

Concomitant with these concerns for achievement and skills is the frequently voiced concern of accreditation and academic rigor. However, as of 2007 most state education departments had adopted standards and procedures for the delivery of distance learning programs. Institutions no longer have the lengthy applications for every program, but can usually be qualified as a whole. This qualification results from demonstrated and documented capacity for institutional technology, distance learning infrastructure, instructional and student support.

As one continues to understand institutional capacity and responsibility in e-learning, the success of these efforts may be viewed from different perspectives. These programs overcome the usual educational restrictions of space limitations, lack of educational personnel, content area experts, or resources, geographical isolation, and limited market reach. CTE e-learning programs offer the capability to "build" a virtual campus that can expand and shrink based on enrollments, but without a large physical footprint. They afford the opportunity to bring technical experts into the classroom via real-time and pre-recorded formats. They also have the potential to consolidate classes from across large geographical spans; so that rare educators with specific expertise can teach a fuller class and everyone enjoy the benefits of the robust dialogue and efficiencies. A final example is the nearly effortless expansion of any CTE e-learning program far beyond its own county or state boundaries. Thus the uniquely equipped CTE program in a remote area can be accessed by students around the world. Conversely, students far from urban centers can still have their choice of multiple CTE programs. Administrators and educators know that in postsecondary education, a key to retention is the fit of the program, therefore having greater student choice, and a wider pool of potential students is to the advantage of every institution.

Teacher Perspective

Design

One model of e-learning is to consider that courses may have different extents of e-learning integration. Therefore, educators may understand the entire spectrum as a continuum moving from web-enhanced classes to hybrid classes and finally to fully distance courses (See Figure 10.1). In one program, some courses are online, while others are face to face. Some work is conducted in traditional settings and certain other assignments, exams, or reports are always submitted online.

Educators can explore how different stages of e-learning integration and try it in comfortable phases of adoption with their classes. For instance, educators may begin by considering the infrastructure available, the needs of your students, program, and accreditation, and then designing what is a good starting point. The next stage will be an improvement, and seasoned distance educators share that they never stop improving.

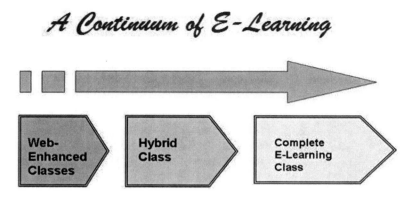

Figure 10.1 Continuum of e-learning, © Kathleen P. King, 2007.

Instruction

Over the years of continued incorporation of research, innovation, trial, and error, the field has come to realize that instructional strategies that are valuable in distance learning include a range of options, which emphasize instructional effectiveness (Brown, 2006). In particular, the examples represented by Brown in his analysis are most relevant for CTE needs. The several e-learning programs he studied focused on one or more of: outcomes based assessment, learning by design approaches, situated learning, and sustaining valuable learning communities. From web-based clinical laboratory classes to Math and Science at a Community College, the successful e-learning programs revealed that even those areas we thought would be most difficult to deliver formats were empowered. In addition, the focus of these efforts on situated learning (Lave & Wenger, 1991) confirms the understanding of CTE educators that students can learn complex material most effectively when it is taught and practiced in context.

The critical role of the instructor in developing effective instructional experiences through e-learning is well described by Brown (2006). In several of these efforts, understanding outcomes based instructional design (Wiggins & McTighe, 1998) was the heart of faculty development. With such a change in perspective and practice, educators were able to transform traditional curriculum into dynamic, effective learning experiences delivered via technology (Brown, Meyers, & Roy, 2003). This conclusion defies the old fear that distance learning could replace educators. E-learning is dependent on the expertise and experience of educators to create new and transform old content, in addition to teaching, dialogue, and assessing student work. In these cases, this instructional model was able to further direct e-learning efforts to integrate available and scalable technology meeting effective, measurable outcomes.

In considering how to assist, educators understand the current practice of e-learning in CTE. One of the primary tenets that emerge is, "One size does not fit all." Reading the analysis provided by Brown (2006) can assist educators to better apprehend the findings of instructional strategies for e-learning across many major distance learning projects in postsecondary education. His focus on instructional effectiveness across these very different e-learning endeavors, confirms the continual need to match learner needs, context, and technology. The focus is not the technology; *the focus is the learners and learning.*

Technology

The advantage of using e-learning today and in the future is that increasingly relevant technology is familiar, available, accessible and affordable. Therefore, rather than looking at another program and class and trying to entirely replicate it, sample several and examine the benefits. Build upon the expertise you have developed as a specific CTE content expert and educator to combine that with the potential of the e-learning resources made available.

Nonetheless, this section is the last under "teacher perspectives" because the emphasis for dynamic e-learning is more on learners, and less on technology. Instead, one should find technologies that function so easily they are nearly transparent. The point of educator's work and interaction with the students should not be the glitz of the technology, but the content, the objectives, and the outcomes. The technology serves the purpose of bringing us all to that place. We as educators use our expertise to make those choices, to craft and design learning *experiences* that will have impact on learners' lives and minds.

In some classes, students are engaging in blogging, are publishing their work, their art, music, and technical drawings for a global audience. Rather than confining their dialogue and display to the four walls of the classroom, or a private virtual classroom, these students are keenly aware that their work will be on a global display and intend to share the work with families and friends. Some schools even provide blog updates, and family can watch the development of a project or field trip as it unfolds. Students' levels of performance can reach new dimensions when they are focused on specific audiences (King, 2008; King & Gura, 2009; Powers & Dallas, 2006).

Another level of technology use is for teachers and students to create materials which can be used again. Basic digital audio can also be created for free as schools usually have an inexpensive microphone available and digital audio software is free. Projects of this sort might include student presentations of projects for employers, oral histories of projects, or supplemental materials teachers create to support differentiated instruction needs. King and Gura (2009) have documented many examples of curricular applications of digital audio which provide an alternative to text-only formats.

Previously in the chapter, the power of simulations was described; these cannot be underestimated (e.g., SimCity™, Spore™). Such virtual experiences bring learning into different senses and levels of consciousness at time. Dialogue and collaborative group projects can engage students in exploring new spaces. For instance, they may explore different terrain for construction sites in Second Life, or varied organizational roles as class members engage in an academic Role Playing Game (RPG), or participate in global learning through dedicated educational social network sites. Even when separated by time and space, students can be actively engaged in meaningful collaborative group work. Digital natives understand the globe is their world; adding the virtual and global dimensions of participation to learning will increase their ownership and investment in problem based learning. Critical problem-solving, higher order thinking, analysis and assessment flow freely throughout these activities.

RECOMMENDATIONS/STRATEGIES USE FOR TEACHING AND LEARNING

Formative Development

In addition to the practices described above in the context of discussing the current state of e-learning in CTE, this section provides some principal concepts to guide the development, delivery, facilitation, and assessment of e-learning courses and programs. As with traditional courses, the creation and improvement of e-learning courses never ends. Instead, educators continually assess what works best, what else is possible, how to improve and align content with what students need to learn. Educators are always striving to reach the objectives and skill sets therein in better ways.

I enjoy the evolving and continuing process of instructional design and prefer to refer to it as formative development—a reference in part to formative assessment—that continues throughout a project, so that it can guide, shape, and form the best results (King, 2002). I find such a dynamic perspective of e-learning to be most dynamic and powerful for students, teachers and institutions as it continually moves us forward to be the best.

Learning Community

One of the dominant themes which emerged in distance learning literature since the 1990s has been that of the learning community (Brown, 2006; Palloff & Pratt, 1999, 2001, 2004, 2007). When e-learning makes effective use of learning communities, it unleashes a power that is rarely tapped in traditional classrooms settings.

Educators know learning communities are powerful learning experiences because many times they are associated with situated learning (Lave & Wenger, 1991), workplace learning, collaborative learning, and/or communities of practice (Wenger, 1999). Indeed the trend of the 21st century is that social networking and learning communities are a major force in many facets of life including not only work (Dufour & Eaker, 1999; Tapscott & Williams, 2006), but also politics, national and sector economics, entertainment, and media (Tapscott & Williams).

Therefore, using learning communities in e-learning settings provides valuable skills, literacies, and experiences that students will carry with them into further adult workplace and professional experiences. In addition, learning communities provide a powerful vehicle for experiencing peer learning, peer dialogue, peer facilitation, teacher facilitation, which are all in-depth instructional strategies. Moreover, this approach can cultivate critical thinking, critical inquiry, technology literacies, information literacy, interpersonal skills, and collaborative learning skills, to name a few essential CTE skills (King & Griggs, 2006; King & Sanquist, 2009; Wonacott, 2001).

Multimedia in E-Learning

At a time when every K–16 education institution seems to be eying strategies to enter the e-learning arena (Carr-Chellman, 2005), using multimedia is critical. Rather than the situation, we described previously of posting lecture notes on the web and maybe launching a student discussion forum to encourage students to "talk among themselves," this approach requires, planning, instructional design and effort.

When e-learning courses are designed with mixed media and multiple learning modes integrated as an instructional plan, the effects are much greater than when single modes of content presentation are used (Metri Group, 2008; Stansbury, 2008). Recent research confirms what most teachers have experienced; video, text, graphics, and experience make for a greater breadth of learning, and therefore greater outcomes. In the context of e-learning, the tools available to use this well proven instructional strategy are numerous, often free (or inexpensive), easy to use, convenient, and motivating for teachers and learners alike.

Consider the opportunity to augment your class presentation about computer aided design (CAD) with video clips of CAD/CAM operators at worksites, explanations from professionals about the nature of their work and simulations of 3D figures that can be transformed on various planes and parameters (Gura & King, 2007). In addition, educators can create portable digital audio tutorials to reinforce lessons that students may need to review or for students who miss classes (King & Gura, 2009).

Certainly multiple intelligences and different learning styles have a lot to do with the power of multi modes of learning, but the point here is that technology, and specifically e-learning afford a powerful, easy platform to make the most of this effective approach. From teacher created materials to student created materials, text, video, audio, simulations, virtual experiences (e.g., Second Life, Google Earth), and more, we can extend the flat screen of the computer into a more holistic experience than often perceived. Educators stand as the most powerful potential innovators for this purpose.

Feedback Emphasis

If one is involved in e-learning today, it is a great surprise to hear people discuss the "isolation" in distance learning. Indeed, today K–16 students today are invested in social networking via technology, they prefer to text and Instant Message (IM), rather than phone their friends. Their social worlds are embedded in the virtual spaces of Myspace.com, Facebook.com, ClubPenguin.com, LiveJournal.com, and scores of other sites.

Indeed, the virtual sometimes "morphs" with face to face. For instance, students who are in class every day together will spend copious amounts of time texting, and IMing together outside of school. However, they also have a much larger circle of friends, which easily may span the globe. Today the world of K–16 students is *their* community and the *means* of communicating is technology. Technology does not isolate them- it connects.

Certainly, in some instances students can become so computer focused that they forget about the interpersonal skills needed for face-to-face communication. However, overall reports such as Growing Up Online (WGBH, 2008) and the enduring concept of Digital Natives (Prensky, 2001) reveal that K–16 students are much more adept at cross walking their relationships, vocabulary, persona, and approaches from virtual to face to face environments than older adults are. They fluidly traverse between these two worlds because both are their native habitats.

Given this context, the opportunity to conduct teacher/student dialogue, feedback, and assessment via e-learning is not a barrier for the students. Students are accustomed to the concept and the modality. Some tools may be different, but many are the same. In most cases, the educators need to ramp up their comfort level, but once they do, the depth and extent of feedback escalates. In fact, most educators quickly find they need to put limits on their feedback activities because, it can become entirely time consuming and dominating their lives inside and outside of work hours.

What are some of the options available for e-learning feedback, which are especially applicable for CTE? Consider that office hours might be held online in a private group chat room at scheduled times, or in a group forum much like a WEB-Ex® platform with an electronic whiteboard for displaying content. Educators might provide comments regarding written work via narrative format in email responses, using comment or tracking features in word processors, or sending a digital audio message to the student via email. Student advising can be done via email, phone, virtual chat, or online discussion board (for groups). These are a few of the simple ways that assignment feedback in e-learning can guide students in their work, and give encouragement and direction.

In fact, the grading system transparently provides students with additional focus and abundant documentation for formalized feedback. Rubrics are valuable for communicating expectations and grading criteria. Educators may break down course requirements into several components. For example, discussion board participation might be graded every week or two weeks- and not only at the end of the semester (such as class participation often is in traditional classes. By providing feedback formatively in most areas of assessment, students have greater opportunities to clarify what is expected, raise their level of performance and get on track for better understanding (Heron & Wright, 2006).

ON THE HORIZON: TRENDS AND FUTURE

Problem-Based Learning

Problem-based learning is a powerful vehicle for CTE learning in general and is a proven, effective strategy for e-learning. Nonetheless, the majority of CTE educators are likely just beginning to explore the ease of use and the possibilities for further advancing their face-to-face problem-based learning activities into alternative digital delivery formats (Sundberg, Sunal, & Mays, 2006).

Indeed, with their vast experience and expertise in problem-based learning across its history (Wang, King, & Nafukho, 2008), and the work already accomplished by CTE K–16 in this area, it is easy to anticipate that CTE also will lead the way in this e-learning innovation. Resources to support problem-based learning extend to such user friendly and convenient web-based technologies as blogs, wikis, predesigned simulations, configurable simulations, instructional simulations, concept mapping, CAD, conversion calculators, videoconferencing, and global collaborative learning communities, virtual and cloud computing, to name a few. In addition, online formats of many classroom experiential and problem-based learning activities are now available including robotics, life science and earth science laboratories, computer repair and programming design and trouble shooting laboratories (sandboxes), and many other constructivist platforms for science, math, technical study, programming, language arts, engineering, mechanics, and agricultural studies, for instance.

Assessment as Learning

Of course, whenever we want to know the direction and impact of educational efforts, assessment is critical at all stages. During planning stages, we assess learner and organizational needs. While delivering instruction, we use formative assessment to ascertain the progress of students, and course instruction in order to provide correction as needed. Finally educators use summative evaluation/assessment to determine the results of instruction, both immediately and sometimes on a longer-term basis.

In the case of e-learning in CTE, we have multiple options available to leverage these assessment efforts with the power, ease, and consistency of technology (Heron & Wright, 2006). For instance, course surveys, student pre- and posttests, and student practice tests may all be designed within an online course environment, administered, and scored. In addition, through a simple interface, educators may allow students to take retests at whatever frequency and interval they determine is needed. From the students' perspective, more assessment means more opportunities to evaluate their understanding and determine what they need to improve upon. In addition, practice tests are a great favorite of students, while they may be cumbersome for educators to develop, administer, and score. Technology formats break through these barriers and e-learning takes the time required beyond the precious little traditional of classroom "seat time" and makes it the students' choice. As educators and students alike become more adept with the potential for e-learning assessment in general, and its authentic assessment alternatives (Powers & Dallas, 2006), CTE educators stand to develop exciting new meaningful advancements. This area to watch for advancement in coming years, especially in our understanding of the need for student feedback, and accountability for all: students, teachers, and schools.

Multimodal Learning

As informed educators we know the background for the success of "multimodal learning" is in part that learners may have varying tendencies for different learning styles, and multiple intelligences. However the research about brain development and changes and its relationships to learning provides many new connections in this area (Metri Group, 2008; Stansbury, 2008).

Given the great value placed on brain research and learning today in our schools, and the linkage to the trend above, using multiple technology tools and media will also likely be an important future direction for CTE e-learning. The approach needs to be validation because educators need professional development time to explore instructional design resources, opportunities, and strategies. When administrators and school boards realize this multimodal e-learning will have great impact on their e-learning programs, they will be more ready to invest the fiscal resources needed.

Professional Development

CTE educators need e-learning professional development (PD) for every stage of planning and developing. Proven, effective PD models include one or more of the following characteristics:

- Engage educators individually and collaboratively in order to facilitate the development of communities of practice within schools and departments/grade levels (Covington, Petherbridge, & Warren, 2005).
- Focus on faculty needs for technology learning and instructional design with adult learning principles (Cranton, 1996; King, 2002).
- Develop faculty ownership of e-learning, planning and design (King 2002; Yanes, Pena, & Curts, 2006).
- Address instructional needs through outcomes based design (Brown, 2006; Brown, Meyers, & Roy, 2003; Wiggins & McTighe, 1998).

The expertise and experience of CTE educators will lead us into a new wave of innovation in e-learning for many reasons. Professional development, which centers on educators' needs and builds on their strengths will have a solid foundation of pedagogy and practice which is consistent with our understanding of the strengths of e-learning.

CONCLUSION

Understanding the foundational connections of e-learning to CTE reveals the central place CTE can play in 21st century learning. Building upon teacher expertise and experience means greater strength for effective and dynamic e-learning in CTE than many other disciplines.

Current and creative practices discussed in this chapter provide a strong foundation for instruction, teachers and institutions alike. Recommendations and future trends reveal the directions which many best focus current and future CTE e-learning programs. In conclusion, *CTE learners' needs can be powerfully served through the medium of e-learning.*

REFERENCES

Allen, E., & Seaman, J. (2008). *Online nation: Five years of growth in online learning.* Needham, MA: Sloan-C. Retrieved September 8, 2008, from http://www.aln. org/publications/survey/pdf/online_nation.pdf

ASTD Public Policy Council (American Society for Training and Development). (2006). *Bridging the skills gap.* Alexandria, VA: ASTD Press. Retrieved September 3, 2008, from http://www.astd.org/NR/rdonlyres/D43B0459-E5F9–4BC0-9275-FA33FF927637/0/SkillsGapWhitePaper.pdf

Bancino, R., & Zevalkink, C. (2007). Soft skills: the new curriculum for hard-core technical professionals. *Techniques: Connecting Education and Careers 82*(5), 20–22.

Benson, A. D., Johnson, S. D., Taylor, G. D., Treat, T., Shinkareva, O. N., & Duncan, J. (2004). *Distance learning in postsecondary career and technical education.* Columbus, OH: National Research Center for Career and Technical Education. (ERIC Doc. Reproduction No. ED 493 603)

Boutelle, M. (2007, Summer). Building bridges and mastering "soft skills." *California Schools Magazine.* Retrieved September 3, 2008, from http://www.csba. org/NewsAndMedia/Publications/CASchoolsMagazine/2007/Summer/InThisIssue/BuildingBridgesAndMastering%20SoftSkills.aspx

Brown, G. (2006). New perspectives on instructional effectiveness through distance education. In K. P. King & J. K. Griggs, (Eds.), *Harnessing innovative technology in higher education: Access, equity, policy and instruction* (pp. 97–110) Madison, WI: Atwood.

Brown, G., Meyers, C., & Roy, S. (2003). Formal course design and the student experience. *Journal of Asynchronous Learning Networks.* Retrieved September 8, 2008, from http://www.aln.org/publications/jaln/v7n3/pdf/v7n3_myers.pdf

Carr-Chellman, A. (2005). Introduction. In A. Carr-Chellman (Ed.), *Global perspectives on e-learning: Rhetoric and reality* (pp. 14–17). Thousand Oaks, CA: Sage.

Covington, D., Petherbridge, D., & Warren, S. (2005, Spring). Best practices: A triangulated support approach in transitioning faculty to online teaching. *Online Journal of Distance Learning Administration, 8*(1). Retrieved September 6, 2008, from http://www.westga.edu/~distance/ojdla/spring81/covington81.htm

Cranton, P. (1996). *Transformative learning in professional development*. San Francisco: Jossey-Bass.

Dufour, R., & Eaker, R. (1999). *Professional learning communities at work*. Bloomington, IN: Solutions Tree.

Gura, M., & King, K. P. (Eds.). (2007). *Classroom robotics: Case stories of 21st century instruction for millennial students*. Charlotte, NC: Information Age.

Heron, J., & Wright, V. (2006). Assessment in online learning. In V. Wright, C. Sunal, & E. Wilson (Eds.), *Research on enhancing the interactivity of online learning* (pp. 45–64). Charlotte, NC: Information Age.

International Education and Resource Network. (2008). *iEARN Media Gallery*. Retrieved September 1, 2008, from http://media.iearn.org/

Jashik, S. (2008, April 7). Distance ed continues rapid growth at community colleges. *Inside HigherEd 4*(7). Retrieved September 5, 2008 from http://www.insidehighered.com/news/2008/04/07/distance

Johnson, S. D., Benson, A. D., Duncan, J., Shinkareva, O. N., Taylor, G. D., & Treat, T. (2003, October). *Distance learning in postsecondary career and technical education*. Minneapolis, MN: National Research Center for Career and Technical Education.

King, K. P. (2001). Educators revitalize the classroom "bulletin board:" A case study of the influence of online dialogue on face-to-face classes from an adult learning perspective. *Journal of Research on Computing in Education 33*(4), 337–354.

King, K. P. (2002). *Keeping pace with technology: Educational technology that transforms Vol. 1*. Cresskill, NJ: Hampton Press.

King, K. P. (2008, May). Introducing new media into teacher preparation. *ISTE SIG Handheld Computing (ISTE SIGHC) 3*(4), 4–7. Retrieved September 13, 2008, from http://www.iste.org/Content/NavigationMenu/Membership/SIGs/SIGHC_Handheld_Computing/SIGHCnewsletter0508.pdf

King, K. P., & Griggs, J. K. (Eds). (2006). *Harnessing innovative technology in higher education: Access, equity, policy and instruction*. Madison, WI: Atwood.

King, K. P., & Gura, M. (2009). *Podcasting for teachers: Using a new technology to revolutionize teaching and learning* (Rev. 2nd ed). Charlotte, NC: Information Age.

King, K. P., & Sanquist, S. (2009). 21st century learning and human performance. In V. Wang, & K. P. King, (Eds.), *Fundamentals of human performance and training. SERIES: Adult education special topics: Theory, research and practice in lifelong learning* (pp. 61–88). Charlotte, NC: Information Age.

Lave, J., & Wenger, E. (1991). *Situated learning: Legitimate peripheral participation*. Cambridge: Cambridge University Press.

Metri Group. (2008). *Multimodal learning through media: What the research says*. San Jose: Cisco. Retrieved May 20, 2008, from http://www.cisco.com/web/strategy/docs/education/Multimodal-Learning-Through-Media.pdf

Moore, M. G., & Kearsley, G. (1996). *Distance education: A systems view*. Belmont, CA: Wadsworth.

Palloff, R., & Pratt, K. (1999). *Building learning communities in cyberspace*. San Francisco: Jossey Bass.

Palloff, R., & Pratt, K. (2001). *Lessons form the cyberspace classroom*. San Francisco: Jossey Bass.

Palloff, R., & Pratt, K. (2004). *Collaborating online: Learning together in community.* San Francisco: Jossey Bass.

Palloff, R., & Pratt, K. (2007). *Building online learning communities.* San Francisco: Jossey Bass.

The Partnership for 21st century Skills. (2004). Framework for 21st century learning. Tucson, AZ: The Partnership for 21st century Skills. Retrieved August 28, 2008, from http://www.21stcenturyskills.org/documents/frameworkflyer_072307.pdf

Powers, S., & Dallas, L. (2006). Authentic assessment through problem-based learning in the online environment. In V. Wright, C. Sunal, & E. Wilson (Eds.), *Research on enhancing the interactivity of online learning* (pp. 65–78).Charlotte, NC: Information Age.

Prensky, M. (2001). Digital natives, digital immigrants. *On The Horizon, 9*(5), 1–6. Retrieved September 8, 2006, from http:// www.marcprensky.com%2Fwriting%2FPrensky%2520-%2520Digital%2520Natives%2C%2520Digital%2520Immigrants%2520-%2520Part1.pdf

Stansbury, M. (2008, March 26). Analysis: How multimedia can improve learning. *eSchool News.* Retrieved May 20, 2008, from http://www.eschoolnews.com/news/top-news/?i=53243

Stone, M. R. (2007, May 1). E-learning applications for career and technical education. *Techniques: Connecting Education and Careers.* Retrieved September 7, 2008, from http://www.thefreelibrary.com/E-learning applications for career and technical education-a0163705821

Sundberg, C., Sunal, D., & Mays, A. (2006). Problem solving and coping strategies used in online environments. In V. Wright, C. Sunal, & E. Wilson (Eds.), *Research on enhancing the interactivity of online learning* (pp. 175–196). Charlotte, NC: Information Age.

Tapscott, D., & Williams, A. D. (2006). *Wikinomics: How mass collaboration changes everything.* New York: Portfolio.

Yanes, M., Pena, C., & Curts, J. B. (2006). An emerging hybrid model for online learning. In V. Wright, C. Sunal, & E. Wilson (Eds.), *Research on enhancing the interactivity of online learning* (pp. 27–44).Charlotte, NC: Information Age.

Wang, V., King, K. P., & Nafukho, F. M. (2008). Historical perspectives of the different components of vocational education. In V. Wang & K. P. King, (Eds.), *Innovations in career and technical education: Strategic approaches towards workforce competencies around the globe* (pp. 49–68). Charlotte, NC: Information Age.

Wenger, E. (1999). *Communities of practice.* Cambridge: Cambridge University Press.

WGBH. (2008, Jan. 22). Growing up digital. *Frontline.* Retrieved September 3, 2008, from http://www.pbs.org/wgbh/pages/frontline/kidsonline/

Wiggins, G., & McTighe, J. (1998). *Understanding by design.* Alexandria, VA: ASCD. ERIC Reproduction No. ED 424 227).

Wonacott, M. E. (2001). *Implications of distance education for CTE* (ERIC Digest No. 227). Columbus, OH: ERIC Clearinghouse on Adult, Career, and Vocational Education. Retrieved September 10, 2008, from http://www.cete.org/acve/docs.dig227.pdf

Woods, P. (2001). *The U.S. Department of Education and student financial aid for distance education: An update.* Washington DC: ERIC Clearinghouse on Higher Education. ERIC Reproduction Doc No: ED 457 762

Zirkle, C. (2004). Distance education and career and technical education: A review of the research literature. *Journal of Vocational Education Research 28*(2). Retrieved September 2, 2008, from http://scholar.lib.vt.edu/ejournals/JVER/v28n2/zirkle.html

CHAPTER 11

TRAINING
AND DEVELOPMENT

Victor C. X. Wang
California State University, Long Beach

INTRODUCTION

Graduates of career and technical education (CTE) will be hired by various organizations, including but not limited to: regional occupational programs (ROP in California), adult schools, community colleges, public schools, the military, police and firefighter agencies, and human resource departments. Organizations seek the skills and knowledge these graduates have acquired from taking core courses in career and technical education. Once hired, graduates of CTE will be provided orientation programs that will assist in their transition into the workplace. The skills and knowledge they have acquired from taking courses in CTE may enable them to do some entry level jobs in these organizations. Employers may need graduates of CTE to perform more sophisticated jobs, requiring the orientation programs and in-depth training programs to be developed in tandem with any strategic objectives or in concert with other HR programs and/or critical operational areas of the organization. To perform well on their jobs in the organization, employees must seek to understand the entire organization and how the organization views them as employees. To most organizations,

Building Workforce Competencies in Career and Technical Education, pages 213–232
Copyright © 2009 by Information Age Publishing
213

employees are considered human assets and training and development is seen as an ongoing investment in these assets.

As employees' behavior and performance are considered important elements that will add value to organizations, the value of training and development as a major strategic issue for organizations cannot be underestimated (Mello, 2006). In addition, rapid changes in technology continue to cause increasing rates of skill obsolescence (Knowles, 1978). In order to remain competitive, organizations need to continue training their employees to use the best and latest technologies available. Continuous learning is needed among CTE graduates and practitioners in such a turbulent environment. Without continuous learning, CTE graduates and practitioners would find it hard to survive in this turbulent environment. Below Mello (2006) discusses the necessity of training and development in relationship to this kind of turbulent environment:

1. The redesign of work into jobs having broader responsibilities requires employees to assume more responsibility, take initiative, and further develop interpersonal skills to ensure their performance and success. Employees need to acquire a broader skill base and be provided with development opportunities to assist with team work, collaboration, and conflict management.
2. Mergers and acquisitions have greatly increased. These activities require integrating employees of one organization into another having a vastly different culture. When financial and performance results of merger and acquisition activity fall short of plans, the reason usually rests with people management system rather than operational or financial management systems.
3. Employees are moving from one employer to another with far more frequency than they did in the past. With less loyalty to a particular employer and more focus on the employees' own careers, more time must be spent on integrating new hires into the workplace.
4. The globalization of business operations requires CTE graduates and practitioners to acquire knowledge and skills related to language and cultural differences. (p. 402)

Indeed, if organizations wish to remain competitive in this knowledge-based society and global economy, they must underscore promotion from within, the career development of existing employees, and continual training and development opportunities of new hires (Wang, 2008). Above all, training and development programs must be aligned with organizations' goals and objectives (Robinson & Robinson, 1996). Without aligning these programs with organization's goals and objectives, employees will fail to understand the entire organization and their place in it. Organization's goals and objectives can set specific directions for training and development programs for employees in the organization. Employees are hired to contribute to the organization's goals and objectives and training and development programs will help them reach those goals and objectives (Mello, 2006). Goals and objectives and training and development have formed a dialectical relationship in any organizations.

With the passing of the *No Child Left Behind* legislation, training and development is being required to move to an "accountability" and "standards-based" orientation (Glatthorn, Boschee, & Whitehead, 2006). If programs in training and development are not effective, the *No Child Left Behind legislation* will remain on paper that cannot be implemented. Only when training and development moves to accountability and standards-based, will we see whether this legislation supports tangible training outcomes, hence resulting in a working dialectical relationship between goals and objectives and training and development. Translated into organizational strategies, training and development must be measured in behavioral terms (Tyler, 1949, 1950, 1957). In other words, organizational goals and objectives must be reached via training and development programs that will foster employees' abilities to contribute to these goals and objectives.

The goal of strategic training and development is to help develop a knowledgeable and flexible workforce (Gray & Herr, 1998; Robinson & Robinson, 1996). One of the benefits that training and development can provide is that well trained employees help improve bottom-line operating results, in other words, company performance, in addition to being more attractive targets of competitors' recruiting efforts. The next section of this chapter will address key characteristics of training, learning and development and their differences and then cover benefits of training and development. What will be covered may be generic. However, it is these generic features of training, learning and development and benefits of training and development that are covered in almost all textbooks for undergraduate and graduate students in the field of career and technical education. It is these generic features of these basic elements regarding training and development that can help lay a solid foundation for students in career and technical education before they enter the world of work.

TRAINING, LEARNING AND DEVELOPMENT— KEY CHARACTERISTICS AND DIFFERENCES

While training is defined as helping employees do their current work better, development is defined as preparing individuals for the future and focusing on learning and personal development (Ivancevich, 2007). In addition, training is the systematic process of altering the behavior of employees in a direction that will achieve organization goals. Training is related to present job skills and abilities. It has a current orientation and helps employees master specific skills and abilities needed to be successful. As training makes an attempt to improve employees' current or future performance, Ivancevich (2007) emphasizes the following specific points about training:

- A formal training program is an effort by the employer to provide opportunities for the employee to acquire job-related skills, attitudes, and knowledge.
- Learning is the act by which the individual acquires skills, knowledge, and abilities that result in a relatively permanent change in his or her behavior.
- Any behavior that has been learned is a skill. Therefore, improvement of skills is what training will accomplish. Motor skills, cognitive skills, and interpersonal skills are targets of training programs. (p. 399)

Significant points derived from Ivancevich's (2007) key points about training comply with the three domains of educational objectives: Psychomotor, Cognitive and Affective. Indeed, after each training session, trainers can ask such questions as "Can trainees do differently? Can trainees think differently? Can trainees feel differently" If the answer to each question is a positive yes, then the three domains of educational (or training) objectives are achieved. While training involves employees acquiring knowledge and learning skills that they will be able to add value to organizations, employee development involves learning that will aid the organization and employee later in the employee's career. It is true the term learning is used rather than training to emphasize the point that the activities engaged in as part of this developmental process are *broad-based* and involve much more than straightforward acquisition of manual or technical skills (Bierema, 2002).

Learning is more emphasized for the training of CTE graduates and practitioners because the ideas of Abraham Maslow (1908–1970) about human motivation have been and are still influential in the United States. According to Maslow (1970), human needs can be ordered in a hierarchy from lower to higher: physiological, safety and security, belongingness, esteem, and self-actualization. In order for a higher need to appear, it is necessary that that lower needs have been satisfied up to a certain extent. A starving person, one whose physiological needs are not at all satisfied, will not be motivated by anything else than the quest for food, and so forth. The top of Maslow's hierarchy, often pictured as a pyramid, is taken by the motive of self-actualization: realizing to the fullest possible extent the creative potential present within the individual. This can be the supreme motivation in an individualist society like the United States (Hofstede & Hofstede,

2005, p. 108). Without a doubt, learning is directly associated with Maslow's hierarchy of human needs and it is learning that can add to employees' skills and knowledge to meet the challenges the organization faces from its external environment. Realizing one's fullest potential in CTE not only involves learning the basic survival skills in the field, but also *life wide and life long learning* so that future employees of any organizations will add to their employees' skills and add meaning to life (Lamdin & Fugate, 1997). Given the above analysis, the emphasis on learning instead of on training seems to be justified. Since the bottom line in organizations is profitability, it seems understandable that the current focus on learning instead of training emphasizes results rather than process, making such an approach more palatable to senior executives. If we take into consideration Maslow's hierarchy of human needs and developmental process rather than mere acquisition of manual and technical skills, we should rely more on learning than on just training in CTE.

BENEFITS OF TRAINING AND DEVELOPMENT

Training and development provide multiple benefits for organizations. Among the many benefits, Noe, Hollenbeck, Gerhart and Wright (2008, p. 266) singled out the following:

Training and development can

- Increase employees' knowledge of foreign competitors and cultures, which is critical for success in foreign markets.
- Help ensure that employees have the basic skills to work with new technology, such as robots and computer-assisted manufacturing processes.
- Help employees understand how to work effectively in terms to contribute to product and service quality.
- Ensure that the company's culture emphasizes innovation, creativity, and learning.
- Ensure employment security by providing new ways for employees to contribute to the company when their jobs change, their interests change, or their skills become obsolete.
- Prepare employees to accept and work more effectively with each other, particularly with minorities and women.

Whether we agree with the above authors on these benefits or not, the benefits they discussed are general benefits that most employers and employees embrace with wide open arms. To add to these benefits, Mello (2006) posits that training involves some kind of change for employees: changes in how to they do their jobs, how to relate to others, the conditions under which they perform, or changes in their job responsibilities (p. 404). Again, Mello's concept on change as a result of training does not deviate too much from the three domains of educational (training) objectives, namely, psychomotor, cognitive and affective. Change involves change in one's knowledge (cognitive), skills (psychomotor) and attitudes (affective). The kind of change Mezirow (1991), Cranton (1994) and King (2005) were interested in promoting was change in one's perspectives as a result of learning or training. While some employees may find any kind of change threatening, others welcome change that training and development can bring about.

Strategically targeted training in critical skills and knowledge bases will result in employees' marketability and employability security that is critical in the current environment of rapidly developing technology and changing jobs and work processes (Decenzo & Robbins, 2007). Companies strive to seek out and hire knowledge workers rather than workers with narrowly defined technical skills. Training and development will add to the "well-rounded" education a new hire has received from career and technical education. Training can help enhance bottom line and general efficiency and profitability measures when it can create more flexible employees who can assume varied responsibilities and have a more holistic understanding of what the organization does and the role they play in the organization's success (Mello, 2006, p. 405). Those companies that can provide employees with broader knowledge and skills and supporting and nurturing ongoing employee development help make employees more accountable for results. In addition, strategic training enables HR and training professionals to get intimately involved with the business, partner with operating managers to help solve their problems, and make significant contributions to organizational results (Mathis & Jackson, 2008, p. 262). Worthy of note is the fact that it was Mello (2006) who first began to address strategic training among so many authors who write about training and development. Indeed, strategic training must make employees accountable for results. Otherwise, it should not be termed as strategic training. If organizations view training as having short-term effects rather than long-term effects, they are less likely to create and support a culture that fosters employee development. Although training alone can not solve most employee or organizational problems, well targeted training, especially aligned with strategic training, can not only address specific needs but also minimize the need to conduct any extensive or remedial training among new employees (Mello, 2006).

TRAINING NEEDS ASSESSMENT

One important approach to developing successful training programs involves four basic steps: *needs assessment* (Witkin & Altschuld, 1995), *the estab-*

lishment of objectives and measures, delivery of the training, and *evaluation.* This approach is in agreement with Ralph Tyler's (1949) rationale. Although needs assessment was covered in the chapter on curriculum development in the book, needs assessment in this chapter entails a somewhat different approach. Ivancevich (2007, p. 399) indicates that needs assessment is a process that is used to determine if and what type of training is necessary. It usually involves an organizational, person, and task analysis. Traditionally, needs assessments addresses what it is and what it should be in order to determine the gap between the present level of trainees and the desired level of trainees.

Based on Ivancevich's approach, first of all, needs assessment places training within an appropriate organizational context. Training objectives must be identified among three levels: organizational, task, and individual. In terms of organizational level, culture, politics, structure and strategy must be considered. This analysis must consider how the training will help the organization in meeting its objectives and training may affect day-to-day workplace dynamics within the organization (Robinson & Robinson, 1996). Task level is not unfamiliar to graduates in CTE as they have usually taken a course titled *Occupational Analysis* (this course has been offered by most programs in career and technical education throughout the country) which looks at specific duties and responsibilities assigned to different jobs and the types of skills and knowledge needed to perform each task (French, 2007). Furthermore, students in CTE are taught how to break down the task into steps of procedures, which can be found in *Dictionary of Occupational Titles* to assist workers/employees with task analysis (See also Chapter 5 in the book).

According to Taylor (1911), the father of scientific management, this level of task analysis is conducted to achieve better control of employee performance on the job. It is true task analysis is conducted so that the job can be redesigned to provide the employee with direct feedback on his or her performance (Berman, Bowman, West, & Wart, 2006). The individual level of analysis requires an assessment of employees' present level of knowledge and skills relating to their learning styles (Knowles, Holton, & Swanson, 2005), personality (Rogers, 1951, 1961, 1969, 1980), and interpersonal styles in interacting with others. In some organizations, employers conduct a survey developed by McGregor (1960, 1967) to determine whether employees are X-type oriented or Y-type oriented. See McGregor's comparison of assumptions about human nature and behavior contained in Table 11.1 below.

Assumptions about theory X persons and theory Y persons (Wang, 2006) have great implications for training and development. Rogers (1972) made meaningful connections between McGregor's assumptions about human nature and behavior and assumptions relevant to training and develop-

TABLE 11.1   A Comparison of Assumptions about Human Nature and Behavior

Theory X assumptions about human nature (McGregor Controlling)	Theory Y assumptions about Human Nature (Releasing)
The average human being inherently dislikes work and will avoid it if he can.	The expenditure of physical and mental effort is as natural as play or rest.
Because of this characteristically human dislike of work, most people must be coerced, controlled and threatened in the interest of organizational objectives.	External control and threat of when punishment is not the only means for bringing about effort toward organizational objectives. Man will exercise self-direction and self control in the service of objectives to which he is committed.
The average human being prefers to be directed, wishes to avoid responsibility, has relatively little ambition, wants security above all.	Commitment to objectives is a function of the rewards associated with their achievement.

Source: McGregor, 1960, 1967

TABLE 11.2   Rogers' Assumptions Based on Theory X Persons and Assumptions Based on Theory Y Persons

Assumptions implicit in training and development based on controlling (Theory X)	Assumptions relevant to training and development based on releasing (Theory Y)
The trainee cannot be trusted to pursue his own learning.	Human beings have a natural potentiality for learning.
Presentation equals learning.	Significant learning takes place when the subject is perceived by the trainee as relevant to his own purpose.
The aim of education is to accumulate brick upon brick of factual knowledge.	Much significant learning is acquired through doing.
The truth is known.	Learning is facilitated by trainee's responsible participation in the learning process.
Creative citizens develop from passive learners.	
Evaluation is education and education is evaluation.	

Source: Rogers, 1972

ment. His connections are still evident and helpful today. Table 11.2 addresses Rogers' (1972) assumptions derived from McGregor's original assumptions about human nature and behavior (as cited in Knowles, 1978, p. 102).

TABLE 11.3 Levels of Needs Assessment

Organizational level
- How does the training relate to organizational objectives?
- How does the training impact day-to-day workplace dynamics?
- What are the costs and expected benefits of the training?

Task level
- What responsibilities are assigned to the job?
- What skills or knowledge are needed for successful performance?
- Should the learning setting be the actual job setting?
- What are the implications of mistakes?
- How can the job provide the employee with direct feedback?
- How similar to or different from the training needs of other jobs?
- What are the needs of this job?

Individual level
- What knowledge, skills, and abilities do trainees already have?
- What are the trainees' learning styles?
- What special needs do the trainees have?

Both McGregor's survey and Rogers' assumptions about training and development will assist in conducting a needs assessment among employees of various organizations. Conducting successful needs assessment on the three levels involves asking pertinent questions. Mello (2006, p. 406) summarizes these questions in a table (see Table 11.3).

TRAINING OBJECTIVES

Objectives should flow directly from the assessed needs (Ivancevich, 2007) and must be expressed in behavioral terms (p. 407). In other words, objectives must be observable and measurable from management's perspective. By using behaviorally based objectives, the intent of the training program is identified. A vague and ambiguous objective might suggest that the training purpose is not important. Taylor's (1911) scientific management aims at accurately measuring and evaluating employees' performance. The more employers know about how employees' jobs are performed, the more accurately employers are able to measure and evaluate employees' performance. If an organization's objectives are written in vague terms, employees' performance cannot be accurately measured or evaluated. Should organizations have no plan for measuring organization's objectives, training programs are of little value to the organization in the long run. The next question to ask is where can we find an organization's objectives? They can be found in the organization's performance management system. They can be derived from the performance deficiencies of an organization's em-

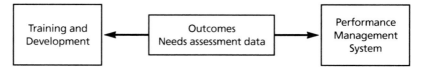

Figure 11.1 Relationship between training and development and performance management. *Source:* Adapted from Mello, 2006, p. 446.

ployees. The purpose of performance management is to facilitate employee development. Mello (2006, p. 446) supports this view by stating,

> By assessing deficiencies in performance levels and skills, an organization can determine specific training and development needs. In fact, the performance feedback process can be designed to provide information to fuel the organization's training and development programs. Assessing individual and team strengths and weaknesses can allow employee and team development plans to be established.

For a visual effect of the relationship between training and development and performance management, see Mello's (2006, p. 446) figure (Figure 11.1).

TRAINING DESIGN AND DELIVERY

Prior to its delivery, critical issues revolving around the design of the training must be considered. One critical issue that comes to mind is that of learners' prior experience. Over the years, employees have accumulated a rich reservoir of experience from their former education, training and jobs. Prior experience does not mean that an experienced learner will learn faster. Often times, prior experience or learning has established habits act as a block or obstacle in the learning process. In such a situation, trainers' job is to make learner's prior experience as the best resource for learning instead of barrier to learning. This is often easier said than done as learners have formed a fixed mindset. Mello (2006) has this observation, "the more experience someone has in behaving in a certain way, the more difficult it may be to modify the response they display. When individuals are stressed, they tend to revert to conditioned behavior" (p. 407). One example to illustrate how prior experience may serve as a barrier to learning can be: the new law in California requires drivers to use a hand-device to assist them in making a phone call from their cell phones while driving on highways. Since many drivers have had this conditioned behavior (calling without a hand-free device) for a long time, common sense tells us CHP officers will issue many tickets to violators of this new law before drivers can fully abide by it.

Another issue that must be considered is transfer. Transfer is defined as whether the trainee or learner can actually perform the new skills or use the new knowledge on the job. Mello (2006) defines transfer as the extent to which the trainee or learner is able to "transfer" the learning to the actual job setting. The reason transfer has become an important issue is that some training programs are not conducted on the jobs although 60 percent of training occurs on the job (Ivancevich, 2007, p. 408). However, some 40 percent of training programs are conducted in the classrooms as emphasized by the Russian training system in the book (this was estimated from Ivancevich's book).

One interesting approach to training and development is rotation (Ivancevich, 2007) which allows new hires to sample different kinds of work within the organization and determine an optimal fit between their needs and interests and those of the organization. Rotation programs can be expensive in the short run but they represent a longer-term investment in employees that can provide significant benefits to an organization (Mello, 2006, p. 404). Employees who have gone through rotation programs and cross trained not only understand their individual jobs better, but also can be reassigned as business and organizations conditions change. Indeed, a number of methods can be used to deliver training programs once they are designed. Mathis and Jackson (2008) remind trainers to take into consideration a number of variables when selecting training approaches. Worthy of note are the following common variables that trainers must look into before finalizing a specific training approach:

- Nature of training
- Number of trainees
- Self-paced vs. guided
- E-learning vs. traditional learning
- Time allotted
- Subject matter
- Individual vs. team
- Training resources/costs
- Geographic locations
- Completion timeline

Given the ubiquitous nature of the computer, many training programs are conducted online (See Chapter 10, *"E-learning in CTE"* in this book.). In other words, the conditions under which employees are trained are vastly different from those in which they actually work. If trainees or learners fail to apply their skills and knowledge acquired via training programs from different work sites, training would be useless. Those responsible for training must ensure that training provides maximum transfer. Once issues revolving around the design of training are solved, the next item that comes to mind is the delivery of the training. Although novel training approaches have been experimented with and introduced, the traditional job instruction training (JIT) methods as given in the War Manpower Commission's bulletin "Training within Industry Series" in 1945 has been used by most organizations (as cited in Ivancevich, 2007, p. 408). See Figure 11.2.

Here is what you must do to get ready to teach a job:
1. Decide what the learner must be taught in order to do the job efficiently, safely, economically, and intelligently.
2. Have the right tools, equipment, supplies, and material ready. Think about the Russian training method covered in Chapter 5 in the book.
3. Have the workplace properly arranged, just as the worker will be expected to keep it.

Then, you should instruct the learner by the following four basic steps: The following four basic steps are also called "four step instruction" by industry standards by other authors (Wang, 2008). Four step instruction reflects one's behavioral teaching philosophy and student learning outcomes must be written in behavioral terms. Four step instruction method may clash with other teaching philosophies such as progressive and humanistic philosophies as emphasized in adult education by adult education leaders. Regardless, four step instruction has proved to be effective especially for on the job training, adult basic education.

Step I—Preparation (of the learner)
1. Put the learner at ease.
2. Find out what he or she already knows about the job.
3. Get the learner interested and desirous of learning the job.

Step II—Presentation (of the operations and knowledge)
1. Tell, show, illustrate, and question in order to put over the new knowledge and operations.
2. Instruct slowly, clearly, completely, and patiently, one point at a time.
3. Check, question, and repeat.
4. Make sure the learner really knows.

Step III—Performance tryout
1. Test the learner by having him or her perform the job.
2. Ask questions beginning with why, how, when, or where.
3. Observe performance, correct errors, and repeat instructions if necessary.
4. Continue until you know that the learner knows.

Step IV—Follow up
1. Put the employee on his or her own.
2. Check frequently to be sure the learner follows instructions.
3. Taper off extra supervision and close follow-up until the person is qualified to work with normal supervision.

Remember—if the learner hasn't learned, the teacher hasn't taught. Note the last reminder of this table. The four step instruction does not focus on self-directed learning on the part of learners. In fact, leading adult educators such as Rogers (1951, 1961, 1969, 1972, 1980) and Knowles (1978) posit that we cannot teach another learner, and that we have to facilitate his or her learning.

Figure 11.2 Job Instruction Training (JIT) methods. *Source:* Adapted from Ivancevich, 2007, p. 408.

The delivery of the training will not be effective unless it is conducted within a larger supportive organizational environment. From workers, supervisors to CEOs, everyone must have a positive attitude towards training programs. If coworkers publicly express negative concerns about the training, this may cause learners to be predisposed against the training. It is natural that some coworkers have prejudice against training programs. This may have resulted from culture, politics, and organizational structure. When this happens, trainers need to create a positive learning environment where learning can best occur.

Transfer can be facilitated by delivering the training in an environment that stimulates the actual conditions as much as possible. Hofstede and Hofstede (2005) indicated that in this individualist country, USA, self-actualization by every individual is an ultimate goal. Therefore, training teaches the honest sharing of feelings. To achieve greater independent self, learners must be challenged as much as possible in training. In some cases, it may be feasible to provide direct, on-the-job training where the employee is trained under the exact working conditions in which he or she will be expected to perform. This falls squarely in line with the principles and philosophy of career and technical education as emphasized by Prosser in chapter two of this book (Building workforce competencies in career and technical education, 2009).

In other cases, on-the-job training may not be possible. Therefore, the Russian training system must be used. The Russian training method takes place in a classroom whereby instructors increase the difficulty level of graded exercises based on students' learning abilities (See Chapter 5, "*Comparing the Russian, the Sloyd, and the Arts and Crafts Movement Training Systems*" for detail). Fire fighters do not learn to put out fires by putting out real fires and being told what to do. Their training involves extensive exposure to simulated fire conditions, which test their learning and ability to react to a variety of situations. The same thing can be said about training police officers trying to deal with terrorist attacks on the streets. One more example is the fact that emergency management officers do not learn to handle crisis situations in real crises such as earthquakes, hurricanes, or tornadoes. Rather, they learn to complete their jobs in simulated conditions. In addition, according to Mello (2006), off-the-job training allows learners to focus on their learning by minimizing interruptions or distractions that might take place in the actual work environment. By conducting training in a classroom, case studies, role-plays, interactive and experiential methods of learning can be used (Dessler, 2008). The traditional JIT supports the behaviorist techniques. Based on the different learning objectives, two other training methods may be useful. Towards this end, Ivancevich (2007, p. 413) shares a definitive figure (See Figure 11.3) with trainers and trainees.

Techniques			
Objective	**Humanist**	**Cognitivist**	**Behaviorist**
Knowledge Transmit Information	Inductive discussion Inductive game Debrief experience Relevance discussion Active elaboration	Lecture/film Graphic illustration Panel/interview SME Class presentation Reading Question and answer Review	Multiple-choice Memorization Association
Verify information **Skill**	Confirmatory discussion	Test	Question with answer
Induce reponse	Discuss action Visualize action Inductive case study	List steps Demonstration Success stories	Behavioral model Behavioral samples Prompting/cueing
Strengthen response (practice)	Mental rehearsal Project	Case study	Worksheets Skill drill (game) Simulation Role playing
Apply the skill	Action plan Planning guide Elaboration (skit) Contract	Coaching/feedback	Realistic practice Job aid prompts On-job reinforcement
Attitude	Self-assessment Encounter experience Discussion of beliefs Reverse role playing Guided reflection Group decision	Authority statement Vicarious experience Debate Testimony	Assessment Pleasant experience Reinforcement

Figure 11.3 Objectives of three approaches to learning. *Source:* Adapted from Ivancevich, 2007, p. 413.

Another excellent delivery method is the organizational training conducted online with the advent of computer technology. The Internet also offers learning and training environment in which trainers and learners can assume either a directing relationship or helping relationship (Wang, 2005). Those who oppose training online fail to recognize the following potential benefits:

1. It can be self-paced, allowing different individuals to learn and absorb material at their own level of comfort and understanding (Mello, 2006).
2. It can be designed so that it is adaptive to different needs and can be customized for different employees (Brown, 2006).

3. It can be designed to be easy to schedule: For instance, an employee may turn on a computer at the office or at home to participate in a webinar or webacast. There is no need to leave one's desk or coordinate schedules with trainers or trainees, nor a need to have trainers and trainees in the same physical space (Mello, 2006).
4. Computer-based training can also reduce travel costs, and therefore, can be less expensive to administer for organizations when units are geographically dispersed (King & Griggs, 2006).

Of course, training online is not all rosy. The major barriers must be considered. First, learners must be internally motivated and take both initiative and responsibility for learning (Knowles, Holton, & Swanson, 2005). In adult learning, this principle is defined as self-directed learning. And research demonstrates that when learners/trainees are not internally/intrinsically motivated to learn, training online does not succeed and has a lower retention rate.

For example, consider if one is delivering a self-paced distance education course, instead of an instructor-guided course. When trainers deliver online training in one location, who will support and facilitate trainees' learning (if they are not internally motivated to learn) in other locations, especially remote locations or in different countries?

Second, the cost of producing quality online training, interactive materials can be very expensive. Adequate financial resources to develop online training materials are needed. Therefore, organizations need to appropriate sufficient funds and resources to fund and develop these instructional materials. The lower quality, the less interactive, the less dialogue based courses, will result in lower outcomes and retention (Brown, 2006; King & Griggs, 2006).

Third, trainers have to update their training content on a regular basis; if it becomes stagnant people will find it irrelevant. Therefore, one cannot have a false expectation that once created, instructional materials are never to be invested in again. They need continued re-evaluation and re-design (Brown, 2006).

Fourth, online training is not for everyone. Although technology makes it possible for trainers and trainees to "see" each other via videos, two-way communication is limited given the fact that not every trainee can afford to use advanced technology. However, with the increasing availability of low cost and in some cases, free solutions for videoconferencing, changes are coming in this issue which will eventually reach training and development.

Of course, the above observations have been used in business and may not apply towards online training in educational settings such as training in CTE. For a fuller discussion on E-learning for CTE students, please refer to Chapter 10 of the book. Chapter 10 offers more in-depth discussion on e-learning, particularly for CTE students.

EVALUATION

Training evaluation refers to evaluation of training comparing the post-training results to the pre-training objectives of managers, trainers, and trainees. The most common questions training evaluation can be: Can employees think differently? Can employees feel differently? Can employees act differently? These three questions are closely related to the three domains of educational objectives: Cognitive, Affective and Psychomotor. Some scholars (Mathis & Jackson, 2008) criticize training as being conducted with little thought of measuring and evaluating it to see how well it worked. The reality has been that training objectives are bound by behaviorist philosophy. In other words, objectives must be measured in behavioral terms. Scholars and practitioners have invented formative and summative evaluation techniques to measure training objectives to determine whether training should be continued in its current form, modified, or eliminated altogether (Mello, 2006). Of the many evaluation models, Kirkpatrick's four levels of training evaluation have been highly regarded and practiced in the field of training and development.

According to Kirkpatrick (1994), training evaluation can take place on four levels and these levels form a hierarchy, meaning that lower levels are prerequisites for higher levels. This hierarchy is similar to Bloom's (1956) taxonomy. According to this taxonomy, lower order thinking skills (characterized by knowledge, comprehension, and application) are prerequisites for higher order thinking skills (characterized by analysis, synthesis and evaluation) (Wang & Farmer, 2008). Like Bloom's taxonomy, the evaluation of training becomes successively more difficult as it moves from measuring reaction to measuring learning to measuring behavior and then to measuring results. By the way, Kirkpatrick (1994) identified four levels of training evaluation: *Reaction, Learning, Behavior and Results.* Given the four levels of training evaluation, most employers would view training as a strategic performance contributor if the training affects behavior and results rather than reaction and learning:

> **Reaction:** This first level of trainees can be evaluated by conducting interviews or asking trainees to answer questionnaires. Concrete questions can be: Did the trainees enjoy the training programs, trainers, facilities? Do they think that the training program was useful? What can be improved?

Learning: This second level of trainees can be evaluated by measuring how well trainees have learned facts, ideas, concepts, theories, and attitudes. Tests are commonly used. A concrete question that can be asked can be: To what extent do trainees have greater knowledge or skill after the training program than they did before?

Behavior: This third level measures what trainees can do on the job after the training. Trainees can be interviewed and evaluators can observe their job performance. The most common question can be: Are trainees behaving differently on the job after training. Another concrete question can be: Are they using the skills and knowledge they learned in training?

Results: Employers evaluate results by measuring the effect of training on the achievement of organizational objectives. Results can be productivity, turnover, quality, time, sales, and costs. The difficulty with measuring results is pinpointing whether changes were actually the result of training or of other major factors (Mathis & Jackson, 2008). The concrete question can be: Is the organization or unit better because of the training?

Regarding the value to organizations and how easy or difficult the levels of training evaluation can be, Mathis and Jackson (2008, p. 282) provide a figure (See Figure 11.4).

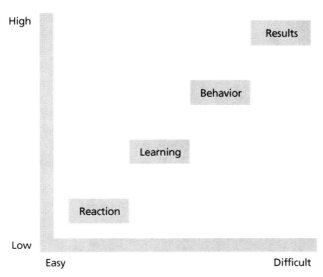

Figure 11.4 Levels of training evaluation. Source: Adapted from Mathis and Jackson, 2008, p. 282.

PERFORMANCE CONSULTING TREND

Starting in the 1990s, there was a new trend in training and development, that is, organizations focus more on performance consulting than on the traditional model (Robinson & Robinson, 1996). (See Chapter 8, *"Training in China"*). Performance consulting refers to the process in which a trainer and the organizational client work together to determine what needs to be done to improve organizational and individual results. Performance consulting may be useful when the traditional model does not provide solutions to organizational or individual performance problems. According to Mathis and Jackson (2008, p. 263), performance consulting takes a broad approach by:

- Focusing on identifying and addressing root causes of performance problems.
- Recognizing that the interaction of individual and organizational factors influences employee performance.
- Documenting the actions and accomplishments of high performers and comparing them with actions of more physical performers.

CONCLUSION

Graduates of career and technical education may tend to think that they have been well educated and trained and that they will be able to perform any job in any organization. The truth is there is always a gap between what students learn and what employers want in the workplace. While organizations offer training opportunities to assist in employees' transition into the workplace, career and development opportunities will depend on employees' own learning. For instance, self-directed learning which may be used for their continued professional learning throughout their lives in both personal and professional realms, may lead to full self-actualization in Maslow's terms (1970).

Training and development of employees is a key strategic issue facing any organization. Although scholars and practitioners bitterly debate what training approaches would best improve organizational performance, the traditional model of training has endured. First and foremost, trainers must address benefits of training and development. Second, a needs assessment must be conducted to determine whether there is a gap between the present level of employees and the desired level of employees. If no gap is identified, no training is needed. Third, once a gap is determined, clear and measurable training objectives must be written. Fourth, design of training and delivery of training must revolve around training objectives. Finally, evaluation must be conducted to decide whether training has worked to improve company performance.

Regardless of the multiple new trends in training and development, which will come and go over the years ahead, the traditional model covered in this chapter will continue to prove to be useful. This chapter provides skills and knowledge bases necessary for training and development to achieve strategic objectives. Many changes will continue to occur in organizational contexts. To cope with change, organizations mandate that specific, targeted, strategic training and development initiatives should be conducted as a pre-requisite for continued success.

REFERENCES

Berman, E. M., Bowman, J. S., West, J. P., & Wart, M. V. (2006). *Human resource management in public service: Paradoxes, processes, and problems* (2nd ed.). Thousand Oaks, CA: Sage.

Bierema, L. L. (2002). A feminist approach to HRD research. *Human Resource Development Review, 1*(2), 244–268.

Bloom, B. S. (Ed.). (1956). *Taxonomy of educational objectives.* London: Longman.

Brown, G. (2006). New perspectives on instructional effectiveness through distance education. In K. P. King & J. K. Griggs (Eds.), *Harnessing innovative technology in higher education: Access, policy, & instruction* (pp. 97–110). Madison, WI: Atwood.

Cranton, P. (1994). *Understanding and promoting transformative learning.* San Francisco: Jossey-Bass.

Decenzo, D. A., & Robbins, S. P. (2007). *Fundamentals of human resource management* (9th ed.). Hoboken, NJ: John Wiley & Sons.

Dessler, G. (2008). *Human resource management* (11th ed.). Upper Saddle River, NJ: Pearson Prentice Hall.

French, W. L. (2007). *Human resource management* (6th ed.). Boston: Houghton Mifflin.

Glatthorn, A. A., Boschee, F., & Whitehead, B. M. (2006). *Curriculum leadership: Development and implementation.* Thousand Oaks, CA: Sage.

Gray, K. C., & Herr, E. L. (1998). *Workforce education.* Boston: Allyn & Bacon.

Hofstede, G., & Hofstede, G. J. (2005). *Cultures and organizations: Software of mind* (2nd ed.). New York: McGraw-Hill.

Ivancevich, J. M. (2007). *Human resource management* (10th ed.). New York: McGraw-Hill Irwin.

King, K. P. (2005). *Bringing transformative learning to life.* Malabar FL: Krieger.

King, K. P., & Griggs, J. K. (Eds.) (2006). *Harnessing innovative technology in higher education: Access, policy, & instruction.* Madison, WI: Atwood.

Kirkpatrick, D. L. (1994). Four steps to measuring training effectiveness. In D. L. Kirkpatrick (Ed.), *Evaluating training programs: The four levels* (pp. 19–25). San Francisco: Berrett-Koehler.

Knowles, M. S. (1978). *The adult learner: A neglected species* (2nd ed.). Houston: Gulf.

Knowles, M. S., Holton, E., & Swanson, A. (2005). *The adult learner* (6th ed.). Boston, MA: Elsevier Butterworth Heinemann.

Lamdin, L., & Fugate, M. (1997). *Elderlearning: New frontier in an aging society.* Phoenix, AZ: ORYX Press.

Maslow, A. H. (1970). *Motivation and personality* (2nd ed.). New York: Harper & Row.

Mathis R. L., & Jackson, J. H. (2008). *Human resource management* (12th ed.). Mason, OH: Thomson South-Western.

McGregor, D. (1960). *The human side of enterprise.* New York: McGraw-Hill.

McGregor, D. (1967). *Leadership and motivation.* Cambridge: The Massachusetts Institute Press.

Mello, J. A. (2006). *Strategic human resource management* (2nd ed.). Mason, OH: Thomson South-Western.

Mezirow, J. (1991). *Transformative dimensions of adult learning.* San Francisco: Jossey-Bass.

Noe, R. A., Hollenbeck, J. R., Gerhart, B., & Wright, P. M. (2008). *Human resource management: Gaining a competitive advantage* (6th ed.). New York: McGraw-Hill Irwin.

Robinson, D. G., & Robinson, J. C. (1996). *Performance consulting: Moving beyond training.* San Francisco: Berrett-Koehler.

Rogers, C. R. (1951). *Client-centered therapy.* Boston: Houghton-Mifflin.

Rogers, C. R. (1961). *On become a person.* Boston: Houghton-Mifflin.

Rogers, C. R. (1969). *Freedom to learn.* Columbus, OH: Merrill.

Rogers, C. R. (1972). Bringing together ideas and feelings in learning. *Learning Today, 5,* 32–43.

Rogers, C. R. (1980). *A way of being.* Boston: Houghton-Mifflin.

Taylor, F. W. (1911). *The principles of scientific management.* New York: Harper & Bros.

Tyler, R. (1949). *Basic principles of curriculum and instruction.* Chicago: University of Chicago Press.

Tyler, R. W. (1950). *Basic principles of curriculum and instruction.* University of Chicago Press.

Tyler, R. W. (1957). *The curriculum then and now. In Proceedings of the 1956 Invitational Conference on Testing Problems.* Princeton, NJ: Educational Testing Service.

Wang, V. (2008). Learning organizations versus static organizations in the context of e-HRM. In T. Torres, & M. Arias (Eds.), *Encyclopedia of human resources information systems: Challenges in e-HRM* (pp. 617–622). Hershey, PA: IGI Global.

Wang, V. C. X. (2005). Perceptions of Teaching Preferences of Online Instructors. *Journal on Excellence in College Teaching, 16*(3), 33–54.

Wang, V. C. X. (2006). A Chinese work ethic in a global community. *International Journal of Vocational Education and Training, 14*(2), 39–52.

Wang, V. C. X., & Farmer, S. J. (2008). Adult teaching methods in China and Bloom's taxonomy. *International Journal for the Scholarship of Teaching and Learning, 2*(2), 1–15. Retrieved September 20, 2008, from http://academics.georgiasouthern.edu/ijsotl/v2n2/articles/_Wang/index.htm

Witkin, B. R., & Altschuld, J. W. (1995). *Planning and conducting needs assessments: A practical guide.* Thousand Oaks, CA: Sage.

CHAPTER 12

PERSPECTIVES OF A HEALTHY WORK ETHIC IN A 21ST-CENTURY INTERNATIONAL COMMUNITY

Ernest Brewer
The University of Tennessee

Gregory C. Petty
The University of Tennessee

Traditionally, we have attributed the development of the work ethic to historic and ancient values and mores spawned by religious and socially acceptable beliefs. The 21st century, however, is creating a world society based on instant communication and global competition. Young people in developing countries are rapidly catching up with their peers in industrialized countries with regard to their use and adaptation of technology and their expectations for leisure and luxury and better safety and health practices

Building Workforce Competencies in Career and Technical Education, pages 233–245
Copyright © 2009 by Information Age Publishing

on the job. We need to explore these perspectives and the dynamics of developing a work ethic in a modem world.

INTRODUCTION

The nature of work and the manner for which young people develop a healthy work ethic is changing (McCortney & Engels, 2003; Pogson, Cober, Doverspike, & Rogers, 2003). Changes in the global nature of jobs, diversity in the workplace, unemployment, and possibly even changes in personalities of individuals themselves are creating work ethic havoc. Today we are a world market economy. With instant (and sustained) communication, prevalent outsourcing of jobs, and international competition, all of us are tied to an international workforce community (Hudelson, 1992; McCortney & Engels). Worldwide recognition and response to the disaster of the Asian Tsunami, events of September 11, 2001, and the recent corporate ethics failures of Enron and Martha Stewart and others has altered the landscape of working-class citizens (Baker, Jacobs, & Tickle-Degnen, 2003). Perhaps what we have adopted and have known as the Protestant Work Ethic as first recognized and identified by Max Weber is an ideal not acceptable to 21st-century workers (Baker et at, 2003; McCortney & Engels, 2003; Niles & Harris-Bowlsbey, 2002).

Today it is important for us to reflect on the forces affecting workers from all parts of the world. To better understand the complex nature of how a positive work ethic is developed, many professionals, particularly baby boomers, need to change their perspective of the world of work (McCortney & Engels, 2003). The concerns of business leaders and workforce educators alone are not enough to improve a young worker's work ethic (Clark, 2003; Petty, 1997).

To better prepare young people for work, it seems proper to review why we work, the value and meaning of work, and how we can foster and develop a positive work ethic. With a view to the history of vocational education and training and the work ethic and to the roots of our profession, perhaps we can improve the future.

WHY WE WORK

People work because they need to work. This observation seems to be a commonly held tenet for work. For some, work provides an important sense of achievement and belonging. It brings meaning to the day and provides some level of self-efficacy. For others, work is a means to an end. People work to earn money and to accumulate property. The need may be driven by several factors, foremost of which is economic.

However, economic needs do not explain the emotional needs expressed by the increasing numbers of retirees who return to work to fulfill intrinsic, even therapeutic needs (Brewer, Campbell, & Petty, 2001). This is but one of the issues regarding the value and meaning of work that complicates its study.

SEVEN VIEWPOINTS ON WORK

An overview and analysis of work reveals seven basic tenets of work. Everyone has a different viewpoint toward work. If the task is pleasurable or is performed among mends and family, work becomes an enjoyable experience. However, if work is drudgery providing little or no emotional satisfaction, it can pose a negative impact for the worker.

Seven viewpoints toward labor relations and workforce education and development suggest that: (a) work is continuous and leads to additional activity, (b) work is productive and produces goods and services, (c) work requires physical and mental exertion, (d) work has socio-psychological aspects, (e) work is performed on a regular or scheduled basis, (f) work requires a degree of constraint and, (g) work is performed for a personal purpose (intrinsic or extrinsic).

WORK RATIONALE

For our discussion we will start with the basic premise in life: Everyone must work. Philosophers have argued that the purpose of work is to distinguish leisure time from other forms of personal time. Some may work because they must make a living whereas others work to maintain a lifestyle or to fulfill obligations. Work can bring great personal pleasure as well as help other people in the process.

One perspective of work comes from Fedorov (1990), a Russian philosopher, who spoke primarily of the learned and the unlearned and that human property (extrinsic rewards) and human dignity (morality and happiness) is the inner spiritual life given power of work itself. This perspective implies the dichotomy of work-it is both extrinsic and intrinsic.

Karl Marx, the German Philosopher, did not believe that all people worked the same way, or that how one works is entirely personal and individual. Instead, he argued that work is a social activity, and that the conditions and forms under and through which people work are socially determined and change over time (Whelan, 1999).

Looking at the literature over time may reveal some insight into our own beliefs about work. Indeed, we are not the first to explore the value and meaning of work. The ancient Greeks were reported to have published much on the subject.

THE MEANING OF WORK IN EARLY CIVILIZATIONS

Greeks

How did individuals from early civilizations come to view work? From Homer, who we learned much about human development, archaeological as well as sociological, we can explore early ancient Greek culture. Homer recorded the Greek belief that the gods hated humankind and out of spite and condemned humanity to toil (Bennett, 1926; Mosse, 1969). To the ruling classes of ancient Greece, work was a curse. Tilgher (1930) quotes Xenophon as calling work the painful price that the gods charged humankind for living (Hill, 1996).

The early Greeks, whose political organization was structured around the city-state, believed that the citizens should own businesses or supervise their own agricultural efforts (Seaford, 2004). Farming, being a necessary factor for the survival of society, became exempt from the stigma attached to other forms of work (Borow, 1973). They deplored the mechanical arts, which they thought brutalized the mind because the mind would be unfit for the thinking of great truths or the practicing of virtue (Bennett, 1926; Brewer & Marmon, 2000; Mosse, 1969). Free artisans and craftsmen were scorned and the mechanical and menial tasks were done by slaves. Slavery itself, in the classic civilization, was not regarded as wrong, morally or otherwise. In fact, slavery was considered to be in the same vein as using beasts of burden such as donkeys and was a means of getting the bulk of the heavy, undesirable labor done (Dougherty & Kurke, 2003; Envy, Spite, & Jealousy, 2003; Kazanas, Baker, Miller, & Hannah, 1973).

Romans

The Romans conquered the Greeks and as a consequence learned much from them. The Romans assimilated most of the Greek's attitudes about the arts, science, and social values into their own culture. Cicero, a notable Roman philosopher and statesman, recited two occupations worthy of a free man. The first was agriculture and the second was commerce, with all other pursuits (of work) being vulgar and dishonoring. Handcraft, the work of artisans, and the crafting of material goods were held in low-esteem (Ermatinger, 2004; Tilgher, 1930).

Hebrews

In the Western world we know much about the Hebrews, who like the early Greeks, considered work to be a painful drudgery. However, whereas the Greeks could see no reason why humanity should be condemned to labor other than at the whim of the gods, the Hebrews felt that work was necessary to make amends for the original sin committed by Adam and Eve in their earthly paradise (Bennett, 1926; Tilgher, 1930).

Early Christians followed the Hebrew belief that not only was work necessary to provide expiation and the existence of many of the necessities, but it was a means for accumulating enough to share with one's fellow human being (Borow, 1973; Brewer & Marmon, 2000). Upon work, then, was reflected some of the divine light that stems from charity. Riches shared with the poor were considered to bring God's blessing upon the giver (Tilgher, 1930).

Early Christians

Early Christian doctrine recognized no separation between mental, bodily, or physical work. To work and share the products of work with others (charity) was desirable. To eliminate the middleman and to allow the recipient of the sharing to share directly in the work was even more desirable. Thus, it became the duty of the Christian brotherhood to give work to the unemployed so that no man need remain in idleness. A refusal to work resulted in the offender being cast out of the community for the good of both the community and the offender (Kazanas et al.,1973; Tilgher, 1930). Despite these foundations, no intrinsic value was yet recognized in work. Therefore, work remained a means to a worthy end (Borow, 1973; Tilgher).

Artisans and craftsmen were not tied to the land; therefore, they were free to sell their services to the highest bidder. By keeping the processes and methods highly guarded secrets of their trade, they were able to control, to an extent, the commerce and the trades. Early Christian leaders generally held a low opinion of physical labor. Thus, greater diligence led to a degree of wealth that enabled a middle class to form about commerce and the trades (Mosse, 1969; Tilgher, 1930).

THE PROTESTANT ETHIC OF WORK

The first great Protestant reformer, Martin Luther, believed that work was both the universal base of society and the real distinction between social classes. It is said he had little sympathy with commerce because it was a means of using work to pass from one social class to another. Luther believed that to rise in the social hierarchy was against God's laws (Borow, 1973). But, Luther believed there was just one best way to serve God, and that was to do most perfectly the work of one's calling (Borow; Tilgher, 1930). To promote this concept, Bennett (1926) portrays Luther as having promoted formal schooling in religious matters for all classes.

Calvinism adopted a new attitude toward work. They borrowed from Luther's concept of religion and believed that it was the will of God for all, including the rich and noble, to work. Further, it was their belief that it was man's obligation to God to extract the maximum amount of wealth from his work. Sweat and toil only had value as a means to establish the kingdom of God on earth (Tilgher, 1930). In addition, no one should lust after the fruits of their labor-wealth, possessions, or luxurious living. The element of profit was therefore added to the Protestant ethic (Hill, 1996).

In a short time, Calvinists discovered that the principles of profit could produce for the secular arm great wealth, position, and other desirable things. These concepts also pleased non-Calvinists and subsequently modern business began. From the religious convictions of the protestant merchant was spawned the businessman who was strong-willed, active, austere, and hard working. According to Hill (1996) it was common to shun idleness, luxuriousness, prodigality, and other extravagances that resulted in the softening of either the muscles or the soul.

The Protestant work ethic developed during this era was a foundation to the success of the modern factory. The diligent application of humanity's energy, regardless of the project on which the efforts were spent, was an essential ingredient of the Industrial Revolution (Tilgher, 1930).

THE PROTESTANT ETHIC OF WORK IN THE WEST

In the western hemisphere, particularly in America, several conditions existed that were beneficial to the establishment and strengthening of the work ethic and became a powerful concept in society. The colonies (America) were largely peopled by those who had everything to gain and comparatively little to lose. These individuals (primarily immigrants) had strong feelings regarding the benefits of diligent work and prosperity that were ingrained in both their moral and religious fiber (Ringer, 2004). Another factor was the vast opportunity in land and natural resources that could enable almost anyone to succeed who was willing to put forth the effort (Barlow, 1967). Even the concept of indentured servitude was but a postponement of the probability of ultimate success. It provided a means of getting to the land where success was so probable (Barlow).

In America, however, another factor entered into the evolving work ethic. This was the factor of education and training. Partly because of the availability of wealth, the established Protestant ethics, the ingrained social attitudes and regard for diligent work, and the social mobility possible in a culture without distinct and traditional cultural castes, many colonists wished for their sons and daughters better training and education than they had received (Barlow, 1967; Bennett, 1926). Colleges, universities, mechanics institutions, and other forms of formal education appeared throughout the colonies (Bennett). Education and wealth were the means to social ascension (Barlow). This upward mobility was impossible in other societies, but was made possible in America. Therefore, the American working class achieved what no other working class had achieved in history. The working class became the middle class and the more they worked, the more and greater success and upward mobility they enjoyed (Balmer, 2002; Eby, 1952; Ringer, 2004).

THE EFFECTS OF THE INDUSTRIAL REVOLUTION AND AUTOMATION ON THE VALUE OF WORK

In the Western world large factories were established where labor could be divided so that semiskilled individuals could perform repetitive elements of a job using apprentices. This led to the development of a working class. With the advent of the Industrial Revolution and the vast flooding of the metropolitan areas with unemployed rural population, the old values (such as the lord of the land exhibiting a degree of kindness and care) were eliminated. Bennett (1926) and Tilgher (1930) indicated that with the money economy, factory lords found a way to get around the traditional burden of responsibility through the payment of wages.

The factory-dominated society led to the metamorphosis of serfs to workers creating a lower class (workers). Culturally, this complemented the middle class, which was composed largely of artisans and merchants, and an upper class composed of the landed and titled nobility and the wealthy. However, through hard work, luck, and diligence a worker could move, by virtue of accruing wealth, from the lowest class to within the limits of the upper class (Bennett, 1926; Runes, 1951; Tilgher, 1930).

A number of authors have pointed out that one of the results that affected working during the Industrial Revolution was the intensification of the division of labor (Brewer et al., 2001; Venn, 1964). The implications of the intense division of labor for the purpose of increasing production were to bring specific work processes to an ever-increasing fragmentation. This removed the worker further and further from participating in the final product (Venn, 1964). This factor resulted in the change in work attitudes from those that existed in the 16th, 17th, and 18th centuries to the emerging new work attitudes of today. Ironically, those very changes that have increased our potential for work productivity, such as mass production, automation, cybernation, and occupational technology, have resulted in making the work ethic, in its classic form, less meaningful and seemingly less appropriate for the individual worker. It is easily observed from a comparison of the production processes of the early 17th century and modem procedures that work has changed; however, the extent and the type of change in the work ethic is not as easily seen.

As work and society changed, the work ethic also changed. Decreased manual labor and reduction in the hours of work contributed to the increased prosperity and freedom from toil experienced by most workers. However, depriving workers of both their involvement in the total production process as well as the possibility of self-realization through work has presented problems far beyond those imagined by the people who felt they were freeing the worker for more honorable labors.

The erosion of the traditional work ethic began with the willingness of immigrants to provide cheap labor and ultimately advance in anew society (Dowd, 2003; Jardine, 2004). Immigrants from countries undergoing political revolution, famine, or vast social pressures in the 17th, 18th, and 19th centuries would literally sell themselves into servitude, oftentimes with their entire families to move to the new world (Barlow, 1967; Bennett, 1926; King, 2001; Timmins, 2000). These immigrants gladly lived in crowded tenements, worked for substandard wages and worked under less than desirable conditions for the sole purpose of providing themselves a means of transportation to the new world (Petras, 2003). Even today, this trend continues with recent immigrants from third-world countries (including Mexico) who move to America to participate in our economic marvel.

STAGES OF HUMAN DEVELOPMENT AND THE WORK ETHIC

So, how does the work ethic develop today? Some researchers think that instilling professionalism is one way of accomplishing this difficult task. It is believed that professionalism leads to a positive value and meaning of work, ergo a positive work ethic. These investigators studied learning and psychological development by exploring thought and behavioral processes within a chronological system (Haines, 2003). Researchers such as Benja-

TABLE 12.1   Effects of Five Stages of Life on Work Ethic

Stage	Age	Effects related to work ethic
1	Growth (birth to 14years old)	Child moves from sensory and tactile identity is established and the child explores interests related to future career potential, and later develops adult motor and critical thinking skills.
2	Exploration (15–24 years old)	Psychosexual identity matures as young man/woman develops goals and career objects, moving from early adulthood, man or woman develops work ethic and pursues career objectives and experiences psychosexual and career development.
3	Establishment (25–44 years old)	Represents a period of domestication and settling down, with planning for future, retirement, and long-term needs/goals with career advancement, change, and renewal; continued planning and long-term goal assessment.
4	Maintenance (45–64 years old)	The apex of worker achievement; family development in flux, workforce advancement is stifled; some anxieties from aging process with preretirement and income reduction concerns, some identity problems for workers in transition from work to retirement.
6	Decline (65+ years old)	Period of worker retirement, financial, and health concerns with some quality of life disruption and anxiety over health issues, family dislocation, and mortality.

min Bloom, Jean Piaget, and Erik Erikson linked behavior to age cycles (Bloom, 1956; Brewer et al., 2001; Erikson, 1964).

To better explain human development, researchers have divided the human life cycle into periods or stages. It is thought that these different levels may offer some ideas of how behavior or physical characteristics, even cognitive and affective development, affect a person's work ethic. The five stages of life suggested in Table 12.1 demonstrate how a chronology of life in years reflects in specific changes in men and women what might affect our work ethic.

CONCLUSIONS

So, where are we today with the struggle to develop and instill meaning and value to work, ergo the work ethic? Surely, global competition has created a lot of pressure for establishing and sustaining a positive work ethic. Traditionally, a person's work ethic was related to production and historically has been established during the postindustrial revolution period and the change from an agrarian society to an industrial society. Workers in developed countries were engaged in the making of something of value and learned to develop their work ethic from this basis.

When a worker creates a product or delivers a service the intrinsic satisfaction resulting from this professional endeavor leaves a feeling of satisfaction and a positive work ethic. Unfortunately, though, production work is being outsourced from so-called first-world countries to developing third-world countries where labor is cheaper. Outsourcing is leaving the preponderance of jobs to a more educated, technologically skilled workforce. This global transfer has created new fields of work that are not directly related to creation satisfaction. This transfer lends credence to Marx's position that work is a social activity and changes over time (Whelan, 1999). Perhaps this can partially explain the changing work ethic.

Another factor that is causing a change in the work ethic is the great rise of service workers in such fields as teaching, police and fire protection, medical assistance, as well as many others. These jobs have a recognized place in our society and as a result of modem technology have become very specialized. Service workers also include the areas of convenience, leisure, and entertainment. In the western world this transference of jobs from industrial production to service has resulted in increased productivity along with an increased standard of living and pay rate. This change, however, carries with it the baggage of decreasing the personal involvement of the worker in earning a living (Petty, 1995a). Consequently, the situation has been established to gradually erode the traditional work ethic by lessening the personal involvement and commitment to work. Work then becomes more and more a means of financing entertainment, a high standard of living, and other nonwork activities (Miller, Woehr, & Hudspeth, 2002). This changes our perception of the work ethic.

The traditional work ethic, is undergoing a radical transformation, especially in the minds of young workers. Changing attitudes of young people in conjunction with changing economic times and conditions are presenting greater demands for change. Herzberg, Mausner, and Snyderman (1959) supported the concept of change 4 decades ago. However, they also felt that for industrial workers, in which work is a means of providing the way of life rather than the thing desired in itself, the traditional work ethic is being replaced by an avoidance ethic. Today these thoughts are not supported by others, who contend that although there are differences in the work ethic of young people and adults, there is no conclusive evidence supporting the erosion of the work ethic (Miller et al., 2002; Petty, 1995b; Pogson et al., 2003).

By most indications the work ethic is changing and is being challenged by several forces of modem society (McCortney & Engels, 2003). Some studies (Csikszentmihalyi, 2003; Petty 1995b; 1997) indicate that many workers in the industrialized western world appear to reject the notion that work is good in and of itself and has intrinsic value. Evidence of this is that more and more people are retiring early in both the blue-collar and white-collar categories. More emphasis is being placed on nonwork or leisure activities as a distraction to the drudgeries of work. Today we are experiencing increased rates in standards of living. Personal health and job safety have come to the forefront of concerns expressed by today's workers. Although these immediate concerns of workers are a manifestation of a progressive, modem society, they may jeopardize the heritage of the traditional work ethic, which states that work in itself is important and has value (Csikszentmihalyi).

REFERENCES

Baker, N. A., Jacobs, K., & Tickle-Degnen, L. (2003). A methodology for developing evidence about meaning in occupation: Exploring the meaning of working. *Occupation, Participation and Health, 23*(2), 57–66.

Balmer, R. H. (2002). *Protestantism in America.* New York: Columbia University Press.

Barlow, M. L. (1967). *History of Industrial Education in the United States.* Peoria, IL: Charles A. Bennett.

Bennett, C. A. (1926). *History of Manual and Industrial Education Up to 1870.* Peoria, IL: Charles A. Bennett.

Bloom, B. (1956). *Taxonomy of educational objectives; The classification of educational goals, by a committee of college and university examiners.* New York: D. McKay.

Borow, H. (Ed.). (1973). *Career guidance for a new age.* Boston: Houghton Mifflin.

Brewer, E. W., Campbell, A. C., & Petty, G. C. (2001) *Foundations of workforce education.* Dubuque, IA: Kendall/Hunt.

Brewer, E. W., & Marmon, D. (2000). *Characteristics, skills, and strategies of the ideal educator.* Boston, MA: Pearson.

Clark, R. (2003). Fostering the work motivation of individuals and teams. *Performance Improvement, 42*(3), 21–29

Csikszentmihalyi, M. (2003). The evolving nature of work. *North American Montessori Teacher's Association Journal, 28*(2), 87–107.

Dougherty, C., & Kurke, L. (Eds.). (2003). *The cultures within ancient Greek culture: Contact, conflict, collaboration.* New York: Cambridge University Press.

Dowd, D. F. (2003). *Capitalism and its economics: A critical history.* Ann Arbor, MI: Pluto Press.

Eby, F. (1952). *The development of modern education, in theory, organization, and practice.* New York: Prentice-Hall.

Envy, Spite, and Jealousy (2003). *The rivalrous emotions in Ancient Greece.* Edinburgh: Edinburgh University Press.

Erikson, E. H. (1964). *Childhood and society.* New York: Norton.

Ermatinger, J. W. (2004). *The decline and fall of the Roman Empire.* Westport, CT: Greenwood Press.

Fedorov, N. F. (1990). *What was man created for?* In E. Koutiassov, & M. Minto (Eds.), *The philosophy of the common task: Selected works* (pp.12–36). Lausanne, Switzerland: Honeyglen/L'Age d'Homme.

Haines, A. M. (2003). Work. *North American Montessori Teacher's Association Journal, 2,* 49–58.

Herzberg, F., Mausner, B., & Snyderman, B. (1959). *The motivation to work.* New York: John Wiley.

Hill, R. B. (1996). *Historical context of the work ethic.* Retrieved March 4, 2005, from http://www.coe.uga.edul-rhill/workethic/hist/htm

Hudelson, D. (1992). Roots or reform: Tracing the path of workforce education. *Career and Technical Education Journal, 67*(7), 28–29, 69.

Jardine, M. (2004). *The making and unmaking of technological society: How Christianity can save modernity from itself.* Grand Rapids, MI: Brazos Press.

Kazanas, H. C., Baker, G. E., Miller, F. M., & Hannah, L. D. (1973). *The meaning and value of work* (Information Series No. 71). Columbus, OH: The Center for Vocational Education (ERIC Document Reproduction Service No. ED 091 504).

King, S. (2001). *Making sense of the Industrial Revolution.* New York: Manchester University Press.

McCortney, A. H., & Engels, D. W. (2003). Revisiting the work ethic in America. *The Career Development Quarterly, 52*(2), 132–40.

Miller, M. J., Woehr, D. J., & Hudspeth, N. (2002). The meaning and measurement of work ethic: Construction and initial validation of a multidimensional inventory [Monograph]. *Journal of Vocational Behavior, 60,451–489.*

Mosse, C. (1969). *Le Travail en Grece et a Rome* [The ancient world at work] (Janet Lloyd, Trans.). New York: Norton. (Original work published 1969)

Niles, S. G.,& Harris-Bowlsbey, J. (2002). *Career development interventions in the 21st century.* Upper Saddle River, NJ: Prentice Hall.

Petras, 1. F. (2003). *A system in crisis: The dynamics of free market capitalism.* New York: Zed Books.

Petty, G. C. (1995a). Adults in the work force and the occupational work ethic. *Journal of Studies in Technical Careers, 15*(3), 133–140.

Petty, G. C. (1995b). Vocational-technical education and the occupational work ethic. *Journal of Industrial Teacher Education, 32*(3).

Petty, G. C. (1997). Employability skills. In C. P. Campbell (Ed.), *Best practices in workforce development* (pp. 122–145). Lancaster, PA: Technomic.

Pogson, C. E., Cober, A. B., Doverspike, D., & Rogers, J. R. (2003). Differences in self-reported work ethic across three career stages. *Journal of Vocational Behavior, 62*(1), 189–201.

Ringer, F. K. (2004). *Max Weber: An intellectual biography.* University of Chicago Press.

Runes, D. D. (1951). *The Hebrew impact on Western civilization.* New York: Philosophical Library.

Seaford, R. (2004). *Money and the early Greek mind: Homer, philosophy, tragedy.* New York: Cambridge University Press.

Tilgher, A. (1930). *Homo faber: Work through the ages* (D. C. Fisher, Trans.). New York: Harcourt Brace.

Timmins, G. (2000). *Understanding the industrial revolution.* New York: Routledge.

Venn, G. (1964). *Education for work: Postsecondary career and technical and technical education.* Washington, DC: American Council on Education.

Whelan, F. (1999). *Karl Marx (biography of Marx).* London: Fourth Estate.

CHAPTER 13

LAUNCH OUT

Building Workforce Competencies in Career and Technical Education

Kathleen P. King
Fordham University

Cherish your vision and your dreams as they are the children of your soul;
the blueprints of your ultimate achievements.

—Napoleon Hill (attributed)

INTRODUCTION

True to our innovative perspective of adult learning, we designed this chapter very differently from the rest of the book. This content and format enables the chapter to serve as a reflective guide for the individual reader. Small groups, professional development teams, or classes may use the chapter's materials as pre-reading, or post-reading discussion starters.

While synthesizing some of the highpoints of the chapters, the chapter provides several series of questions/prompts to guide deeper reflection and consideration. Specifically, the chapter includes reflective activities,

Building Workforce Competencies in Career and Technical Education, pages 247–258
Copyright © 2009 by Information Age Publishing

vision setting suggestions and activities, goal development and planning, and encouragement through quotes and suggestions. We look forward to hearing how this chapter serves to meet your needs in building workforce competencies in CTE.

LAUNCH OUT

Having traversed and experienced foundational chapters of CTE history and practice, global perspectives, future visions, and critical issues, this chapter provides an opportunity to briefly reconsider the highpoints which impressed you the most, and consider what they mean for your involvement in CTE. Therefore, the concluding chapter of our volume is entitled, *Launch Out: Building Workforce Competencies in Career and Technical Education.* This brief, but important, chapter assists you in reflecting on your reading experience, integrate your learning, and develop a vision and practice of building workforce competencies in right where you are in your career.

Our title emphasizes the concept of launching out as we consider the *landscape* of career and technical education in the context of the world today. Much like pioneers of the past, we need to look to the past, gain a vision of the future and step forward to discover new possibilities. From our perspective, CTE is powerfully positioned to impact the expanse of the P–16 continuum (King, 2009) and corporate training. Our educators and programs have vast experience in coping with changing workplace demands, addressing real-life competencies and cultivating lifelong learners. By recognizing, and validating this illustrious past, we gain strength to realize the valuable expertise and perspective CTE field offers.

As professional educators and trainers, we are committed to serving learners, developing excellence and lifelong learning (ACTE Online.org, 2008). Educators who are invested in discovering strategies and solutions to serve learners, are reflective practitioners (Giroux, 1988; Schon, 1983, 1990). Such educators seek opportunities and resources, such as this book, to deepen their learning, consider its meaning, and develop relevant application for their practice (Schon, 1990). Reflective practitioners are also willing to explore deeper meaning and question assumptions. Rather than being satisfied to have their classes and programs continue the same way always, regardless of need, they instead actively seek resources, assessment and dialogue with other professionals to develop new visions of teaching and learning and to inform their practice.

BUILD UPON THE PAST

While reading this book, you encountered several chapters, which discussed the long and varied history of CTE. With such a widespread history across the entire world, one no doubt discovers new examples and connections. Consider the following lists of questions potential reflective prompts or discussion starters (groups). However, never be confined to the questions we provide

Please note that these question lists are only samples, and your past and current experiences are necessarily different from others; therefore, you might have additional questions to ask, or different ways to consider them. Everyone will have many specific, valuable questions to consider.

Explore this list and let your mind develop new connections as you think back through the chapters (See Box 13.1) You might turn the pages of the book as you go through the list, to help you think of specific examples. To record your responses you might write them down on paper, create a word processing document, or even start a journal for continued professional reflections.

BOX 13.1   REFLECTIVE ACTIVITY FOR *BUILDING WORKFORCE COMPETENCIES IN CTE*

INSTRUCTIONS: Use this list to allow your mind to develop new connections as you reflect upon the chapters of *Building Workforce Competencies in CTE* (Wang & King, 2009). To help you think of specific examples, you might turn the pages of the book as you work through the list. To record your responses you might write them down on paper, create a word processing document, or even start a journal for continued professional reflections.

HISTORY

- Revisit the roots of your discipline.
- What and how are you connected? Where are you different?
- New synergies: What other components of CTE offer your perspective and practices?
- *What else do you want to learn about CTE history and practices?*

INTERNATIONAL EXAMPLES

- Cross cultural and international lessons?
- Why do we have this practice, this view, and these expectations?

- Do the other angles give new ideas, what can you gain from this new perspective?
- *What else do you want to learn about international perspectives of adult learning and CTE?*

EDUCATIONAL PHILOSOPHY

- What is your educational philosophy?
- How is it different from others that you read about or about which you know?
- What can you gain from this reflection to do differently?
- *What else do you want to learn about educational philosophy?*

E-LEARNING

- How has e-learning been used in your content area and organization for CTE?
- What resources are available within your organization to support e-learning?
- Based on the experiences shared in this book, how could your learners benefit from e-learning?
- *What else do you want to learn about e-learning?*

CURRICULUM DEVELOPMENT

- What are the foundational models of curriculum design for CTE?
- To which major theories and philosophies are they connected?
- How does an educator develop instructional objectives and what should be included in them?
- How does this learning compare to your practice? To your program's processes?
- What can you do to improve your practice?
- What resources are available to help learn more about this topic?
- *What else do you want to learn about curriculum development?*

TRAINING AND DEVELOPMENT (T&D)

- What are the foundational models of training and design?
- To which major theories and philosophies are they connected?
- How do organizations plan for, design and deliver T&D?

- Do your classes and programs incorporate elements of T&D? If so, which? If not, would they benefit from it?
- What resources are available to help learn more about this topic?
- *What else do you want to learn about training and development?*

WORK ETHIC

- What is the role and importance of work ethic in CTE?
- What do Petty and Brewer identify as central historical points and characteristics of this concept?
- How has work ethic changed in the last 25 years? How has it affected your area of CTE?
- Based on this book, how could your CTE learners and program benefit from revisiting concepts in work ethic?
- What resources are available within your organization to support changes or integration of teaching work ethic?
- *What else do you want to learn about work ethic?*

© 2009 Kathleen P. King

At this point, continue to read this chapter to understand how we suggest conceptually applying your questions, and understanding for action. Alternatively, you may choose to stop and conduct this first exercise in full, or in part. Once you are ready, proceed to the next section, *"Develop a Vision,"* to discover how one may use reflective practice to create a larger vision.

DEVELOP A VISION

What is vision and what possible roles can it play for individual performance and direction? Consider this salient quote from Covey:

> Vision is seeing with mind's eye what is possible in people in projects, in causes and in enterprises. Vision results when our mind joins need with possibility... When people have no vision, they neglect the development of the mind's capacity to create, they fall prey to human tendency toward victimization." (Covey, 2004, p. 65)

As adults, professionals and educators, we know intuitively the power of vision in providing broad strokes of direction. Thus, today, we experience a continuing, central emphasis on mission and vision of all organizations, and even educational programs (Anderson, 2006; Caffarella, 2001; Senge, 2006; Yorks, 2005). Indeed, most management and inspirational speakers/ writers emphasize broad strokes of one's vision for action as a minimum to guide our steps and steer our choices (e.g., Covey, 2004; Drucker, 1990).

Pause to reflect upon these additional following popular quotes regarding the importance of vision, as we turn to developing your vision of CTE, present and future:

> If you don't have a vision, then your reality will always be determined by other's perceptions.—Melanee Addison (attributed)

> Achievers can almost literally taste success because they imagine their goals in such vivid detail. Setbacks only seem to add spice and favor to the final taste of victory.—Denis Waitley (attributed)

More specifically, within the realm of education, Senge articulates the grounding philosophy and understanding behind our dedication, even obsession with mission and vision today:

> You cannot have a learning organization without shared vision. Without a pull toward some goal, which people truly want to achieve, the forces in support of the status quo can be overwhelming. Vision establishes and overarching goal. The loftiness of the target compels new ways of thinking and acting. . . . Learning can be difficult, even painful. With a shared vision, we are more likely to expose our ways of thinking, give up deeply held views, and recognize personal and organizational shortcomings. (Senge, 2006, p. 195)

The question we pose in this chapter to you as readers is:

Based on your experience, reading in this volume, and reflection, what do you envision for the future of CTE?

As educators, we need to consider many factors in considering and designing your personal general and specific vision for the future. You might find the following activity helpful in guiding you in developing a response to our question to you. (See Box 13.2).

As you use the CTE Vision Activity, answer each question as best you can at this point in time. Do not overly labor on your responses. Instead, try to express your current convictions and desires. This is an activity you can revisit many times in the future, to hone your vision more specifically. Unless instructed otherwise, this activity is for your personal development, thoughtfully and honestly take advantage of the opportunity to consider your deeper values, and beliefs about teaching and learning, how you can help build workforce competencies in CTE, etc.

BOX 13.2   CTE VISION ACTIVITY

FOUNDATIONAL PILLARS FOR YOUR EDUCATIONAL VISION

As you respond to the questions below:

- Respond from the perspective of our beliefs, the mission of your organization and the context in which you teach.
- Be specific to the organization, or situation you are describing. That is, you might develop a personal vision: a vision for your work at school XYZ and your professional vision of participation in the profession.
- Think in positive terms and use inspiring phrases.
- Be open to change and do not "box yourself in" to the current organizational structure and limitations- change can happen: "think big" and innovatively.

CURRENT CONDITIONS

- Describe what you see as the future dimensions and trends in CTE regarding one of those listed below (or another topic related to this volume).
  - Instructional changes
  - Problem-based and skills based learning
  - Models of practice
  - Curricular design
  - Distance learning
  - Accountability
  - Global markets
  - International identities
  - Lifelong learning and training and development
  - Strategic Partnerships
- What is emerging? What is fading? (List as many as applicable.)
- Prioritize the points you have listed.
- What connections or synergies do you see among these characteristics, trends or issues? (Describe in words, diagrams, etc.)
- Does a pattern or relationship emerge among the items you identified in the previous step? If so, what is it?
  - Write and/or draw as complete a description and diagram of this pattern as possible.
  - Think about, and then write out an example of where you have seen this pattern in action already. Be sure to include the conditions, action and results in your narrative.

KNOWLEDGE, BELIEFS AND PHILOSOPHY

- Describe your knowledge of the issue/s or trends you have identified.
- What is your underlying perspective and philosophy on this issue?
- List only two enduring principles or models related to your vision development: which ones are the most central and must be included?
  - How might they influence teaching, learning, programs, and the workplace?
- Determine the relevant organizational philosophy, culture, and perspective on this issue as well. You might have to examine organizational documents, such a procedures, protocols and handbooks. Look about your building and listen to people talk about various topics to find spoken, written, and/or unspoken and unwritten evidence of these philosophies.
- Repeat the step above for personal and organizational beliefs on the related topic.
  - For instance, do you believe it is possible to change this characteristic/trend? Why or why not?
  - Do you believe individuals can affect change in this respect? Why or why not?

FOCUS

- What is the vision you see for your critical issue or trend in CTE education?
- Draft the first version of your vision in simple bullet points.
- Organize and expand upon your bullet points to develop your first draft of a vision statement.
- Edit your vision statement to improve these characteristics
  - Focused, and not too broad.
  - Specific and descriptive.
  - Inspiring.
  - Purposeful and directional.
  - Innovative, new thinking, breaks outside of customary mode of thinking, and action.
  - Curricular and pedagogically sound.
  - Concise.
- Write your final version of the visions statement (for this session).
- Post your vision statement in as prominent a location with which you are comfortable.

© 2009 Kathleen P. King

At first, developing this vision statement can be a brief activity. We suggest revisiting it frequently in order to effectively include your new thoughts, understandings, and experiences in it. If you have a group of professionals or friends to share your vision statement with, you will find many benefits. By discussing our visions, we benefit from putting our thoughts into more descriptive words and explaining them. As we know from educational theorists, such social dialogue provides a powerful opportunity for greater reflection, clarity and development (Giroux, 1988; King, 2005; Schon, 1990).

By creating a vision statement and continuing to develop it, you will likely be surprised at how much more focused your efforts may become. Rather than being subject to the needs of the moment alone, you have a planned, guiding course in which you know is consistent with your core values and commitments. In a rapidly changing and tumultuous world, having a navigational map can provide a personal mooring to guide our way for advancement, which affords strength and direction. More importantly, your vision statement will map out what specifically you will do to help build workforce competencies in CTE once you have confirmed your core values and commitments.

FORWARD INTO NEW POSSIBILITIES

Based on the vision statement you have created in this chapter, now you are positioned to take strategic action and implement change. Consider the vision statement you wrote and then begin to list the actions that emerged from it. If you truly believe in what you have said, you will see that there are changes needed to reflect the issues and trends you identified. As in all other fields, we need change in CTE and change should be the constant in all fields of study.

You may start with a brainstorm of possibilities, writing everything that comes to mind, related to you vision, or you may start with the list below and see if any of the items apply to your vision and plan. This list is a jump-start and is by no means comprehensive, nor directive. (See Table 13.1.)

With your list identified, of course the next step is to prioritize the points listed according to the most critical needs. Most people would choose to pause to implement the most necessary changes first, however, there might be reasons this cannot be done. Instead, wise educators will assess the organization environment and climate, consider changes needed, contingencies, resources, obstacles, opportunities, and use that information to develop a strategic plan for implementation.

TABLE 13.1 New Possibilities List: Building Workforce Competencies in CTE

New possibilities list: Building workforce competencies in CTE

• Evaluate current programs	• Revise a program
• Develop new programs	• Integrate new technologies
• Redesign using technology	• Offer hybrid options
• Offer e-learning	• New professional development efforts—organizational level
• New instructional strategies	• Personal, professional development
• New collaborations	• New partnerships
• Innovations	• Redesigns
• New student assessments	• New teaching evaluation system
• New teacher rewards and promotion incentives	• Do a new needs assessment
• New training models	• Add soft skills to the curriculum
• Student support	• Increase/include student dialogue
• Peer learning	• New student assessment strategies
• New workplace integrations	• Student participation and responsibility in educational planning
• Other:	• Other:
• Other:	• Other:
• Other:	• Other:

LAUNCH OUT

In this chapter, we have guided you through several reflective activities to consider how this book might assist you consistently and strategically in building workforce competencies. We strongly believe that theory and research, which remains isolated, disconnected from practice, is ineffective. Instead, explicitly throughout this volume, we use many examples from different countries and contexts, and in this final chapter, we provide means to assist you in connecting your reading to practice.

Our hope is that this book has been a thoughtful learning process as you revisit and reflect upon the broad and illustrious history and future of CTE. As said many times in the book, we believe that CTE educators are uniquely positioned to continue to lead powerful innovation and advancement across educational settings. We are proud to be part of this movement and to be part of the CTE community. This book demonstrates that we stand with you, and seek to support our CTE colleagues and field.

However, the future is now in your hands, literally, because you likely have at least the beginning of a vision statement and goals of what you would like to see changed in CTE practice. Making the choice to be one of the scores of leaders needed to effect this change is a very important role. Will you join with us as we push through the demands of daily life and look beyond your vision, raise your eyes to the possibilities of greater things?

If you hesitate, we ask you to consider your learners. Consider the lives and opportunities they might not have aside from CTE programs. The work we do is essential, it is vital, and it is unmatched by any other sector of the educational field. If we are not the change agents, then those who do not have grassroots expertise may seek to take control for other advantages. Our students and our globe need critical thinkers, lifelong learners, and problem solvers with CTE skills to lead us into the next decades and centuries of innovation and change (Allen & Seaman, 2008; Anderson, 2006; Gardner, 2007; Partnership for 21st Century Skills, 2008). Let us together work to meet this unprecedented need. Individually and collectively, we have the ability like no one else. When needed, we can share, consolidate and leverage resources. Will you make the choice to launch out and put your heartfelt convictions into action? From the long history of CTE, which we have visited in this book and elsewhere, we know you will; and we will be there with you (ACTE Online.org, 2008).

REFERENCES

ACTE Online.org. (2008). *History of CTE.* Retrieved September 15, 2008, from http://www.acteonline.org/career_tech/ctehistory.cfm

Allen, E., & Seaman, J. (2008). *Online nation: Five years of growth in online learning.* Needham, MA: Sloan-C. Retrieved September 8, 2008, from http://www.aln.org/publications/survey/pdf/online_nation.pdf

Anderson, C. (2006). *The long tail: Why the future of business is selling less for more.* New York: Hyperion.

Caffarella, R. (2001). *Planning programs for adult learners* (2nd ed.). San Francisco: Jossey-Bass.

Covey, S. (2004). *The 8th habit: From effectiveness to greatness.* New York: Free Press.

Drucker, P. (1990). *Managing the non-profit organization.* New York: Harper Collins.

Gardner, H. (2007). *Five minds for the future.* Cambridge, MA: Harvard Business School Press.

Giroux, H. A. (1988). *Teachers as intellectuals: Towards a critical pedagogy of learning.* Westport, CT: Bergin & Garvey / Greenwood.

King, K. P. (2005). *Bringing transformative learning to life.* Malabar, FL: Krieger.

King, K. P. (2009). Bridging the gap in K–12 education with career and technical education: The view from adult learning. In *Building workforce competencies in career and technology education. SERIES: Adult education special topics: Theory, research and practice in lifelong learning* (pp. 129–158). Charlotte, NC: Information Age.

Partnership for 21st Century Skills. (2008). *Moving forward.* Retrieved Sept. 18, 2008, from http://www.21stcenturyskills.org/documents/p21_brochure_-final4.pdf

Schon, D. (1983). *The reflective practitioner.* New York: Basic Books.

Schon, D. (1990). *Educating the reflective practitioner.* San Francisco: Jossey-Bass.

Senge, P. M. (2006). *The fifth discipline: The art and practice of the learning organization* (Rev.). New York: random House, Inc.

Yorks, L. (2005). *Strategic human resource development.* Mason, OH: Thomson.

ABOUT THE AUTHORS

Victor C. X. Wang, Ed.D., is an assistant professor/credential coordinator of CTE and adult education at California State University, Long Beach (CSULB). Wang's research and writing activities have focused on workforce education, the foundations of adult education, adult teaching and learning, training, transformative learning, cultural issues in vocational and adult education, distance education and curriculum development. He has published more than 70 journal articles, book chapters and books during his 6 years at CSULB and has been a reviewer for 4 journals. In addition, he is the editor in chief of the International Journal of Adult Vocational Education and Technology. He has won many academic achievement awards from different universities in China and in the United States. He taught extensively as a full professor in Chinese universities prior to coming to study and work in the United States in 1997. He has taught adult learners English as a second language, Chinese, computer technology, vocational and adult education courses, research methods, administrative leadership, human resource management and curriculum development for the past 19 years in university settings. In addition, he has served as a translator/narrator for national and international leaders both in China and in the United States. The videotapes and DVDs he published for national and international leaders are played all over the world for both educational and investment purposes. He coedited two books (*Comparative Adult Education Around The Globe; Innovations in Career and Technical Education: Strategic Approaches Towards Workforce Competencies Around the Globe*) with Fordham University's Professor Kathleen P. King, which have been adopted as required textbooks by major universities in the United States and in China.

Building Workforce Competencies in Career and Technical Education, pages 259–260
Copyright © 2009 by Information Age Publishing
All rights of reproduction in any form reserved.

Kathleen P. King, Ed.D., is Professor of adult education and human resource development at Fordham University's Graduate School of Education in New York City. King's major areas of research have been transformative learning, professional development, distance learning, and instructional technology. She is also an award winning author of 16 books, popular keynote and conference speaker, editor, mentor, and private consultant. She has been widely recognized for her research, service, and contribution to the fields of adult learning. Her experience in adult learning has spanned these fields in diverse organizations including community based organizations, business, higher education, career and technical education and numerous partnerships. Most recent endeavors continue to explore and develop learning innovations and opportunities to address equity, access and international issues. Dr. King is the founder and co-editor of *Perspectives, The New York Journal of Adult Learning* and research board member for several national and international academic journals. In addition to receiving numerous academic and professional awards in the field of adult learning, her co-edited book about distance education, *Harnessing Innovations Technologies in Higher Education*, received the Frandson Book Award from the University Continuing Education Association in 2007, and she has received numerous other international and national awards for her leadership, research and innovation in adult learning, adult education and distance learning. Dr. King was included as one of 50 adult educators highlighted in *North American Adult Educators: Phyllis M. Cunningham Archive of Quintessential Autobiographies for the 21st Century* published by Discovery House in 2007.

ABOUT THE CONTRIBUTORS

Ernest Brewer, Ed.D., is Professor and Principal Investigator/Director of Pre-College Enrichment Programs at The University of Tennessee, Knoxville. He is the editor of *International Journal of Vocational Education and Training*. He is the author of numerous articles and books in career and technical education and has received numerous academic honors and awards. He is a successful grant writer and grant administrator and has brought millions of dollars to the university. Dr. Brewer's current research interests, which are frequently intertwined, include job satisfaction, occupational stress, and job burnout. In his current capacity as a professor, he chairs masters and doctoral committees at the university.

Gregory C. Petty, Ph.D., is Professor at the University of Tennessee, Knoxville. For the past two decades, he has focused on the study of the occupational work ethic, that is, the scientific exploration of behavioral factors and motivation of workers. His unique and original research has led to the design of a psychometric instrument, the Occupational Work Ethic Inventory, OWEI ((c) Petty, 1992) to determine an individual's occupational work ethic. He teaches undergraduate and graduate courses in Health and Safety. His primary research areas are work ethic for a healthy life, behavioral issues for safety and health including occupational stress and psychometric measures of performance, attitude, and self efficacy. He has contributed to and/or written various grants funded by the Department of Health and the Department of Labor and has been a consultant to private industry for organizational behavior and management. His academic work includes directing 24 Doctoral Dissertations and 20 Master's Theses; publishing 43 peer reviewed publications and 53 scholarly refereed papers at national conferences.

Building Workforce Competencies in Career and Technical Education, page 261
Copyright © 2009 by Information Age Publishing
261

INDEX

A

Adult learning case study, 129
  CTE bridge, 130–132, 153–154
  findings, 149–152
  future study directions, 156
  Phase One, 136
  Phase One/findings (standards and
    adult learning), 137–140
  Phase One/method and analysis,
    137
  Phase Two, 140–141
  Phase Two/findings and discussion,
    142–149
  Phase Two/method, 141–142
  Phase Two/participants, 141
  recommendations, 154–156
  research questions, 131
  study limitations, 152–153
  See also NCCTE standards
Adult learning principles, 132–133
  build on learners' experience, 135,
    139, 145–146
  climate of respect, 135, 139–140, 148
  cultivating collaborative skills, 135–
    136, 139, 146–147

involving learners in active learning,
  134, 139, 144–145
involving learners in planning, 133,
  140, 148–149
self-directed learning, 133, 139, 146
Agriculture education
  courses, 68
  developments in, 45–46
  instructional programs, 65–68
Albertson, Ralph, 58
Ancient Egyptian civilization
  medical practices, 48
  vocational education examples, 2–3
Ancient Greece
  education, 4
  meaning of work in, 236
  medical practices, 48
Andragogical mode of instruction, 108
Apprenticeship-training programs, 51,
  53
  first reference to, 3
Arts and Crafts Movement, 54, 90,
  91–92, 96–97, 161
  advantages, 97, 98
  disadvantages, 97–98
Assessment, as learning, 206–207
Assyrians, 3

Building Workforce Competencies in Career and Technical Education, pages 263–269
Copyright © 2009 by Information Age Publishing
All rights of reproduction in any form reserved.

CPSIA information can be obtained at www.ICGtesting.com
Printed in the USA
BVOW040714231111

276452BV00003B/16/P

9 781607 520290